CONTENTS

INSURANCE

4th Edition

Julia Holyoake

William Weipers

institute of financial services

Apart from any fair dealing for the purpose of research or private study, or criticism or review, as permitted under the Copyright, Designs and Patents Act 1988, this publication may only be reproduced, stored or transmitted, in any form or by any means, with the prior permission in writing of the publisher, or in the case of reprographic reproduction in accordance with the terms and licences issued by the Copyright Licensing Agency. Enquiries concerning reproduction outside those terms should be addressed to the publisher's agents at the undermentioned address:

CIB Publishing
c/o The Chartered Institute of Bankers
Emmanuel House
4-9 Burgate Lane
Canterbury
Kent
CT1 2XJ
United Kingdom

Telephone: 01227 762600

CIB Publishing publications are published by The Chartered Institute of Bankers, a non-profit making registered educational charity.

The Chartered Institute of Bankers believes that the sources of information upon which the book is based are reliable and has made every effort to ensure the complete accuracy of the text. However, neither CIB, the author nor any contributor can accept any legal responsibility whatsoever for consequences that may arise from errors or omissions or any opinion or advice given.

Typeset by Kevin O'Connor

Printed by Selwood Printing, Burgess Hill, West Sussex

© Chartered Institute of Bankers 1999

ISBN 0-85297-555-4

Contents

Contents

Insurance

Introduction

Insurance

The Concept of the Course

This is a practical course written for students studying for banking and finance qualifications and for practitioners in the financial services who are looking for a practical refresher. The framework of this study text is structured so that many will find it to be the most coherent way of learning the subject.

Each chapter or unit of the Study Text is divided into sections and contains:

- learning objectives

- an introduction, indicating how this subject area relates to others to which the reader may have cause to refer

- clear, concise topic-by-topic coverage

- examples and exercises to reinforce learning, confirm understanding and stimulate thought

- often a recommendation on illustrative questions to try for practice.

Exercises

Exercises are provided throughout to enable you to check your progress as you work through the text. These come in a variety of forms; some test your ability to analyse material you have read, others see whether you have taken in the full significance of a piece of information. Some are meant to be discussed with colleagues, friends or fellow students.

A suggested solution is usually given, but often in abbreviated form to help you avoid the temptation of merely reading the exercise rather than actively engaging your brain. We think it is preferable on the whole to give the solution immediately after the exercise rather than making you hunt for it at the end of the chapter, losing your place and your concentration. Cover up the solution with a piece of paper if you find the temptation to cheat too great!

Examples can also often be used as exercises, if not the first time you read a passage then certainly afterwards when you come to revise.

Each of the main units consists of study notes designed to focus attention upon the key aspects of the subject matter. These notes are divided into convenient sections for study purposes. Following each small group section there is a 'Student Activity' session, which is intended to encourage student to think about what they have studied in the preceding few sections and to consolidate their knowledge. In the main, these Student Activity sessions comprise a series of short questions, for each of which a reference is given to the precise part of the preceding text where the answer may be found. Students are strongly encouraged to use these Study Activity sessions in order to test their understanding of the material. They should also note their areas of weakness and re-read the relevant parts of the text.

At the end of each unit there are self-assessment questions. These comprise a number of short answer questions and sometimes multiple-choice questions, and a full specimen examination question. The answers to all of these questions are to be found at the back of the book. Further examination questions are to be found in the workbook and the revision section may be used as a mock examination, although students should remain aware of the fact that the examination itself will comprise questions drawn from across the whole Chartered Institute of Bankers syllabus; the key sections of which for this subject are:

Scope and Purpose of Insurance

Insurance Contracts

Classes of Insurance

Authorization and Regulation of Intermediaries

Although the workbook is designed to stand alone, as with most topics certain aspects of this subject are constantly changing. Therefore it is of great importance that students should keep up to date with these key areas.

It is anticipated that the student will study this course for one academic year, reading through and studying approximately two units every three weeks. However, it should be noted that as topics vary in size and as knowledge tends not to fall into uniform chunks, some units in this workbook are unavoidably longer than others.

The masculine pronoun 'he' has been used in this Workbook to encompass both genders and to avoid the awkwardness of the constant repetition of 'he and/or she'.

Study Guide

In the next few pages, we offer some advice and ideas on studying, revising and approaching examinations.

Studying

As with any examination, there is no substitute for preparation based on an organized and disciplined study plan. You should devise an approach that will enable you to get right through this Study Text and still leave time for revision of this and any other subject you are taking at the same time. Many candidates find that about six weeks is the right period of time to leave for revision, enough time to get through the revision material, but not so long that it is no longer fresh in your mind by the time you reach the examination.

This means that you should plan how to get to the last chapter by, say, the end of March for a May sitting or the end of August for an October sitting. This includes not only reading the text, but making notes and attempting the bulk of the illustrative questions in the back of the text.

We offer the following as a starting point for approaching your study.

- Plan time each week to study a part of this Study Text. Make sure that it is 'quality' study time: let everyone know that you are studying and the you should not be disturbed. If you are at home, unplug your telephone or switch the answerphone on; if you are in the office, put you telephone on 'divert'.

- Set a clearly defined objective for each study period. You may simply wish to read through a chapter for the first time or perhaps you want to make some notes on a chapter you have already read a couple of times. Do not forget the illustrative questions.

- Review your study plan. Use the study checklist a couple of pages on to see how well you are keeping up. Do not panic if you fall behind, but do think how you will make up for lost time.

- Look for examples of what you have covered in the 'real' world. If you work for a financial organization, this should be a good starting point. If you do not, then think about your experiences as an individual bank or building society customer or perhaps about your employer's position as a corporate customer of a bank. Keep an eye on the quality press for reports about banks and building societies and their activities.

Revising

- The period which you have earmarked for revision is a very important time. Now it is even more important that you plan time each week for study and that you set clear objectives for each revision session.

- Use time sensibly. How much revision time do you have? Remember that you still need to eat, sleep and fit in some leisure time.

- How will you split the available time between subjects? What are your weaker subjects? You will need to focus on some topics in more detail than others. You will also need to plan your revision around your learning style. By now, you should know whether, for example, early morning, early evening or late evening is best.

- Take regular breaks. Most people find they can absorb more if they attempt to revise for long uninterrupted periods of time. Award yourself a five minute break every hour. Go for a stroll or make a cup of coffee, but do not turn the television on.

- Believe in yourself. Are you cultivating the right attitude of mind? There is absolutely no reason why you should not pass this exam if you adopt the correct approach. Be confident, you have passed exams before so you can pass this one.

The Day of the Exam

- Passing professional examinations is half about having the knowledge, and half about doing yourself full justice in the examination. You must have the right technique.

- Set at least one alarm (or get an alarm call) for a morning exam.

- Having something to eat but beware of eating too much; you may feel sleepy if your system is digesting a large meal.

- Do not forget pens, pencils, rulers, erasers and anything else you will need.

- Avoid discussion about the exam with other candidates outside the exam hall.

Tackling the Examination Paper

First, make sure that you satisfy the examiner's requirements.

Read the instructions on the front of the exam paper carefully. Check that the exam format has not changed. It is surprising how often examiners' reports remark on the number of students who attempt too few - or too many - questions, or who attempt the wrong number of questions from different parts of the paper. Make sure that you are planning to answer the right number of questions.

Read all the questions on the exam paper before you start writing. Look at the weighting of marks to each part of the question. If part (a) offers only 4 marks and you cannot answer the 12 marks part (b), then do not choose the question.

Do not produce irrelevant answers. Make sure you answer the question set, and not the question you would have preferred to have been set.

Produce an answer in the correct format. The examiner will state in the requirements the format in which the question should be answered, for example as a report or memorandum. If a question asks for a diagram or an example, give one. If a question does not specifically asks for a diagram or example, but it seems appropriate, give one.

Second, observe these simple rules to ensure that your script is pleasing to the examiner.

Present a tidy paper. You are a professional and it should always show in the presentation of your work. Candidates are penalized for poor presentation and so you should make sure that you write legibly, label diagrams clearly and lay out your work professionally. Markers of scripts each have dozens of papers to mark; a badly written scrawl is unlikely to receive the same attention as a neat and well laid out paper.

State the obvious. Many candidates look for complexity which is not required and consequently overlook the obvious. Make basic statements first. Plan your answer and ask yourself whether you have answered the main parts of the question.

Use examples. This will help to demonstrate to the examiner that you keep up-to-date with the subject. There are lots of useful examples scattered through this study text and you can read about others if you dip into the quality press or take notice of what is happening in your working environment.

Finally, make sure that you give yourself the opportunity to do yourself justice.

Select questions carefully. Read through the paper once, then quickly jot down any key points against each question in a second read through. Reject those questions against which you have jotted down very little. Select those where you could latch on to 'what the question is about' - but remember to check carefully that you have got the right end of the stick before putting pen to paper.

Plan your attack carefully. Consider the order in which you are going to tackle questions. It is a good idea to start with your best question to boost your morale and get some easy marks 'in the bag'.

Read the question carefully and plan your answer. Read through the question again very carefully when you come to answer it.

Gain the easy marks. Include the obvious if it answers the question and do not spend unnecessary time producing the perfect answer. As suggested above, there is nothing wrong with stating the obvious.

Avoid getting bogged down in small parts of questions. If you find a part of a question difficult, get on with the rest of the question. If you are having problems with something the chances are that everyone else is too.

Do not leave the exam early. Use your spare time checking and rechecking your script.

Do not worry if you feel you have performed badly in the exam. It is more likely that the other candidates will have found the exam difficult too. Do not forget that there is a competitive element in exams. As soon as you get up and leave the exam hall, forget the exam and think about the next - or , if it is the last one, celebrate!

Do not discuss an exam with other candidates. This is particularly the case if you still have other exams to sit. Put it out of your mind until the day of the results. Forget about exams and relax.

1

THE NATURE OF RISK

Objectives

After studying this unit, you should be able to:

- relate the ideas incorporated in the meaning of risk;

- clarify the concept of risk using various criteria;

- state the extent of risk in various areas (for example at work, crime, bad accidents, fire);

- describe the basic components of risk management (that is identification, analysis, control).

1.1   Introduction

The starting point for any course on insurance must be the concept of **risk** itself and our understanding of it. What exactly is meant by the word risk? The word is certainly used frequently in everyday conversation and seems to be well understood by those using it.

To most people, risk implies some form of uncertainty about an outcome in a given situation. An event might occur and if it does, the outcome is not favourable to us; it is not an outcome we look forward to. The word risk implies both doubt about the future, and the fact that the outcome could leave us in a worse position than we are in at the moment.

It is interesting to contrast this with the use of the word **chance**. Chance also implies some doubt about the outcome in a given situation, the difference is that the outcome is normally a favourable outcome. We talk about the **risk** of an accident, the **risk** of losing our job, but we talk about the **chance** of winning a bet, the **chance** of passing an examination.

For many people the analysis of what we mean by **risk** stops there. In fact we have probably gone beyond the level of thought which most people give to the word. However, as students of risk and insurance, and practitioners in the insurance marketplace, we cannot be content with this relatively brief analysis of the concept.

Our understanding of the word is made more difficult by the variety of ways in which it is used in the world of risk management and insurance. Throughout this text and in common business conversations, we will come across the word risk used to mean different things. For example:

Risk as the cause

We use the word risk to refer to the cause of an outcome. In this way we speak about fire as a risk, theft as a risk, personal injury as a risk. We may use the phrase 'the risk of fire', meaning the risk of fire damage but we are still referring to potential causes.

Risk as the likelihood

We often talk about 'the risk of something happening', meaning the probability or likelihood of it occurring. We sometimes modify this by referring to a high or low risk of some event. Leaving the keys in a car results in a high risk of theft, locking the car in a garage results in a lower risk of theft. The implication is that there are levels of risk, degrees of likelihood.

Risk as the object

When we talk about 'going to see a risk' we do not mean that we are going to look at a storm. In this context we mean the object or person at risk. The factory, plane, machine or ship might be referred to as the risk and we might send someone to look at it.

Risk as loss

Taking a risk does not mean that we are going to take a fire or storm, or take a ship or a factory. What we mean in these cases is that we place ourselves in a situation or position where there is some doubt about the future outcome.

Risk as a verb

Finally, we use the word risk not only as a noun but also as a verb. We might risk crossing the road between traffic lights or risk investing some money in a new venture. This is the act of positively placing oneself in a situation where a loss could occur.

This is all part of the jargon of the world of risk and insurance and shows how the use of the word goes far beyond its use in everyday language.

1.2   The Meaning of Risk

Writers, particularly in the USA, have produced a number of definitions of risk. These are usually accompanied by lengthy arguments to support the particular view they put forward.

Consider some of these definitions:

- risk is the possibility of an unfortunate occurrence;
- risk is a combination of hazards;
- risk is unpredictability - the tendency that actual results may differ from predicted results;
- risk is uncertainty of loss;
- risk is the possibility of loss.

Given the brief discussion we have had on the nature and use of the word risk, we can imagine that academics and others have found considerable scope for intellectual discussion.

However, looking at the definitions there does seem to emerge some kind of common thread running through each of them. Firstly, there is the underlying idea of uncertainty, what we have referred to as doubt about the future. Secondly, there is the implication that there are differing levels or degrees of risk. The use of words such as **possibility** and **unpredictability**, does seem to indicate some measure of variability in the effect of this doubt. Thirdly, there is the idea of a result having been brought about by a cause or causes. This does seem to tie in nicely with the working definition we used earlier of **uncertainty about the outcome in a given situation**.

The value of having a single definition is questionable, because it is likely to be limited in its ability to capture the comprehensive flavour of risk. It is more valuable to dissect the idea of risk and consider its component parts.

We shall look at the three common threads that we have detected. In doing this we may be able to move towards a more comprehensive and practical understanding of the meaning and nature of risk than would be the case if we stuck rigidly to one or two definitions.

Uncertainty

We have used the word uncertainty several times already. In our first attempt at a working definition of risk, we said that it was uncertainty about the outcome in a given situation. Uncertainty is at the very core of the concept of risk itself, but are we clear what we mean by it when we use the word?

We could take the rather philosophical view and say that uncertainty is, like beauty, in the eye of the beholder. We could go a step further than this and say that there is no real uncertainty in the natural order of things in our world. This point is worth exploring a little further as part of our consideration of the nature of risk.

An argument can be put which says that there is no uncertainty, that it does not exist in the natural order of things. You may well respond to this by saying that there are a number of outcomes that are uncertain. For example, the weather for the Test Match, the possibility of being made redundant, the risk of having an accident. There is surely uncertainty surrounding all of these events - or is there?

We may say that there is a risk of rain, a risk of being made redundant or a risk of being in an accident. We use the phrase almost suggesting that the event may or may not happen. The fact is that the event will or will not occur, there is no doubt about that. What we are really expressing is the fact that **we** have some doubt as to whether the event will occur or not. We have **imperfect information about the future**, and this imperfection in our knowledge is what leads to the doubt and hence to the uncertainty which we express.

This rather places the idea of uncertainty, and consequently risk, with the individual and supports the view that uncertainty is in the eye of the beholder. However, we must be careful not to go too far down that road. Are we to say that uncertainty exists only when an individual recognizes that he has some doubt about the future? To say that risk and uncertainty exist only when they are recognized by an individual would discount certain situations where we would all agree uncertainty was present, even if not recognized by anyone.

Consider a child playing in the middle of a busy road; a workman using a machine while being unaware that it is faulty and dangerous; pedestrians unaware that a wall running alongside a pavement is in a dangerous condition and about to collapse. In each of these situations there is an element of risk and uncertainty. The child may escape free of injury, the machine may hold out until the workman has finished using it and the wall may not collapse and injure passers-by. Alternatively, there could be serious injury in each case.

The people involved in each of these examples are unaware of the uncertainty, but does this mean that there is no uncertainty? Most people would agree that uncertainty is present, even if it is not recognized by the people who could be affected. We conclude that uncertainty can exist in the abstract, it is not dependent on being **recognized** as existing by those who may be most directly involved. Uncertainty is linked more to the event itself rather than to any personal perception of the existence of uncertainty.

Now, can we go as far as to say that uncertainty exists even when there is no possibility of personal involvement? If the wall we mentioned earlier is on a deserted island, is there still uncertainty, is this a risky situation? The difference of course is that nobody can be injured. There is no **potential** for an unfortunate outcome and this is probably the important point. Under such circumstances it is hard to argue that uncertainty exists.

To bring this philosophical discussion to some conclusion, we could say that the concept of uncertainty implies doubt about the future based on a lack of knowledge, or imperfection in knowledge. Uncertainty exists regardless of whether this doubt has been recognized by those who may be most directly involved.

The reason for looking at uncertainty was that it formed one of the components of the concept of risk. Going back to the broader idea of risk, and using our understanding of uncertainty, we could say that the basis of risk is lack of knowledge, regardless of whether the state of lack of knowledge is recognized. If we always knew what was going to happen there would be no risk. We would know for certain if our house was to burn down this year, if we were to have an accident, if the burglars were to select our house, if our car was to be stolen, and so on. We do not have this knowledge and hence operate in an uncertain or risky environment.

We can therefore say that risk exists outside the individual; it may be recognized as existing but this is not a prerequisite. In this sense it is objective and not dependent on any one individual. People often do in fact place their own subjective assessments on the existence and level of risk in given situations.

Level of Risk

The second component of risk is the idea that there are different levels of risk. We cannot make the assumption that all risks are equally likely to occur: some will be more or less **risky** than others. What exactly do we mean when we use the word 'risky'? What do levels of risk mean?

Consider an example: There is a house by the side of a river which is known for a tendency to overflow its banks. We might use the word risky to describe this situation. There is doubt about the future outcome, there is uncertainty about whether or not the river will flood and cause damage to the house. The fact that the river is known for flooding has heightened the prospect that damage will occur, in fact we may say that the frequency of damage will be high. We use the term risky to denote this heightened possibility.

We can see this clearly if we imagine a second house, which is farther from the river bank and on a slight hill. This second house would be described as being in a less risky situation. The prospect of the river flooding its banks has not altered in any way, but the possibility of damage being caused to the house as a result is much lower.

However, our judgement may alter by considering the value which is at risk. Let us say that the first house, on the river bank, is a holiday home rarely used and in a poor state of repair, with a value of no more than £5,000. The second house, on the other hand, is a luxury house valued at more than £200,000. We might want to modify our view about which house represents the higher risk, in view of the higher potential severity.

This example highlights two important concepts in the consideration of the level of risk, and we will look at each in turn.

Frequency and severity

We must recognize that risk is a combination of the likelihood of an event and the severity should the event occur. In the example of the two houses, we can see that the frequency of damage by flooding will be higher for the house on the bank of the river than for the house on the hill. However, the severity of damage, should a flood occur, will be higher for the second in view of its higher value.

When we turn to the measurement of risk, in later units, we shall see that the distinction between frequency and severity of risk is important from an insurance point of view. The reason for this can be illustrated by thinking back to the idea of uncertainty and lack of knowledge about the future. If an event has occurred often in the past, then our knowledge about the future begins to increase and an element of certainty begins to creep in.

Shop-lifting is an example of this kind of high frequency risk. In many shops there will be a high incidence of shop-lifting. The risk is predictable in the sense that the owners of the shop know that a certain volume of goods will be stolen each year and hence the uncertainty has been reduced by the frequency of the event. An insurance company can predict events more accurately, if the frequency of occurrence is high. This means that the premium they charge is more likely to be accurate than if the event was very rare. The individual running the risk must decide if insurance is the best mechanism for financing the potential losses. He may be better advised to meet the cost of the risk himself rather than insure. This may seem strange, but if the risk is predictable the insurance company will have to charge a premium that is sufficient to cover the expected losses and make provision for profit and expenses. The individual would be better to put aside money to meet these almost inevitable losses when they occur, and in this way avoid paying the expenses and profit of the insurance company.

These decisions about insurance could almost be taken in isolation of the severity of individual events, but when we combine frequency and severity we find two relationships that predominate:

● High frequency, low severity.

● Low frequency, high severity.

High frequency, low severity

Figure 1.1 illustrates the profile which many risk situations match.

Figure 1.1: High Frequency, Low Severity

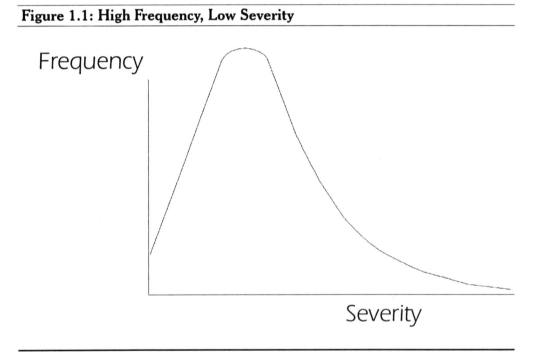

Using fire insurance as an example, there will be a large number of small fires and relatively few large ones. A person may be willing to fund losses which are frequent and not too severe, but is unlikely to consider doing the same for rare events which have the potential for very high costs.

Industrial injury incidents follow a very similar pattern, which is illustrated by Figure 1.2.

Figure 1.2: the Heinrich Triangle

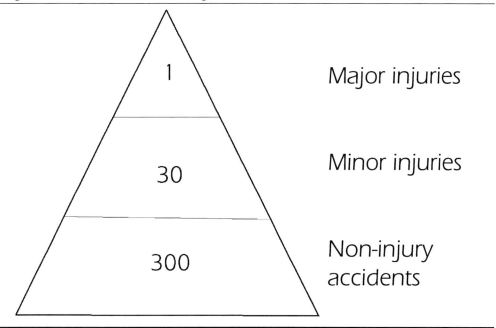

This shows that for every one major injury at work, there are 30 minor injuries and 300 non-injury accidents.

Low frequency, high severity

This profile is illustrated in Figure 1.3.

Figure 1.3: Low Frequency, High Severity

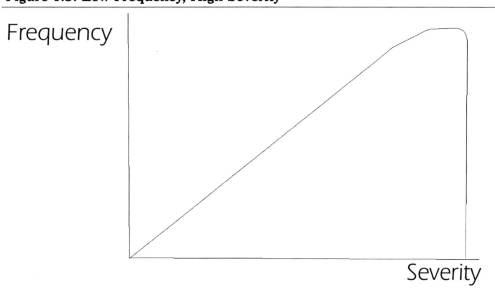

The total number of events will not be as high as in Figure 1.1, but when they occur they will result in very large costs. Accidents involving ships and planes are good examples because, should a loss occur, the cost will be substantial.

Utility

When we introduced the idea of levels of risk we said that there were two aspects which merited consideration. We dealt with the first when we looked at frequency and severity, and now turn to the second issue. This relates more to the measure of risk to which an individual is exposed. We have looked at the number of times an event may occur and the cost should it occur, but we dealt with them as independent components of risk. Utility theory attempts to represent the probability of loss and the cost of loss in the one measurement.

The value that a person attaches to a risky situation is a function of the probability of the loss occurring and the severity should it occur. The point which utility theory stresses is that this cannot be viewed in isolation from the aggregate wealth of the person. For example a person who possesses only £10 would view the risk of losing £8 as extremely serious, whereas a millionaire would not think twice about a potential loss of such a small amount. (There will be some who may argue that the person is a millionaire precisely because he did bother about small amounts!) Even where the probability of losing the £8 is extremely low, the first person would still consider the venture to be very risky in the light of the combination of frequency, severity and his total wealth.

Think back to the problem of the two houses for a moment. We used this example to illustrate the idea that there is both a frequency and severity dimension when we use the word risk. Consider now that the £5,000 house is owned by a man with total assets of only £6,000; the loss of the house would represent financial ruin. Even if it was sited up the hill, farther from the river, the owner might still consider the risk of flood damage to be high. On the other hand, imagine that the £200,000 house is owned by a multimillionaire with 50 houses and several million pounds in the bank. The loss of £200,000 would be serious, but in relative terms it would be much less important then the loss of £5,000 would be to the first person.

Peril and Hazard

We have looked at the notion of uncertainty, the fact that there are different levels of risk, and the final component of risk we will look at is the cause of the eventual loss.

We often use the word risk to mean both the event that will give rise to some loss and the factors that may influence the outcome of a loss. When we think about cause we must be clear that there are at least these two aspects to it. We can see this if we think back to the two houses on the river bank and the risk of flood. The risk of flood does not really make sense, what we mean is the risk of flood damage. Flood is the cause of the loss and the fact that one of the houses was right on the bank of the river influences the outcome.

Flood is the **peril** and the proximity of the house to the river is the **hazard**. The **peril** is the prime cause, it is what will give rise to the loss. Often it is beyond the control of anyone who may be involved. In this way we can say that storm, fire, theft, motor accident and explosion are all perils.

Factors that may influence the outcome are referred to as **hazards**. These hazards are not themselves the cause of the loss, but they can increase or decrease the effect should a peril operate. The consideration of hazard is important when an insurance company is deciding whether or not it should insure some risk and what premium to charge.

Hazard can be **physical** or **moral**. **Physical hazard** relates to the physical characteristics of the risk, such as the nature of construction of a building, security protection at a shop or factory, or the proximity of houses to a river bank. **Moral hazard** concerns the human aspects that may influence the outcome. This usually refers to the attitude of the insured person.

We shall leave the study of the concept of risk itself at this point and move on to examine some of the various classifications of risk.

1.3   Classifications of Risk

We turn our attention now to the classifications into which risk can be placed. This is different from scrutinizing the actual idea of risk; we are now looking at the whole concept of risk and grouping together similar classes of risk. Of the many classifications, we shall look at three:

- financial and non-financial risk;

- pure and speculative risks;

- fundamental and particular risks.

Financial and Non-financial Risk
Financial risk
Outcome can be measured in monetary terms.

Non-financial risk
Measurement in monetary terms is not possible.

We have already said that risk implies a situation where there is uncertainty about the outcome. A financial risk is one where the outcome can be measured in monetary terms.

This is easy to see in the case of material damage to property, theft of property or loss of business profit following a fire. In cases of personal injury, it can also be possible to measure financial loss - by a court when damages are awarded, or as a result of negotiation between lawyers and insurers. In any of these cases the outcome of the risky situation can be measured financially.

There are other situations where this kind of measurement is not possible. Take the case of the choice of a new car or the selection of an item from a restaurant menu. These could be construed as risky situations, not because the outcome will cause financial loss, but because the outcome could be uncomfortable or disliked in some other way. We could even go as far as to say that the great social decisions of life are examples of non-financial risks: the selection of a career, the choice of a marriage partner, having children. There may or may not be financial implications, but in the main the outcome is not measurable financially but by other, more human, criteria.

In the world of business we are primarily concerned with risks that have a financially measurable outcome.

Pure and Speculative Risks

The second risk classification also concerns the outcome. It distinguishes between those situations where there is only the possibility of loss and those where a gain may also result.

Pure risk

Loss or break-even situation.

Speculative risk

Loss, break-even or gain.

Pure risks involve a loss or, at best, a break-even situation. The outcome can only be unfavourable to us or leave us in the same position as we enjoyed before the event occurred. The risk of a motor accident, fire at a factory, theft of goods from a store, injury at work are all pure risks with no element of gain.

The alternative to this is **speculative risk**, where there is the chance of gain. Investing money in shares is a good example. The investment may result in a loss or possibly a break-even position, but the reason it was made was the prospect of gain.

In the world of business there are both pure and speculative risks. Take the case of a food manufacturer. He has a large factory with sophisticated machinery and production lines. He produces a range of foodstuffs for both the home and export markets.

Pure risks:

- there is the whole range of material damage to the factory, machinery and stock. This could be by fire, storm, explosion, malicious damage or any other peril;

- he is also exposed to the risk of theft. This includes theft of the finished stock, the raw materials and even the machinery in the factory. A person does not have to work long in the risk and insurance industry to discover that there is no limit to the ingenuity of the determined criminal;

- liability also poses a potential threat. He may find himself liable to employees at work or visitors to the plant, who may be injured or have property damaged. As a food manufacturer he may also be liable to any consumer who is injured or otherwise suffers as a result of eating one of his products;

- should the factory be damaged by fire, there is the inevitable interruption in the business and the consequential loss of profit;

- as a food manufacturer he is also exposed to the risk of his products being tampered with in some criminal way. There have been a number of cases of this over recent years;

- machinery upon which he depends may break down and take some time to repair or replace. This will involve the cost of repair and a loss of production.

Speculative risks:
- the pricing of the products. The risk being that a wrong price may either render the products uncompetitive or not yield a sufficiently high return to the company. The price is intended to result in a gain for the company;

- marketing decisions all carry a speculative risk. An incorrect interpretation of market needs may cause a loss but a correct decision could be very profitable;

- any decision on diversification, expansion or acquisition could result in substantial gains for the company. They may also, however, cause losses;

- providing credit to customers can be a risky venture. The goods have been sold in the hope of gain, but the customer may not be in a position to pay and the end result is a loss.

These are often referred to as the risks of business.

Looking at these two lists, it is a wonder that anyone should want to be in business in the first place. It may seem that placing his money in a building society or bank would be far less stressful for the factory owner. However, the world of business is a world of risk and uncertainty, and this is the reason why profit can be made. If the result of all business ventures or decisions was certain then there would be little scope for one competitor having an edge over another and taking risks would be impossible. The existence of risk separates the sound from the unsound and in the end is for the benefit of the consumer.

The reason for stressing the difference between pure and speculative risks is to highlight the fact that pure risks are normally insurable whereas speculative risks are not. It is difficult to be dogmatic about this, because practice is changing and the division between pure and speculative is becoming more blurred as time passes. Take the case of the credit risk which we listed under the heading of speculative risks. The goods have been sold on credit in the hope that a gain will result, but a form of credit insurance is available which will meet some of the consequences should the debtor default.

However, insurance is not normally available for those risks where the outcome can be a gain and it is easy to see why this should be so. Speculative risks are entered into voluntarily in the hope that there will be gain. There would be very little incentive to work towards achieving that gain if it was known that an insurance company would pay up regardless of the effort expended by the individual. Using the terminology of hazard, we could say that there would be a very high risk of moral hazard.

However, we should be clear that the pure risk consequences of speculative risks can be insured and that more and more people involved in risk and insurance are being asked to handle speculative risks.

Fundamental and Particular Risks

Fundamental

Impersonal in origin; widespread in effect.

Particular

Personal in both cause and effect.

The final classification relates to both the cause and effect of risk. **Fundamental risks** are those that arise from causes outside the control of any one individual or even a group of individuals. In addition, the effect of fundamental risks is felt by large numbers of people. This classification would include earthquakes, floods, famine, volcanoes and other natural 'disasters'. However it would not be accurate to limit fundamental risk to naturally occurring perils. Social change, political intervention and war are all capable of being interpreted as fundamental risks.

In contrast to this form of risk, which is impersonal in origin and widespread in effect, we have **particular risks**. Particular risks are much more personal both in their cause and effect. This would include many of the risks we have already mentioned such as fire, theft, work related injury and motor accidents. All of these risks arise from individual causes and affect individuals in their consequences.

What is interesting is the way in which risks can change classification. This does support the view that risk is a dynamic concept and that our view of it can be modified as time passes. Much of this movement in classification has been from particular to fundamental.

Unemployment was regarded as a particular risk for much of the early part of this century; there was almost the implication that being unemployed was the fault of the individual. However, the technological unemployment of the 1970s and 1980s has changed that view, and we now talk about people suffering unemployment. As a consequence of changes in our industrial and commercial world, the emphasis has moved away from the individual to society as a whole. The evidence of this is seen in the financial provision made for those who are unemployed, in almost all industrialized countries.

A similar move has taken place concerning injury in motor accidents, injury at work and injury caused by faulty products. In each of these cases society has decided that those who are injured should be able to receive financial compensation. It does this by passing legislation which ensures either that suitable insurance is in force, or that those who are injured need not have the burden of proving fault.

In the main, particular risks are insurable whereas fundamental risks are not, but it is difficult to generalize because views in the insurance marketplace change from time to time. We could say that fundamental risks are normally so uncontrollable, widespread and indiscriminate that it is felt they should be the responsibility of society as a whole. The geographical factor is often important, particularly for natural hazards such as flood and earthquake. In many parts of the world these risks would be regarded as fundamental and not insurable, but in the United Kingdom they are insurable.

The discussion up to this point has been intended to give a rounded view of the nature of the concept of risk itself. It may have seemed rather philosophical at times but it has been useful to explore ideas rather than simply accept definitions. We now move on to the much more practical and objective question of the cost of risk.

1.4   The Cost of Risk

We can look at the cost of risk from a number of different perspectives. Among these are:

- frequency of risk;

- monetary cost or financial severity;

- human cost in terms of pain and suffering.

There is no doubt at all that regardless of how we measure risk, it has had a significant impact on the personal and national life of very many countries. We can see this by looking back over the last 20 years, which could certainly be classed as the decades of disasters. During the 1980s and 1990s we had a number of incidents, the names of which have almost entered into the vocabulary of the world. Names such as:

> *Bhopal, Chernobyl, Kings Cross, Amoco Cadiz, The Challenger Space Shuttle, Hillsborough, Mexico City, Exxon Valdez, Bradford City, Manchester Airport, Zeebrugge, Heysel Stadium, Clapham, Armenia, Lockerbie, San Francisco, Piper Alpha, Kobe, Kegworth.*

These were major risks which certainly hit the headlines when they occurred. However, they are very much the tip of the risk iceberg: there will be very many less serious events for each major incident. It is on this main thrust of risk that most people in the risk and insurance business will spend their time, not events such as those we have listed above. As an example let us look at fire insurance.

Fire

The risk of fire is of major concern not only to private individuals but also to those involved in industry. The total cost of domestic and commercial property claims paid by UK insurers in 1993 was £2,426 million. Of this, £223 million was in respect of domestic fires, and £423 million in respect of commercial fire claims. (Source: *ABI Statistics & Research Review*, January 1995.)

The total figure is reported in the ABI Insurance Statistics booklet with the warning that the figure does not include '. . . losses to the economy caused by disruption of business and employment, lost overseas markets and lost production'. It is impossible to build a full picture of the cost of the fire risk but it will clearly be very substantial indeed.

Student Activity 1

Before reading the next section of the text, answer the following questions and then check your answers against the pages indicated.

1.   Distinguish between peril and hazard.   *(page 8)*

2.   Distinguish between physical and moral hazard.   *(page 9)*

If your answers are basically correct, then proceed to the next section. If significant parts of your answers are wrong, then study the whole of the relevant sections again in detail. Note your areas of weakness, and be prepared for further questions on these areas in the self-assessment section at the end of this unit.

1.5   The Management of Risk

We have looked at the nature of risk, the various classifications into which it can be put and have also attempted to estimate the cost of certain risks. The concept which develops is one of risk as an all-pervasive force in the world: a negative feature in life bringing unfortunate, or unlooked for, outcomes. The various classifications we have used all tend to support the view that risk is to be avoided at all costs. It would be valuable to stop here for a moment and take stock of what this means. Are we to conclude that risk has no beneficial side to it? Is it solely a negative concept, implying loss and not gain? Has the world gained nothing from the existence of risk?

Medical research is in the same category. Many of the great steps forward in medicine have been achieved at the personal risk of those researchers who were prepared to test drugs and treatments on themselves.

There are many other examples in the social history of our world, where people have taken a stand at great personal risk. Suffragettes, prison reformers, emancipation of slavery campaigners, trade unionists and others have all had an impact on our world and our understanding of civilization.

We could argue whether these various achievements are due to risk or to risk taking, but at the end of the day it was the existence of uncertainty, and the desire to overcome it, that has been important.

How can this be translated to the world of business? It enters into all aspects of business life, but does it have any beneficial function at all? One view which could be taken is that risk is at the very heart of any free market economy. Risk enables wealth to be created. It does this in a number of ways:

● it creates the hope for profit. Entrepreneurs are encouraged to take risks of all kinds, in the hope that the reward will be higher than they could achieve by choosing a safer option. Often, this risk-taking will be wealth-creating in the form of employment, goods, services, investment;

● risk is a bar to entry into the marketplace for ventures that are unsound, or likely to be shortlived. The cost of risk will be viewed as too high and potential players in the risk marketplace will look elsewhere for a return. The result should be a more competitive marketplace, which is to the benefit of the consumer and the national economy;

● risk encourages a safety culture. This means safety in its widest sense and includes employees, consumers, the public and the environment. Those who operate in the marketplace cannot afford to run too high a risk.

All these points suggest a slightly more positive side to risk-taking, but we should modify this by including a form of 'Health Warning: Risks can be positive or negative!'. That is, businesses exist in part because there is risk, but this risk can be their downfall. The answer must be to manage the risks to which the business is exposed.

Risk and uncertainty are familiar concepts to those involved in business. Business people are used to dealing with the speculative forms of business risk and we saw some of them when we listed risks for the food manufacturer earlier. Techniques have been developed to manage the risks associated with investing, marketing, offering credit, research and development. However, there is much less experience in responding to the pure risks associated with business, or to those risks which do not neatly fall into one category or another. Over the past few decades we have seen a steady move towards a more managerial response to these forms of risk. What has emerged is the discipline of risk management. We could define **risk management** as:

> *The identification, analysis and economic control of those risks that can threaten the assets or earning capacity of an enterprise.*

This definition is valuable because it highlights the structured approach which is called for if risks in the business environment are to be managed:

● The threefold nature of risk management is highlighted in the definition. Risks must be identified before they can be measured, and only after their impact has been evaluated can we decide on the most effective method of control.

- However we decide to control risk, it must be 'economic'. There is no point in spending £10 to control a risk which can only ever cost £5. There will always be a point where spending on risk control has to stop.

- The definition mentions the assets and earning capacity of an organization. These assets can be physical or human; they are both important, and risk management must be seen to have a part to play in both. However, risks do not only strike at assets directly and for this reason the definition also mentions the earning capacity of an enterprise.

- Finally, note that the definition uses the word 'enterprise' rather than a more restrictive word such as 'company' or 'manufacturer'. The principles of risk management are just as applicable in the service sector as they are in the manufacturing sector, and are of equal importance in the public and private sectors of the economy.

We shall work our way through the idea of risk management by taking each aspect of the definition, and considering it in more detail.

Risk Identification

When considering risk identification we must remember to take the broad view. We are not solely concerned with what can be insured, or even with what can be controlled. We start from the very basic question of:

> *'How can the assets or earning capacity of the enterprise be threatened?'*

Starting from this position does not place any constraint on us as to what kind of risks we are looking for. We must begin the task in an unblinkered manner, willing to identify the whole host of ways in which an organization may be impeded from achieving its objectives.

This is very much easier to say than to put into practice. At a theoretical level, it would be ideal if a gantry could be built above the open-roofed buildings which contain our company. If this were possible, then we would be able to walk along the gantry and see down into all the compartments that make up the organization. We would be able to identify what was done in each compartment, and how the process in one area might be potentially dangerous to the compartment next to it. We would be able to see how each section of the company interacted, where the points of possible conflict emerged, where concentrations of processes existed, and whether there were any dependencies. Not only would we be able to look down on our own company, we would also be able to look outside the plant itself and see the ways in which our activities could be a threat to the surrounding neighbourhood and hence a potential risk to us. We could also see if there was someone close by who was a potential threat to us.

If we could be up there on that gantry, we would see all forms of risk and not just those which we knew to be insurable, or those we had some experience of in the past. For example:

- The company which had been storing all its finished stock in one finished goods store would be able to see the problems that this would pose in the event of a fire or flood or some other form of loss or damage to stock.

- The company whose three production lines all depended on one packaging machine would be helped to see the unwise level of dependence inherent in the system.

- The company with several manufacturing plants, but with the production of its most profitable product limited to only one plant, would see the risks associated with this concentration of activity.

These examples may seem obvious, but they are all based on fact. What we would hope is that, by some form of rigorous risk identification, the whole spectrum of risk would open up before us.

This may be a fine idea but it is only theory! We can see the benefits, but how can they be achieved in reality? In the end we could say that there are at least two essentials if risk identification is to be effective:

Risk identification

Risk identification must be recognized as important within an enterprise and, when this is the case, it is often marked down as a task within the job description of a particular manager. Operating managers within organizations are busy on their own functions, which could be marketing, finance, production, sales, research and development, etc. They do not always have the time to consider, in great detail, the risks their endeavours may be causing. It could be argued that they should be managing risk as a daily part of their normal activities, but the history of major events shows that this is not the case.

In the mid-1970s there was a major explosion at a chemical works in Flixborough, which underlines this point very well. There were four chemical reactors in a row and each was joined by a pipe. When one of these reactors developed a fault, it was removed for repair and a dog-leg by-pass pipe was installed around the faulty pipe, in order that production could continue. However, a flange used to connect this dog-leg pipe was not strong enough and there was a serious explosion – at that time, one of the largest industrial disasters which had been experienced. One passage from the official enquiry into the explosion is relevant to the point we are stressing at the moment. It reads:

> *The key post of works engineer was vacant and none of the senior personnel, who were chemical engineers, were capable of recognizing the existence of what in essence was a simple engineering problem.*

One way to interpret this is to say that nobody had the specific job of risk identification. All the senior managers would be busy with their own jobs and no one was able to stand back and recognize a potential major risk.

Further evidence of this kind of problem was highlighted in the official report of the enquiry into the fire at Kings Cross underground station. Of the 157 recommendations in the report, about 70 refer to the system of managing safety. One extract illustrates this:

> *In truth, London underground had no system which permitted management or staff to identify and then promptly eliminate hazards.*

Taken together, these quotations seem to indicate that more than just good management is required if risks are to be identified. The government has stressed this same point in a consultative document issued by the Department of Energy, on formal safety assessments in the North Sea oil business, when they said:

> *. . . reliance on good engineering practice, the application of approved standards and the certification and inspection regimes do not of themselves comprehensively identify and highlight the hazards and consequences of events that can lead to a major hazard.*

This represents a very clear statement that the identification of risk is a management responsibility and has to be highlighted as such.

The people who carry out the task of risk identification in industry vary a great deal. There are risk managers who are employed by organizations to carry out the whole function of risk management, which includes the identification of risk as the first step. The professional association of risk managers, the Association of Risk and Insurance Managers in Industry and Commerce (AIRMIC), has several hundred members employed in this capacity. In other organizations there may be a reliance on insurers, brokers or risk management consultants to perform the task. The important thing is that it is done.

Industry sophistication

Because industry is becoming more and more sophisticated in its processes, materials and systems of production, it is no longer adequate to walk round a factory, or other plant, and hope to see all the risks. The person responsible for risk identification must be armed with the relevant 'tools of the trade' and must make use of them. These techniques provide the risk manager with a powerful weapon in the struggle towards identifying the risks to which organizations are exposed.

Risk Analysis

The second aspect of our definition of risk management related to the analysis of risk. Once it has been identified that there is a risk, then steps have to be taken to measure the potential impact of that risk on the organization. This leads us into the area of statistical analysis and Units 4, 5, 6 and 7 are devoted to the measurement of risk in various ways.

In a practical sense the measurement of risk starts with the gathering of information, followed by the analysis of past experience, and then moves on to look at what the data tell us about the level of frequency and/or severity of risk to which an organization is exposed. There is a need for accuracy and relevance at each stage and, above all, it is necessary to ensure that the results make sense and can be understood. There is an element of scepticism about the use of statistics and much of this is due to badly presented findings.

Risk Control

The final step in the process is that of risk control. After the risk has been identified and it has been established that it is important enough to be controlled, what can be done? The first thing to say is that the emphasis must be on economic control. There is little point in spending £100 to control a risk which, even in the worst situation, can cost the organization only £75. There can be a tendency to want to spend an unrealistic amount on risk control. There will be a point at which the next pound spent will actually not enhance the profit of the company at all. In fact it may even begin to be a net cost.

Clearly, any amount spent on risk control is intended to add to the profitability of the organization. This may well be the case for low to medium expenditure on risk control. However, once expenditure exceeds a certain amount, the marginal effect on profit may begin to level off and eventually the effect is negative. The logical result, if the company continues to spend money on risk control, is that it will go out of business.

Some people may argue that it is worth spending more and more money, especially where human life is concerned or potential damage to the environment. But even in these cases there will be a break-even point. We may not like to think about risk control in these terms, but it is realistic.

Even individuals have their own break-even point as far as risk control is concerned. Take the example of safety in air travel, particularly safety from terrorist attack. We could eliminate the risk of bombs being carried on to planes in passengers' luggage by not allowing any luggage on planes at all. This would clearly be unacceptable to most people and so we have a kind of break-even point. We all make these judgements and industry must do the same. Figure 1.4 illustrates the possibilities for risk control.

Figure 1.4: Risk Control

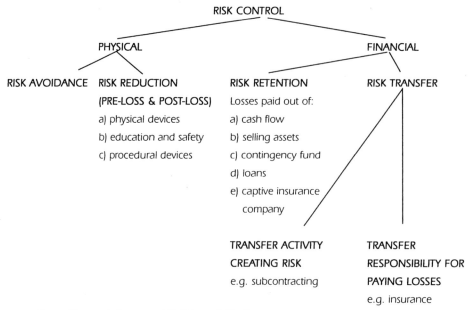

Source:'Success in Insurance,' S. Diacon & R. Carter

Physical aspects of risk control

We are concerned here with physical steps which can be taken in order to control risk. The first step must be to reduce the level of the risk as far as is possible. This means both the chance that something will happen and the severity of the incident, should it occur. There are at least two ways in which we could look at risk reduction.

Pre-loss risk reduction

It is possible to take steps before any event has occurred to minimize risk. The essence of pre-loss reduction of risk is that the effects of the loss are anticipated and steps are taken to ensure that they are kept to a minimum.

Wearing a car seatbelt is a good, personal example of this. There has been no loss but the possible effect of a loss has been anticipated and the pre-loss risk reduction step of wearing a belt has been taken.

The use of safety guards on machinery is an industrial equivalent. There has been no injury, but steps have been taken to reduce the risk of injury.

When we look at the actual transaction of insurance, we will see that the insurance industry does play a role in alerting industry to the most effective forms of risk control.

Post-loss risk control

This form of risk control imagines that the risk has occurred and takes steps to minimize the effect of the loss. The use of automatic fire sprinkler systems fits into this category. Once the fire has started, the sprinklers operate to reduce the impact of the fire.

A more recent development in seeking to minimize the potential loss from a risk is that of disaster recovery planning, which many companies have instigated following the explosion in the City of London in 1992.

Financial risk control

We now turn our attention to financial mechanisms that can be used to control risk. These can be divided into two.

Risk retention

Once the risk has been identified and controlled in some physical way, it will be necessary to consider how the effects are to be financed, should the worst happen.

In certain situations, it may be wise to retain the risk rather than to seek some other form of protection, such as insurance. We have already mentioned the problems associated with insuring high frequency, low severity events and they certainly fall into the self-retention category. The cost of these events could be paid for out of current income and passed on to the customer via the price of the product (or service) which is offered by the organization. Alternatively a fund could be established out of which the losses are to be paid.

Either way, it may not be wise to purchase insurance protection where the losses are reasonably likely to occur. If the organization knows that they will occur, then so will the insurer and the insurer will need to cover expenses in addition to the cost of the losses.

Retaining risk does give organizations a very great incentive to be vigilant in their risk management. They will be able to see a direct relationship between their risk management activity and the eventual cost of risk.

Risk transfer

Alternatively, an organization can transfer the financial effect of the risk to some other party. An example of this would be where a landlord has written into a lease that a tenant is responsible for the risk of damage to the property by fire. However, by far the most common form of risk transfer is that of insurance.

Insurance is a risk transfer mechanism, by which an organization can exchange its uncertainty for certainty. The uncertainty experienced would include whether a loss will occur, when it will take place, how severe it will be and how many there might be in a year. This uncertainty makes it very difficult to budget and so the organization seeks ways of controlling the financial effect of the risk. Insurance offers the opportunity to exchange this uncertain loss for a certain loss; the insurance premium. The organization agrees to pay a fixed premium and, in return, the insurance company agrees to meet any losses that fall within the terms of the policy. This is a risk transfer mechanism and one which is of immense value not only to industry, but also to individuals.

Student Activity 2

Before reading the next section of the text, answer the following questions and then check your answers against the pages indicated.

1.   Give an example of pre-loss risk reduction. *(page 20)*

2.   Give an example of risk transfer other than insurance. *(page 21)*

If your answers are basically correct, then proceed to the Summary. If significant parts of your answers are wrong, then study the whole of the relevant sections again in detail. Note your areas of weakness, and be prepared for further questions on these areas in the self-assessment section at the end of this unit.

Summary

In this unit we have introduced the concept of risk and considered what we mean by it. We have looked at various classifications of risk, in particular identifying those that might be unsurpassable; and by looking at some statistics, we have attempted to place risk in perspective in terms of the economy as a whole.

Finally, we have had a very brief look at risk management.

Self-assessment Questions

Short Answer Questions

1.   Define risk management.

2.   Give an example of a high-frequency low-severity risk.

3.   Give an example of a low-frequency high-severity risk.

4.   What is a pure risk?

5.   What type of risk is a famine?

6.   Give the full name of AIRMIC.

7.   Identify the purpose of a captive insurance company.

8.   What kind of mechanism is insurance?

(Answers given in Appendix 1)

Specimen Examination Question

Discuss the ways in which a risk management strategy, including insurance, will help to secure a business and increase profitability.

(Answer given in Appendix 1)

2

INTRODUCTION TO INSURANCE

Objectives

After studying this unit, you should be able to:

- state the primary function of insurance and how it is achieved;

- explain the benefits of insurance enjoyed by individuals, companies and the country as a whole;

- identify those risks that are insurable and those that are not;

- outline the history of the various classes of insurance, and the common features in their development;

- describe the main classes of insurance that are currently available and the cover provided within each.

2.1   The Functions of Insurance

Let us start by looking at the main functions of insurance and then move on to examine the benefits that can be derived from performing these functions. We can do this by answering the questions: What is the role of insurance? What function does it perform?

We all have some basic notion of how insurance works: a person pays a premium at the beginning of a year and can make a claim if certain events occur. This is true for individuals insuring their private houses at one end of the scale, up to airlines insuring Jumbo jets at the other. Later units will look in some detail at the actual transacting of insurance, but why do we have this service called **insurance** in the first place? We might think we know **how** it works, but **why** does it exist?

Risk Transfer

The primary function of insurance is to act as a risk transfer mechanism. We can see this by considering two examples, the individual and the industrial buyer:

- Think of a car owner. He has a car valued at £12,000, which probably represents one of the largest investments he is ever likely to make. A considerable amount of his savings has been invested in its purchase and even the least risk conscious person would recognize that they are at risk in such a situation. The car could be stolen, damaged in an accident or catch fire. There could be an accident, resulting in serious injury to passengers or other people. How will the owner of the car cope with all of these potential risks and their financial consequences? He has no knowledge of whether or not any of them will materialize and, if they do, what the cost is likely to be. He could get to the end of the year completely free of incident or his car could be totally destroyed tomorrow! Insurance will not, in itself, prevent any of the above risks from occurring but what it will do is provide some form of financial security. The owner of the car can transfer the financial consequences of the risk to the insurer, in return for paying a premium.

● Industry is in exactly the same position. The managing director of a company knows that his firm is exposed to a whole range of risks; we have looked at many of them in the previous unit. He does not know if any of them will materialize and, if they do, what the cost is likely to be. How will he be able to manage his business? If he has a loss of some kind, he will have to recover the cost from his customers by increasing the price of the product he manufactures, or the service he provides. What cost will he pass on? He has no idea whether he will have a loss or not, or the cost of any loss that might occur. The function that insurance performs in this situation is to be a risk transfer mechanism.

The managing director can exchange his uncertainty for certainty. In return for a definite loss, which is the premium, he is relieved from the uncertainty of a potentially much larger loss. The risks themselves are not removed, but the financial consequences of some are now known with greater certainty and he can budget accordingly.

A whole range of benefits flow from this primary function of risk transfer and these are detailed in Section 2.2. Before moving on to examine each one in detail, there are two other functions we should look at: the common pool and equitable premiums. In one sense, we could say that the common pool and equitable premiums represent the way in which the main function of risk transfer is provided. However, the provision of a risk transfer mechanism could be made without the need for either a common pool or equitable premiums, and so they are functions in their own right.

Creation of the Common Pool

In the early days of marine insurance, the various merchants who were having goods carried on a ship would agree to make contributions to those who may have suffered a loss during the voyage, after the loss had taken place. This certainly removed the risk of a total loss from any one merchant, because each one knew that his loss would be shared. What it did not do was to give the merchant any idea of what his loss would be; he knew this only after a voyage. If there had been no losses then he would have nothing to pay, he had agreed to share in any losses which had taken place and the exact amount of these could be determined only after the event.

This was not an entirely satisfactory state of affairs. It would have been far better to know what your share of the loss was going to be, before it took place. This may seem a strange thing to say. How can we calculate the amount of a loss before it takes place? This is where the common pool comes in. The difficulty for any one person is that he can only guess what the future holds in terms of losses. The owner of a £50,000 house does not know if he will have a loss during any one year and, if he does, what it will cost. He could put aside a few hundred pounds in a special bank account to prepare for a loss, but that loss could be several thousand pounds, the complete destruction of the house or nothing at all. However it would be different if he could get together with other people in the same situation.

In order to demonstrate this point, and the function of the common pool, let us concentrate on the risk of his house being totally destroyed and say that there is a one in a thousand chance that this will happen during the year. We could have obtained this figure from past experience of similar houses, or from consulting publicly available statistics. To an individual home owner, this knowledge that one in every thousand houses will be destroyed has no great value; but if we consider a large number of houses, it does begin to mean something. For example if there were one thousand similar houses, then we could say that one of them will probably be destroyed during the year. (This is the one in a thousand chance of a house being totally destroyed.) On average, therefore, the expected total loss would amount to £50,000. Knowing this, the owners of the one thousand houses could all contribute at least £50 into a common pool, and there would then be enough to pay for the one loss.

To be realistic, we would have to say that there is no guarantee that there would only be one loss. This is what was expected, based on our calculations, but there could of course be more than one loss or even no loss. However, the principle remains the same: the losses of the few are met by the contributions of the many, and the mechanism which allowed this to happen was the common pool.

An insurance company sets itself up to operate such a pool. It takes contributions, in the form of insurance premiums, from many people and pays the losses of the few. The contributions have to be enough to meet the total losses in any one year and cover the other costs of operating the pool, including the profit of the insurer. Even after taking all these costs into account, insurance is still a very attractive proposition in very many cases.

In operating the common pool, the insurer benefits from the **law of large numbers**. This says that the actual number of events occurring will tend towards the expected number, where there is a large number of similar situations. This can be seen in a simple illustration with a coin. The flip of a coin could result in a head or a tail. Flipping a coin 20 times could result in any combination of heads and tails, we could get 12 heads and 8 tails, 9 heads and 11 tails, or any other split. On the simple mathematics of the situation we would expect to get the same number of heads and tails, because the chance of getting either one is 50%. However, flipping the coin only 20 times may not give us the result we expected. Had we flipped the coin 10,000 times we would almost certainly get something very, very close to 5,000 heads and 5,000 tails. The law of large numbers would have operated to give a result which was in keeping with the basic underlying probability.

Going back to the house insurance example, we can see the same law at work. The insurer can fairly confidently predict what the final total cost is likely to be in any one year, simply because a large number of similar events are insured and the final number of events will tend to be very close to the expected number. There are one thousand houses and the insurer expects only one of them to be totally destroyed. The cost of this will be £50,000, and a contribution will have to be made to the pool which will cover this expected loss and all the costs and profit of the insurer. The actual outcome in one year may vary from what is expected, but a small provision in the amount collected from each person insuring will take care of this.

The result is that the insurer can fix a premium and the person insuring knows, subject to the type of cover purchased, that he will not have to pay any more at the end of the year.

Equitable Premiums

It is clear that there can be several of these pools; one for each main type of risk. The people who have a house to insure would not contribute to the same pool as those insuring a car. Operating in this way allows an insurer to identify which types of insurance are profitable and which are not. In reality there may be some transferring of funds across the pools, but at this stage it is simpler for us to imagine individual pools for different types of risk.

Even when risks of a similar type are brought together in a common pool, they do not all represent the same degree of risk to the pool itself. That is, the probability of a loss having to be met by the pool is not equal over all those in the pool. For example, a timber-built house represents a different risk from one of standard brick construction; an 18-year-old driver, with a fast sports car, is quite a different risk from a 40-year-old married man, driving a family saloon; an employee using woodworking machinery is probably at greater risk of personal injury than someone who spends his working days in an office.

In each of these examples, the insurer was faced with risks of differing magnitude or hazard. The probability of an event occurring was quite different for each of the pairs, in the examples we quoted. This will have to be reflected in the contributions which each will make to the pool. It would not be equitable to expect the driver of the family saloon to subsidise those who choose to drive fast sports cars. Each person or company, wishing to join the pool, must be prepared to make an equitable contribution to that pool.

Hazard is not the only factor that is important. We could have risks that represent much the same hazard, but would still merit different contributions to the pool. This would happen where the value at risk was different. For example a person with a £250,000 house would have to pay more to the pool than someone with a £35,000 flat. This may seem fairly obvious, but it is still necessary to point it out at this stage. Value, in addition to hazard, plays its part in determining what contribution each risk must make to the pool.

Clearly the ideas of hazard and value are closely linked to frequency and severity. Each risk has the probability with which it occurs, its frequency or hazard. It also has the eventual cost should it occur, the severity or value, as we have termed it in this unit.

It can be seen that the assessment of risk is extremely important. The insurer has to ensure that a fair premium is charged, which reflects the hazard and the value which the person or company brings to the pool. This is a complex enough process, but in addition the premium must also be competitive. There is not just one insurer in the marketplace and hence competition enters into the calculation. If an insurer charge a premium which greatly exceeds that quoted by other insurers, then it will probably lose the business. Charging too little also has its dangers: the contributions to the pool would be less than required and a loss would be made. This loss would have to be recouped at some stage, possibly making the premiums uncompetitive at that time.

2.2   The Benefits of Insurance

The existence of a sound insurance market is an essential component of any successful economy and the proof of this can be seen in many parts of the world. The fact that insurance is much less talked about than other financial institutions (such as banks, merchant banks and building societies) is no reflection of its real importance. Many writers on economic history and the history of insurance comment on the link between a sound insurance market and industrial development. Mehr and Cammack, the American writers on insurance, observe in their book *Principles of Insurance* that the rise of Britain as a great trading nation and the fact that it had good fire insurance facilities during the same period, was no coincidence. The benefits, which prompted these and other writers to make such observations, are still obtainable and we shall look at a number in this section of Unit 2. There is no special significance attached to the order in which they are mentioned.

Peace of Mind

The knowledge that insurance exists to meet the financial consequences of certain risks provides a form of peace of mind. This is important for private individuals when they insure their car, house, possessions and so on, but it is also of vital importance in industry and commerce.

Why should a person put money into a business venture when there are so many risks that could result in the loss of the money? Yet, if people did not invest in businesses then there would be fewer jobs, less goods, the need for even higher imports and a general reduction in wealth. Buying insurance allows the entrepreneur to transfer at least some of the risks of being in business to an insurer, in the manner we have described earlier.

Insurance also acts as a stimulus for the activity of businesses that are already in existence. This is done through the release of funds for investment in the productive side of the business, which would otherwise have to be held in easily accessible reserves to cover any future loss. Medium-sized and larger firms could certainly create reserves for emergencies such as fires, thefts or serious injuries. However, this money would have to be accessible reasonably quickly and hence the rate of interest which the company could obtain would be much less than the normal rate. Quite apart from this is the fact that the money would not be available for investment in the business itself.

Because of the effects of the common pool, the business is able to purchase insurance at a premium which is less than the fund that the company itself would have to retain, even assuming it could retain anything in the first place. The premium can be looked upon as a certain loss to the business, but the firm is now free to continue its business and invest in the knowledge that certain risks are now provided for. With this peace of mind it can develop its business activities.

This peace of mind, or security, has become an important aspect of business activity in many sectors. As we shall see later in this unit, some forms of insurance are compulsory by law and others have to be in force under the terms of contracts. In the case of compulsory insurances, such as injury to employees at work, it is society that has decided it wants the security or peace of mind insurance brings. In the case of insurances being required to satisfy, for example, certain construction contracts, it is another business that wants to have the security of knowing that the people they are doing business with are protected by insurance.

Loss Control

Insurance is primarily concerned with the financial consequences of losses, but it would be fair to say that insurers have more than a passing interest in loss control. It could be argued that insurers have no real interest in the complete control of loss, because this would inevitably lead to an end to their business. This is a rather short-sighted view. Insurers do have an interest in reducing the frequency and severity of losses, not only to enhance their own profitability, but also to contribute to a general reduction in the economic waste that follows from losses. We looked at the cost of risk in Unit 1 and it would be fair to say that insurers have played a major role in loss control over the years. In the case of fire insurance, we can trace the involvement of insurers in loss control right back to the provision of fire brigades. In this instance, insurance companies provided the only form of fire fighting for many years and this is certainly evidence of an active interest in loss control. In modern times, the insurance industry pools its resources and funds ongoing research work into the prevention and control of many forms of loss. A number of individual insurance companies have developed considerable expertise in the technology of different forms of loss control and are regarded as being at the forefront of research in this field.

In a practical way, buyers of insurance normally come into contact with the loss control services offered by an insurer when they meet the surveyor. The surveyor may be employed by the insurer, or indeed the insurance broker, and part of his job is to give advice on loss control. Many insurers employ specialist surveyors in fire, security, liability and other types of risk; others employ people with broader, but less detailed, knowledge.

The surveyor will assess the extent of the risk to which the insurance company is exposed. In doing so he will also offer advice, which could take the form of pre-loss control (minimizing the chance that something will happen) or post-loss control (after an event has occurred).

The best time for a surveyor to be consulted is at the planning stage of a project. He can then incorporate features that may minimize risk and control loss. A good example of this is the installation of automatic fire-sprinkler systems. It is obviously far simpler and cheaper to include a sprinkler system in the design of a building, rather than to alter a building once it has been constructed to add sprinklers. Most builders are alert to the value of fire prevention and control, but the same principle applies to safety and security.

The surveyor's work is mainly at the commencement of insurances; the work of the loss adjuster comes when there has been a loss. The loss adjuster also forms part of the loss control service provided by the insurance industry. He is not employed by the insurer, but will be from an independent company of loss adjusters. The investigation of losses, their causes and values is often a highly technical and complex process, which requires very quick action after a loss in order to assess these factors accurately and to take steps to minimize further loss.

It would be uneconomic for insurers to have large teams of experts in various disciplines, scattered all around the country. Independent firms of adjusters provide loss-adjusting services on a fee basis to insurers. These adjusters contribute greatly to the minimization of losses, by knowing how best to get a business back on its feet after a loss, where to obtain temporary plant, which specialist builders or repairers to approach, where to dispose of salvage at the best price, and so on.

Social Benefits

The fact that the owner of a business has the funds available to recover from a loss provides the stimulus to business activity we noted earlier. It also means that jobs may not be lost and goods or services can still be sold. The social benefit of this is that people keep their jobs, their sources of income are maintained and they can continue to contribute to the national economy. We all know the effects on a community when a large employer moves or ceases operation; the area runs the risk of being depressed, people have less money to spend and the consequences can be far-reaching.

To a lesser extent, a major loss resulting in the closure of a business can have the same impact on a community. It may not be as noticeable as the shutdown of a coal mine or large factory, but when losses are aggregated throughout the country the effect is considerable. It is not suggested that insurance alone keeps people in jobs, but it does play a significant role in ensuring that there are not unnecessary economic hardships.

The three benefits that we have looked at all follow on from the protection offered by insurance. These benefits may be to the buyer of insurance or to the economy as a whole, but they relate in some way to the basic idea of providing a risk transfer mechanism. The final two benefits that we shall consider are in a slightly different category. Firstly, they are benefits that are enjoyed by the overall, national economy and therefore only indirectly affect individual people or enterprises. Secondly, they are not benefits that arise out of the effect of providing the risk transfer mechanism.

Peace of mind, loss control and the social benefits we have looked at do seem to arise directly from the effect of the risk transfer mechanism itself, which is that the financial consequences of certain losses can be met by an insurer. Vast sums of money are involved, by way of total insurance premiums, to bring about this risk transfer and the management of that money then brings its own benefits. The two main benefits derived in this way, which we are going to examine, are the investment of funds and the effect on the balance of payments. We could say that these two benefits arise as a result of there being an insurance market, rather than the existence of any particular form of insurance.

Investment of Funds

Insurance companies have at their disposal large amounts of money. This arises from the fact that there is a time gap between the receipt of a premium and the payment of a claim. A premium could be paid in January and a claim may not occur until December, if it occurs at all. The insurer has this money and can invest it. In fact, an insurer will have the accumulated premiums of all insureds, over a long period of time. In 1993, the Association of British Insurers (ABI) reported that the total value of invested assets was £535,016m.

The actual investments for 1993, as published by the ABI, are shown in Figure 2.1.

Figure 2.1: Insurance Company Investments 1993

	Life Insurance		General	
	£m	%	£m	%
British Government Securities	99,082	21.5	25,426	34.1
Stocks and Shares	15,473	7.2	5,630	13.2
Stocks and Shares	287,325	62.4	26,763	35.9
Mortgages	16,779	3.6	1,389	1.9
Property and Rents	35,264	7.7	3,580	4.8
Other Investments	22,064	4.8	17,362	23.3

From this table, we can see that the value of life insurance investments far exceeds that of general insurance. Given what we have said earlier about the gap in time between the receipt of premium and the payment of claims, this will now seem obvious. One other aspect worth noting is that the pattern of investment is not the same for the two types of insurance funds. Once again, this has much to do with the nature of the risks being run. In life assurance, there is expected to be some time between the receipt of premium and the eventual payment of the claim; as a result, the funds can be invested in longer-term ventures. In general insurance, the money cannot be locked away for so long and therefore has to be spread over long-, medium- and short-term investments.

The use of this money within the economy as a whole is where the benefit lies; both the government and industry have access to a large pool of working money. This money is the result of thousands of different people and organizations paying premiums and, in one sense, the existence of an insurance market really brings about a form of enforced saving. For example, if we consider a person insuring his house. Such a person may not have sufficient free money to be able to purchase shares, buy property or lend money. However, when the premium from that person is added to the premiums from several thousand other people, then a reasonable amount of investment money is made available.

Invisible Earnings

We have already said that insurance allows people and organizations to spread risk among themselves. In the same way, we can also say that countries spread risk. A great deal of insurance is transacted in the UK in respect of property and liabilities incurred overseas. London is still very much the centre of world insurance and large volumes of premium flow into London every year; these are described as invisible earnings.

As a trading, island nation we have to import goods which we need for our people, and by the same token we export goods which other people want to buy.

Where the goods are tangible, a visible trade exists; for example, when goods are shipped to a foreign country and are paid for by that country, these are visible exports. In the case of insurance, goods are invisible but the principle remains the same. Whether goods concerned are visible or invisible, exports are bringing money into the UK and imports are sending money out.

From an economic point of view, it is wise to have a balance between the volume of what we export and import. Importing a much higher amount than we export means that we are spending money that we have not earned. The difference between the value of visible exports and imports is called the balance of trade, and this is often referred to in newspapers and on television. When we export more than we import we have a **surplus** and when imports exceed exports we have a **deficit** on our balance of trade.

In addition to this physical balance, we also have the invisible trade for which the UK is well known. This includes trading in such things as tourism and banking, and we have already considered insurance, which is one form of invisible earnings. Overseas risks are insured in the UK and the money earned on these transactions, once all costs have been met, represents a substantial volume of earnings.

In 1993, invisible earnings from insurance represented £4,623 million and was the largest single earner of all the various UK financial institutions.

Student Activity 1

Before reading the next section of the text, answer the following questions and then check your answers against the sections and paragraphs indicated.

1.   What is the theory behind the law of large numbers?

(page 26)

2.   What are invisible earnings?   *(page 32)*

If your answers are basically correct, then proceed to the next section. If significant parts of your answers are wrong, then study the whole of the relevant sections again in detail. Note your areas of weakness, and be prepared for further questions on these areas in the self-assessment section at the end of this unit.

2.3   The Nature of Insurable Risks

The picture we have painted of insurance so far is one of a valuable service to individuals and industry. The provision of this service results in a number of direct benefits to those who purchase protection, and leads to a number of other, more general, benefits to the nation as a whole. However, there must be limits on the availability of this risk transfer mechanism. For example, it would not be wise to allow people to benefit from their own criminal actions. This could happen if it were possible for a person to insure their neighbour's house and then burn it down, in order to collect the claim money. Even where no criminal intent is present, it does not seem proper for a person to benefit from a fire at a neighbour's house, where he himself had no financial interest at all in the house that was destroyed.

We could compile a list of the types of events that would be acceptable for insurance purposes, but there are at least two problems with this approach:

- The list would be almost endless. There are all kinds of incidents that can occur and would be perfectly acceptable for insurance protection. It would be almost impossible to list them all.

- The list would never be up to date. Risk is dynamic, in the sense that it is always changing, so that any list of events that is suitable for the form of risk transfer we have described would also have to change continually.

However, it is still necessary to have some idea of what can and cannot be insured and, with the above problems in mind, a different approach is called for. Rather than list the events themselves, we have noted the characteristics or nature of insurable risks. This list will not be infinite, as would any list of insurable events, but will still be flexible enough to cope with change.

There is one caveat that should be made at this point: it is not possible, or indeed wise, to be dogmatic about these classifications of insurable risk. The world of business is not a static environment. It changes to adjust to circumstances as they are perceived, and what may be an uninsurable risk today could very well be insurable tomorrow.

Fortuitous

The happening of the event must be entirely fortuitous, as far as the insured is concerned. (The 'insured' is the person, company or organization insured by an insurance company.) It is not possible to insure against an event which will definitely occur because it involves no uncertainty of loss and therefore no transfer of risk would be taking place.

This would rule out inevitable events such as damage caused by wear, tear and depreciation. Any damage or loss inflicted on purpose by the insured would also be ruled out. Purposeful acts by other people would not automatically be ruled out, provided that they were entirely fortuitous as far as the insured was concerned.

Using the terminology of frequency and severity, we could say that the frequency and severity of any risk must be beyond the control of the insured. The one example which may seem to fall outside this rule, and yet is insurable, is the risk of death itself. We all know that it is possible to purchase life assurance, even though death is probably one of the few certainties there are! However, the timing of death is what is fortuitous and it is this with which life assurance is primarily concerned.

Financial Value

The essence of insurance, as we have seen, is to act as a risk transfer mechanism and provide financial compensation for loss. Insurance does not remove the risk, but it does endeavour to provide financial protection against the consequences. If this is the case then the risk which is to be insured must result in a loss which is capable of being measured in financial terms.

In the case of property loss or damage, this is easy to see. The monetary value of property lost can be established and, subject to the terms of the insurance policy, compensation can be provided. The exact value of the loss will not be known at the outset, only after the event has occurred. All material damage to, or theft of, property would fall into this category.

Later in this unit, we shall see that there are many other forms of insurance protection available and each of them is concerned with risks that can result in losses capable of financial measurement. For example, consider the case of injury to people at work. Employers can effect a policy of insurance which protects them against the risk that an employee might be injured at work and succeed in a claim against them for compensation. This is quite different from the case of property loss or damage. The actual financial value cannot be arrived at in the same objective manner. In some cases, the court will decide the level of compensation due to an injured person; in others, the respective lawyers will agree amounts. In either case, it is the legal liability to pay compensation that is the financial value at risk.

In life assurance, the level of financial compensation is agreed at the beginning of a contract. It is impossible to place values on the life of a wife, husband or child, but the financial sum assured can be determined at the commencement of the insurance.

Insurable Interest

The practice of insurance is governed by a number of basic doctrines or principles. One of these doctrines is that of insurable interest. We have already said that one requirement of an insurable risk is that there must be some loss which is capable of being measured in financial terms. It is easy to anticipate situations where a person could insure the property of someone else so that when the property was lost or damaged he, in addition to the owner of the property, would receive compensation. At the extreme, we could even anticipate people visiting local hospitals and effecting life assurance on the lives of people who were very ill.

In both of these cases there would be a financially measurable loss, in terms that we have described. However, both situations seem quite unacceptable. What is missing is any kind of legally recognizable relationship between the insured and the financial loss. A substantial volume of legal precedents has been built up, over very many years, and the study of this is an essential prerequisite to an understanding of the practice of insurance. We will deal with this in a later unit.

Homogeneous Exposures

We have already looked at the impact of the law of large numbers on the operation of insurance. Given a sufficient number of exposures to similar risks, the insurer can forecast the expected extent of their loss.

In the absence of a large number of similar, homogeneous exposures the task is much more difficult. The benefits of the law of large numbers disappear and the calculation of required premiums becomes more of a 'guesstimate' than a statistical calculation.

With these cases, the insurers may or may not be accurate in the setting of a premium, but inevitably will want to protect themselves by charging a premium which should cover even the worst case. Competition will be much less important, because there are not large numbers of the exposure all seeking protection.

While having a large number of similar exposures is a characteristic of an insurable risk, it is possible to cite examples where this was not the case and insurance was still provided. Occasionally there are reports of unusual risks being insured, normally at Lloyd's; we shall look at the operation of Lloyd's later. Film stars' legs or pianists' fingers have featured in such reports and these are possibly newsworthy in some sense, but in practical terms they have little to teach us. A much more topical and realistic illustration of very low numbers of similar exposures would be space satellites. We are seeing more launched every year, but they are still relatively rare and have certainly not been around long enough to enable insurers to build up any kind of statistical base.

However, in normal circumstances an insurer looks for homogeneous exposures, in order to enjoy the benefits of the law of large numbers.

Pure Risks

Insurance is concerned primarily with pure risks. Speculative risks are normally taken in the hope of some gain and the provision of insurance may act as a distinct disincentive to effort. For example if it were possible to insure the profit that a person hoped to gain from an enterprise, then there would be little incentive for some people to do anything to generate the profit. No personal effort to secure the profit would still result in profit, because the policy would pay up in the event that no profit was generated.

The pure risk consequences of speculative risks are certainly insurable, but not the speculative risk itself. Take as an example the marketing of a new line in clothing. The risk that the new line will sell or not is clearly a speculative one. It is a risk knowingly entered into in the hope of financial gain. This, after all, is the very essence of business activity. However, the risk that the line will not sell is not the only risk to which the enterprise is exposed: the factory in which the garments are to be made could be damaged, designs could be stolen, suppliers of essential materials could have fires or other damage resulting in them being unable to supply the raw material. All of these risks are pure risks which are insurable, but they arose directly from the decision to take the speculative risk in the first place.

We are not saying that all pure risks are insurable, just that speculative risks are normally not.

Particular Risks

The division of risks into particular and fundamental was another dichotomy that we looked at in Unit 1. The widespread and indiscriminate nature of fundamental risks has resulted in their traditionally being uninsurable. It is not accurate to say that all fundamental risks cannot be insured, but insurers are very selective in the risks of this type that they are prepared to insure.

What we could say is that those fundamental risks which arise out of the nature of society itself are not usually insurable. This would include war, changing customs and inflation.

Fundamental risks arising out of some physical cause such as typhoons, earthquakes and hurricanes may be insurable. The decision would depend, in these cases, on the geographical location of the property that had to be insured against these risks. The cynic would say that insurance would be available provided the property was in a location where typhoons, earthquakes or hurricanes were known not to occur!

In the main, fundamental risks are looked upon by the insurance industry as the responsibility of society as a whole and not simply those who choose to insure.

Public Policy

We have already seen that the insured must have a financial interest in the loss and that the loss must be fortuitous. This ruled out the possibility of insuring the property of other people, or inflicting damage or loss on purpose in order to benefit from an insurance policy. However, there are still risks that we might all agree should not be insurable.

It is a common principle in law that contracts must not be contrary to what society would consider to be the right and moral thing to do. Contracts to kill a person are unacceptable, as are contracts to inflict damage on the property of people, or to steal from them.

In terms of risk and contracts of insurance, the same principle applies. It would be unacceptable to insure against the risk of a criminal venture going wrong. For example, society could not accept the idea that thieves could effect a policy which would pay them the expected gain from a theft, if they were caught by the police and therefore unable to complete the deed. This may seem a little far-fetched, but what about the risk of incurring a fine? A person could be caught speeding, or worse could be charged with dangerous or drunken driving. The risk he runs is that a large fine could be imposed. The person certainly has a financial relationship with the loss, and it could be argued that the loss is fortuitous as far as he is concerned. However, society would not find it acceptable for a person to be able to avoid the punishment implicit in the fine, simply by taking out insurance.

This list of the nature of insurable risks can only be a guide. In the fast changing world of risk and insurance, it would not be possible or even wise to create hard and fast rules regarding those risks that can and cannot be insured. The list serves to highlight and underline a philosophy of insurability, rather than provide a code of practice.

Insurance is a service industry, it is there to serve the needs of its customers and these needs do change. The underlying service is that of providing a risk transfer mechanism, but the nature of the risks for which this may be necessary will alter as time passes. New products, processes and industrial systems all bring new forms of risk for which consumers, be they corporate or private, will need protection.

2.4   The Development of Insurance

The concept of insurance is not new. A form of insurance existed even in early Rome, where Romans gathered together in burial societies. They all contributed to a fund and the members of the pool had their burial costs met by the society. This was an early forerunner of the common pool which we discussed in Section 1.

To examine the origin of modern insurance is a fascinating area of study in itself. It can also be valuable to those who are embarking upon the study of insurance as it exists today. A knowledge of the origins of a subject is always beneficial, and for insurance we can identify at least three reasons why it is important to look back:

● Many of our modern insurance institutions, such as Lloyd's of London, would be extremely difficult to understand if we did not enquire into their history.

● Insurance companies and Lloyd's have perfected the method of practising insurance over many years and a large part of present-day practice, including certain policy wordings, would prove quite inexplicable if we had no knowledge of its development.

● Insurance has often been a response to some problem faced by society, and an understanding of how insurance companies faced up to and solved these important issues helps to explain many present-day methods.

Figure 2.2 shows the chronological development of 12 of the more common forms of insurance. Rather than treat each form independently, we shall look at just two briefly for illustrative purposes: marine and life.

Figure 2.2: The Development of Insurance

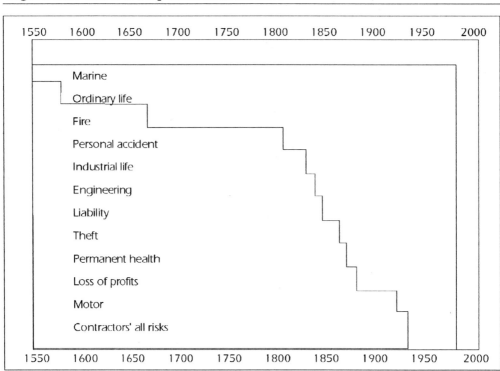

Marine

Since earliest times, people have been fascinated by sea travel. It is not surprising, therefore, that people's first attempt at seeking protection was from the danger posed at sea. Historians have uncovered evidence suggesting that some sharing of losses did exist among seafarers as early as the 9th century BC. In contrast, aviation insurance is of far more recent origin.

Marine insurance development

Lloyd's is probably the most famous insurance market in the world, being the centre for the world's marine insurance and shipping intelligence. In the 17th century, insurance of ships and cargoes was often underwritten by merchants who were willing to carry part of the risk of a voyage in return for part of the premium. Commerce of various types was transacted among the merchants who met each other at various coffee houses around the City of London. Similarly, those wishing to transact insurance would meet in these coffee houses. One of them, owned by one Edward Lloyd, was situated near the River Thames and was frequented by merchants, shipowners and others having an interest in maritime ventures.

'Lloyd's Coffee House' was situated in Tower Street and was in existence by 1688, although the original date of opening is uncertain. Edward Lloyd encouraged the merchants or underwriters (they signed their names at the foot of the insurance contracts), because it brought extra business to his coffee house. He supplied shipping information and published a news sheet in 1696, called *Lloyd's News*. This was superseded some years after his death by *Lloyd's List*, which is London's oldest newspaper.

In 1769, the insurance market transferred its business centre to the 'New Lloyd's Coffee House' in Pope's Head Alley, and in 1771 a committee was formed to seek larger premises. With their membership subscriptions, premises were established in 1774 in the Royal Exchange. The formation of the committee took the running of Lloyd's out of the hands of the coffee house owner (now Thomas Fielding) and into the hands of the insurance fraternity.

The modern Corporation of Lloyd's was formed in 1871 by act of parliament, and more recent statutes have kept the constitution up to date with the needs of a modern insurance market. The present premises are centred in Lime Street, London.

Chartered companies monopoly

In 1720, the London Assurance and the Royal Exchange were granted Royal Charters to transact marine insurance. The act providing for the incorporation of two companies, the Bubble Act, also restricted the provision of marine insurance to these two companies or to individuals. In other words, the two companies had almost gained a monopoly, because only they or individuals could provide marine insurance. Not unnaturally, to achieve this privileged position some amount of backroom work was necessary, culminating in what some historians refer to as bribery, when both companies offered £300,000 for their charter to the King, who was much in need of money at that time.

Because only individuals could provide marine insurance, it is little wonder that the activities in Edward Lloyd's coffee house prospered and, as we shall find later, Lloyd's has developed as a marketplace for insurance provided by individuals.

The monopoly was terminated eventually in 1824, when the Alliance Marine Insurance Company was successful in an application to provide marine insurance.

Marine Insurance Act 1906

The case law that was being accumulated over the years, some 2,000 cases, was incorporated in the Marine Insurance Act 1906; the law relating to marine insurance was codified, that is, brought together in the one statute. The act forms the basis for the operation of marine insurance to this day, and knowledge of its terms is essential to anyone embarking upon a career in marine insurance. Its value goes beyond the boundary of marine insurance, because it is the only code of commercial insurance on the statute book and for that reason is of considerable importance in its own right. Much case law and a variety of international rules and conventions also impact upon current marine insurance practice.

Life, Personal Accident and Health

We commented earlier on the existence of burial societies in the ancient world. This form of activity continued; however they did not take account of the dependants who were left, nor did they provide any compensation to a person who was injured, but not fatally injured.

Ordinary life assurance

The first real evidence of life assurance as we know it dates back to 1583. A policy was taken out on 18 June, on the life of William Gibbons, for a sum of £382.6s.8d.

The contract was for 12 months and the money was to be paid if Gibbons died within the year. In fact he did die on 8 May 1584 and, after a slight dispute over whether 12 months meant 12 x 28 days or 12 calendar months, the money was paid.

The short-term form of policy taken out by William Gibbons was typical of the type of assurance issued in these early days. The provision of life assurance continued unaltered for the next century with the short-term form of policy mentioned above and a form of mutual association, similar in design to the ancient burial societies, where members contributed to a common pool out of which payments were made on death.

One such mutual association that grew in prosperity was the Amicable Society for a Perpetual Assurance Office, founded in 1705 by Royal Charter. The Amicable transacted business on traditional lines, but in 1757 it took the daring step of guaranteeing a minimum sum to be payable on death. This seemed to satisfy a demand, because the company did not suffer by its boldness.

Actuarial principles

Around the turn of the century, at roughly the same time as the 'Amicable' was founded, mathematicians were working on what have become known as mortality tables. Two of the most important contributions were by Edmund Halley, the astronomer, in 1693 (after whom Halley's comet is named) and James Dodson, then mathematics master at the school attached to Christ's Hospital, in 1775. The intention of the mortality tables was, in part, to be able to state in mathematical terms the likelihood of persons of a given age dying. The objective they aimed at is well described by Halley when he wrote '... that the price of insurance on lives might be regulated by the age of the persons on whose life the insurance is made'. Dodson followed this idea and on being refused assurance by the Amicable on account of his age, ' ... determined to form a new society on a plan of assurance on more equitable terms than those of the Amicable, which takes the same premium for all ages'.

He did not have to wait long. In 1762 the Equitable Life Assurance Society was formed and transacted business on the basis suggested by him. It was able to offer life assurance on level premiums, that were dependent upon the age of the person when he took out the policy. This was a significant difference from the previous companies. In addition it offered a whole life policy, which paid the sum assured on the death of the assured person. This was possible because the work of Dodson and others had introduced an element of science into the business of knowing how much to charge. This science is now known as actuarial science and is taught at many universities and colleges; examinations are conducted by the Faculty of Actuaries in Scotland and the Institute of Actuaries in England. Much of what we now know as actuarial mathematics is built upon the early work of Richard Price and his nephew William Morgan, who were both associated with the 'Equitable', Morgan as actuary for more than 50 years.

The next landmark in the development was the passing of the Life Assurance Act 1774, the title of which explains its purpose: 'An act for regulating insurances upon lives and prohibiting all such insurances except in cases where persons insuring shall have an interest on the life or death of the person insured'.

By the end of the 18th century several proprietary companies had been formed where policyholders did not share in profits - as they had with mutual associations. These proprietary companies were spearheaded by the Westminster Society, 1792, and the Pelican Life Office, 1797.

Industrial life assurance

What we have described so far has been the development of what is now known as ordinary life assurance. This is to be contrasted with industrial life assurance. The changing structure of society brought about by the Industrial Revolution produced the beginnings of the 'industrial' classes. The men and women who worked in the new industries were not financially protected against infirmity and the onset of old age as employees are today, and in order to avoid the stigma of the Poor Laws many friendly societies were formed. These societies, thousands of which were in existence before the end of the 18th century, allowed some provision for sickness and funeral expenses. Out of the friendly society grew the concept of industrial life assurance, with companies transacting life assurance that was especially suited to the needs and pockets of the 'industrial' classes.

Liability

This category comprises those risks where the loss suffered by the person insuring is either an amount of money he is to pay as compensation to another, or some loss of his own money.

The development of liability insurance is of more recent origin then fire insurance and certain other forms of insurance in respect of damage to property we have already looked at.

The growth in liability insurance can be dealt with under two headings: employers' and public liability.

Employers' liability

Where an employee is injured by the fault of the employer, the right arises for that injured person to claim compensation, or 'damages' from the employer. Today, this fact is accepted as sound and just, but it was not so some 150 years ago.

During the early part of the 19th century, the industrialization of Britain had brought many people to the towns and cities where work was to be found in the new factories being built there. As has often been portrayed in word and picture, these factories were dark, dismal places where men and women spent long hours in hard and exhausting work. Apart from certain enlightened employers, the drive for more and more production resulted in appalling conditions and a disregard for safety which caused many injuries.

The view, in those days, was that an industrial injury was very much a particular risk and not the responsibility of the employer. The principle applying was one known as *volenti non fit injuria*, which meant that the employee had consented to run the risk of injury by being employed. In addition to this principle, the ordinary employee would have found it extremely difficult to succeed in any claim. This was due to lack of money, poor education and the fact that the law allowed employers to avoid any liability for injury where the injury was caused in part by the employee himself, no matter how little he may have contributed to it. Also, the liability could be avoided where the injury sustained by one employee was caused by another. This latter defence was known as common employment, of which the judge in the case of *Priestley v. Fowler* (1837) said, 'What make a master liable if one of his servants injures another! If this is allowed, where shall we stop?'

In 1880, the Employers' Liability Act placed certain employees in a much better legal position. Railwaymen, miners, labourers and others now found that they could sue their employers with a slightly higher chance of success, but many of the obstacles mentioned above still persisted. 1880 was also the year in which the first specialist insurer was established, the Employers' Liability Assurance Corporation.

A significant step forward took place with the passing of the Workmens' Compensation Act 1897. This provided scale benefits such as £300 on death and half earnings during disablement for up to 31 weeks, regardless of proving fault. The act lasted with alterations until 1946, when the National Insurance (Industries Injuries) Act took its place.

However, there was still no compulsion on employers to carry insurance to provide the funds out of which claims were to be paid, although talk of compulsory insurance can be traced back to 1897. Compulsory insurance eventually came with the passing of the Employers' Liability (Compulsory Insurance) Act 1969, which was effective from 1 January 1972.

Public liability

Little has been reported on the historical development of public liability insurance: the provision of insurance for legal liability to pay claims to those who are injured, but are not employees, or to those whose property is damaged by another person.

The earliest policies, towards the last quarter of the 19th century, related to horse-drawn coaches, and this later developed into motor vehicle insurance, of which more is said below.

There are now a number of different forms of public liability insurance, all of which will be discussed later.

Suretyship, Credit, Loss of Profits

The forms of insurance dealt with under this heading are often referred to as pecuniary insurances because they relate to the loss of money, by one means or another, as opposed to damage to property or legal liability.

Suretyship, or fidelity guarantee, insurance caters for the risk of losing money by the fraud or dishonesty of some other person. People who held positions of responsibility often had others to act as surety, or in other words guarantee to refund any money misappropriated by them in the course of their business.

Providing these sureties was a very hazardous activity, and in 1840 the Guarantee Society was formed to provide surety by the means of a policy of insurance. Five years later in 1845, the British Guarantee Society was formed in Edinburgh and began transacting a similar form of business.

Towards the end of the 19th century, in 1893, another form of pecuniary insurance began to be transacted by the Excess Insurance Company. This attempted to meet the risk that a person might sell goods and the purchaser might not pay for them. This became known as credit insurance and by 1918 a specialist company was formed; it is called the Trade Indemnity Company and is still operating today. For foreign transactions the government established, in 1920, the Export Credit Scheme now known as the Export Credits Guarantee Department.

Loss of profits, or business interruption, insurance is the third form of cover mentioned in the heading and such policies began to appear at the start of the 20th century. These policies endeavour to relieve the hardship associated with consequential loss following fire. The fire policy may cover the material damage and relieve the hardship involved in repair or rebuilding work, but it does not provide any compensation for lost profit or other financial consequences of fire.

A comparatively new form of insurance protection, within the last ten years, is the provision of cover for legal expenses. The risk being faced by a person or company is looked upon as being the uncertainty over whether or not legal expenses may be incurred and, if incurred, what they may amount to. In return for an annual premium, the insured person can be freed from this uncertainty because the insurer agrees to meet legal costs, subject to certain exceptions.

Common Features of Development

On looking back over the development of the different forms of insurance a number of common features are apparent. By way of conclusion we can list the following as being the main common features:

● Each class of insurance developed in response to a demand for protection. The demand for protection was not always motivated by the eventual purchasers – for example, if we had looked at employers' liability and motor insurance we would find that these were made compulsory by statute, thus increasing demand. The moves of parliament in passing the appropriate legislation could, however, be looked upon as the expression of the people's desire to see protection purchased.

● The development of the various forms of insurance was accompanied by a measure of government supervision. We should note the interest with which successive governments have viewed the development of insurance.

In the main, insurance companies started off as specialist companies offering one or two types of insurance only. A feature of insurance development has been the way in which these specialist companies have expanded the forms of cover they wrote. Today there are very few specialist companies other than life and pensions companies, and the majority offer many different forms of insurance.

Today most insurance companies have gathered considerable experience in many forms of insurance. They have also collated statistics and have access to data collected by government and other bodies, which assist in arriving at reasonable premiums to charge. On looking back, however, a feature of the development of insurance was the absence of any reliable statistical information on future losses.

A further feature, perhaps following on from the previous point, has been the way in which insurance companies joined together over the years to pool resources. This had many advantages: the association of insurance companies all offering protection against the same kind of risk could classify the risks, pool statistics and come up with common wordings and rates.

A possible explanation for the relative security of insurers in what were very uncertain times could be the growth of reinsurance. A feature of the development of insurance was the way in which insurance companies themselves sought financial protection. This insurance bought by insurance companies is termed reinsurance, and is now an essential part of the insurance marketplace.

One final feature of the development of insurance is of more recent origin, and refers to the way in which insurance companies began to combine different classes of insurance. Specialist companies began writing other forms of insurance and so became composite insurers. Similarly, these composite insurance companies began combining different forms of cover in one policy. A good example of this is the way companies put fire, theft, liability and other forms of cover together in one policy for the householder and termed it the household combined, or household comprehensive policy. Combined or comprehensive policies are now a common feature with many companies.

2.5   Classes of Insurance

As insurance has developed, the various types of cover have been grouped into several classes which have come about by practice within insurance company offices, and by the influence of legislation controlling the financial aspects of transacting insurance. Insurance offices are generally split into departments or sections, each of which will deal with types of risk that have an affiliation with each other. There is a very wide variety in the way in which companies organize their business, but the following divisions are not unusual:

- fire, including business interruption;

- accident, including theft, all risks, goods in transit, glass, money, credit, fidelity;

- liability, including employers' liability, public liability, products and professional indemnity;

- motor;

- engineering;

- marine and aviation;

- life, health insurance and pensions.

Many of these terms may mean little to you at this point but we shall be looking, in this section, at the classes of insurance available. Depending on the amount of business transacted some branches may split, say, the accident department into several distinct sections or departments, whereas on the other hand if the amount of business written is relatively small the accident and liability departments may be combined. There is also a tendency to create 'personal' departments handling all non-life business for the private individual, thus leaving the other departments to concentrate on the more specialist commercial and industrial risks. Some insurers also have special branches or areas of branches, for the use of brokers. In this way a broker can meet and build up a working relationship with the same insurance official.

Another way of classifying insurance is set down under statute and we shall be looking at this in a later unit. For our purposes at the moment we shall work our way through the various forms of insurance under a number of broad headings.

Ordinary Life Assurance

The term **ordinary life assurance** is used to describe a particular style of doing business and is what many people will recognize as being life assurance. The other style is **industrial (home service) life assurance**, which relates to smaller values and normally involves collection of the premiums from the home of the assured person. Life assurance and pensions are dealt with in detail in Units 12 and 13.

Term assurance

This is the simplest and oldest form of assurance and provides for payment of the sum assured on death, provided death occurs within a specified term. Should the life assured survive to the end of the term then the cover ceases and no money is payable.

Whole-life assurance

The sum assured is payable on the death of the assured whenever it occurs. Premiums are payable either throughout the life of the assured or, more normally, until retirement of the assured at age 60 or 65. Even if premiums cease at, say, age 60 the policy is still in force, and should the person die at age 75 the policy would provide the benefits for his beneficiaries.

Endowment assurance

The sum assured is payable in the event of death within a specified period of between 10 and 30 years. However, if the life assured survives until the end of this period (until the 'maturity date'), the sum assured will also be paid.

Group life assurances

Employers sometimes arrange special terms for life assurance for their employees, with the sum assured being payable in the event of death of an employee during his term of service with the employer. Membership of the scheme is open to all employees working on the inception date, or the anniversary date in future years.

Key person insurance

Key person insurance is a relatively recent form of cover taken out by a company on the life of an employee who is vital to the continued profitability of the business. An example would be a marketing executive who has valuable contacts in overseas countries or the 'ideas' person in a manufacturing company.

It is difficult to assess the sum assured needed in such circumstances, and careful financial underwriting is required. However, the company will be able to effect cover for:

● loss of profits; and

● the costs of finding, securing and training a successor.

The most suitable type of contract is a term assurance, although whole-life policies are sometimes used.

In addition to life assurance, key person permanent health insurance and critical illness cover is also available.

Insured pension schemes

There are over 11 million people in pension and life assurance schemes, or benefiting from them, in the United Kingdom.

These schemes provide a variety of benefits for members, but their main aim is to ensure that some form of pension is available on retirement. Life assurance companies perform a vital role in running such pensions schemes. Those constructing a scheme may approach a company to:

● organize the whole scheme, including installation and documentation, receipt of premium contributions, investment of the funds and administration of the pensions; or

● manage the fund of a pension scheme; or

- provide life assurance benefits for members and their widow(er)s who die before retirement.

Many employers' pension schemes are insured by means of group or master policies issued to the employer or to the trustees of the scheme. These provide retirement pensions and other benefits in respect of the employees who are eligible for the scheme, usually related to their service and salary.

A record-keeping and administration service is usually provided in association with the issue of the policy. The contract may be based on one of the types of policy used in ordinary life assurance, for example endowment assurances, or annuities (as described later), or it may be specially devised for the purpose. The extent to which there is a transfer of risk varies considerably, and in some cases the main emphasis is on the provision of an investment service by the insurance company.

In association with the provision of retirement benefits, policies are usually issued insuring death in service benefits for those employees who do not reach retirement age. These may be in the form of group life assurance as described above, or of widows' and widowers' pensions.

Annuities

Certain of the assurances mentioned above have had the aim of ensuring an income of one form or another. An **annuity** is a method by which a person can receive a yearly sum in return for the payment to an insurance company of a sum of money. This is not life assurance as we have described it, but it is dealt with by life assurance companies and is based on actuarial principles.

Investments

We have already identified the life assurance industry as being of considerable size by considering the number of policies in force and the value of premiums paid each year. These vast amounts of money are held by companies to meet future liabilities and are termed life assurance funds. The total value of such funds for long-term business in 1993 was £412.7 billion.

These funds do not lie dormant waiting for claims to come in; they are invested to provide income for the companies and so assist policyholders and shareholders. Not only do these two groups benefit, but the country as a whole benefits, as we have already seen in this unit.

Industrial Life Assurance

Originally called 'insurance for the masses' the aim of this type of life assurance was to offer protection to those who would usually be unable to afford cover. Premium payments are small and made at frequent intervals, collected at the home of the policyholder by a home service agent. Policies are usually endowment or whole-life assurances and have very low sums assured.

Traditionally, there were many more industrial life policies in force than ordinary life policies, but for much smaller sums assured. However, in the last 20 years there has been a steady decline in new industrial life policies being taken out, with the result that, at the end of 1993, the total number of ordinary life policies in force exceeded the number of industrial policies in force.

Figure 2.3: Policies in Force at End of 1993

	No. in force (000's)	Yearly premium (£m)
Ordinary	60,286	16,918
Industrial	44,451	1,344

Figure 2.4 shows the steady decline in the number of industrial life policies being effected.

Figure 2.4: Number of Life Policies in Force (000's)

	End of 1983	End of 1988	End of 1993
Ordinary	30,207	45,061	60,286
Industrial	68,776	55,524	44,451

These figures illustrate that there was a drop of over 24 million industrial life policies within a ten-year period. During the same period ordinary life policies in force grew by over 30 million.

Disability Insurances

There have been a number of significant developments in the market for disability insurance cover. Composite and specialist offices now offer a range of stand-alone contracts and optional extras to life contracts which cover costs, hardships and financial repercussions resulting from sickness, accident, disability or disease.

Permanent health insurance

This contract provides a replacement of income in the event of long-term disability. It is vital for a self-employed person, but even an employee will need such cover once an employer discontinues salary after three or six months of disablement.

Deferred periods (the time that has to elapse before payments begin) of four weeks, 13 weeks, 26 weeks, 52 weeks or 104 weeks are available to allow the insured to integrate the contract with any employer benefits. The longer the deferred period, the cheaper the premium rate.

Once a claim is made, cover lasts until retirement age, return to work or earlier death. However, benefits are limited to 50 - 60% of pre-disability earnings, including any other disability benefits, in order to maintain an incentive to return to work.

Critical illness cover

Originally known as 'dread disease' cover, this type of contract was developed in South Africa. In 1986, the first critical illness policy was launched in the UK and, since then, the cover has been adapted and extended so that it is now available on a 'stand-alone', 'accelerated payment' or group basis.

The sum assured under the contract is payable on the diagnosis of any of the disorders specified in the policy. These include cancer, stroke, heart attack and major organ transplant, although competition in the market has led to this list being greatly extended.

Long-term care

This is a recent development in the UK market, although it is widely sold in the USA.

Private residential nursing home costs or the costs of caring for a disabled elderly person at home can be extremely high and any state benefit is strictly means-tested.

Long-term care contracts are designed to meet the costs of such care by paying an income when the insured is 'disabled' according to the policy definitions.

Such contracts can be funded in advance or a lump sum can be paid at 'point of need'.

The Department of Health is currently putting forward proposals for long-term care insurance, how this will interact with state benefits, and possible incentives that can be offered by the state to encourage individuals to fund for such care, thereby reducing the state's financial burden. You should ensure that you remain up to date with developments in this area in the future.

Personal Accident Insurance

The intention of the basic policy is to provide compensation in the event of an accident causing death or injury. What are termed capital sums are paid in the event of death or certain specified injuries, such as the loss of limbs or sight, as may be defined in the policy. The policy is usually extended to include a weekly benefit if the insured is temporarily totally or partly disabled due to an accident, usually subject to a maximum payout period of 104 weeks.

In the event of permanent total disablement (other than loss of eyes or limbs) an annuity or capital sum is paid.

In addition to the purchase of personal accident insurance by individuals, it is also possible for companies to arrange cover on behalf of their employees and many organizations arrange 'group schemes' to this end.

Motor Insurance

The minimum requirement by law is to provide insurance in respect of legal liability to pay damages arising out of injury caused to any person. Policies with various levels of cover are available, and will be considered in detail in Unit 16 so far as private car insurance is concerned.

Separate cover is available for motor cycles. The type of policy depends upon the machine, whether it is a moped or a high-powered motor cycle, and on the age and experience of the rider.

Commercial motor insurance

There are many different kinds of commercial motor insurance and it is not intended to deal with these in depth. You should, however, be aware of the scope of commercial motor insurances.

In general, those risks insured in the name of a company will be considered commercial risks (even if the risk represents only private cars). The considerations for those risks that do relate to private cars are similar to those for the private motorist and you should take into account what is said in Unit 17 about such risks. However, there are many risks that are peculiar to 'commercial' areas and these can be summarized:

Commercial vehicles

These range from the small goods van used for the carriage of own goods through to the 32-ton articulated vehicles used for general haulage. A variety of rating structures exists. There is a very small insurance market for the general haulage operator and premiums are very high.

If there are enough vehicles (usually ten or more) a fleet rating is possible. This tends to move away from a 'book rate' to a tailored approach linked more closely to the experience of the individual fleet.

Motor trade

Special considerations apply to motor traders. This arises from the fact that they do not know, from day to day, what vehicles will be in their custody or control. This means that special contracts of insurance are needed. The basis of cover is geared to trade plates, named drivers or a 'points' system which allocates premium to different risk aspects. Cover includes liability for injury and damage while vehicles are on the road, and may include damage to own vehicles in a garage or showroom.

Special types

Many vehicles are used in particular ways. You have only to think of dumper trucks or mobile cranes to realize that many vehicles do not follow traditional patterns. How do you rate a mobile crane worth £40,000 when it is hardly ever on the road? For this reason special policies and premium rates have been developed which seek to deal with these vehicles. One of the most critical aspects for some 'special type' vehicles is the extent to which cover is required while the vehicle is operating as a tool of trade. Value also plays an important part.

Marine and Transport Insurance

Marine policies relate to three areas of risk: the hull, cargo and freight. Although hull and cargo are self-explanatory, the word **freight** may not be: it is the sum paid for transporting goods, or for the hire of a ship. When goods are lost by marine perils then freight, or part of it, is lost; hence the need for cover.

The risks against which these items are normally insured are collectively termed 'perils of the sea' and include fire, theft, collision and a wide range of other perils.

The main types of policy are:

- Time policy

  This is for a fixed period, usually not exceeding 12 months.

- Voyage policy

  Operative for the period of the voyage; for cargo the cover is from warehouse to warehouse.

- Mixed policy

  Covers the subject matter for the voyage and a period of time thereafter, for example, while in port.

- Building risk policy

  Covers the construction of marine vessels.

- Floating policy

  This provides the policyholder with a large reserve of cover for cargo. A large initial sum is granted and each time shipments are sent, the insured declares this and the value of the shipment is deducted from the outstanding sum insured.

- Small craft

  The increasing leisure use of small boats brought about the introduction of a policy aimed at this form of craft. It is comprehensive in style, covering a wide range of perils including liability insurance.

Apart from small-craft policies, which are written and issued by many companies, all marine policies are written on the standard MAR (Marine) form. This is a blank policy form and is added to by various clauses, both for hull and cargo insurances.

Marine cargo

Cargo is usually insured on a warehouse (of departure) to warehouse (of arrival) basis and frequently covers all risks.

Marine liabilities

The custom has been to provide insurance for three-quarters of the shipowner's liability for collisions at sea under a marine policy. The remaining quarter, and all other forms of liability, are catered for by associations set up for the purpose by shipowners and known as Protecting and Indemnity Clubs (P and I Clubs).

Aviation insurance

The use of aircraft as a means of transport is increasing each year and because of the specialist and technical nature of the risks associated with it, plus the high potential cost of accidents, all aviation risks, from component parts to complete Jumbo jets, are insured in the aviation insurance market.

Most policies are issued on an 'all risks' basis, subject to certain restrictions. The buyers of these policies include the large commercial airlines, corporate aircraft owners, private owners and flying clubs. Usually a comprehensive policy is issued covering the aircraft itself (the hull), the liabilities to passengers and the liabilities to others.

Liability for accidents to passengers is governed by a maze of international agreements and national laws around the world. The main ones are the Warsaw Convention 1929, which made signatories liable to passengers without negligence, subject to certain maximum amounts, and the Hague Protocol 1955, which raised some of these limits. The national laws may place higher limits on domestic flights. It is interesting to note that in *Goldman v. Thai Airlines International* (1981), it was held that the limits did not apply when the aircrew were 'reckless' in flying the aircraft. In the aftermath of the Lockerbie disaster, there have been a number of attempts at securing much higher compensation than the agreements lay down. Readers should keep up to date with these developments.

The two international agreements also place limits on liability for goods carried by air. Unless of special risk or value, cargo is usually insured 'all risks' in the marine or general markets rather than the aviation market.

Other groups of persons requiring aviation liability cover are aircraft and aircraft component manufacturers, and airport authorities.

Fire and Other Property Damage Insurance

There are a whole number of different ways in which property can be damaged. One need only think of a small factory unit to imagine all that can be damaged and all the ways in which damage can be sustained. Fire and theft probably come to mind first, but then there very many different forms of accidental damage. Figure 2.5 outlines some of the forms of property cover that are available.

Figure 2.5: Fire and Other Property Damage Insurance

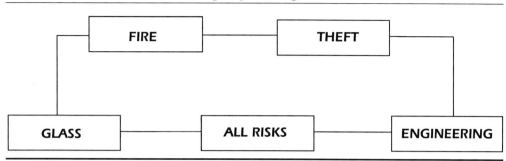

Fire insurance

A standard fire policy is used for many business insurances, with Lloyd's of London also issuing a standard fire policy that is slightly different in its wording.

The basic intention of the fire policy is to provide compensation to the insured person in the event of there being damage to the property insured. It is not possible, in the commercial world, to issue a policy that will provide compensation regardless of how the damage occurs. The insurance company, the insurers, have to know which perils they are insuring against.

The standard fire policy covers damage to property caused by fire, lightning or explosion, where this explosion is brought about by gas or boilers not used for any industrial purpose.

This is limited in its scope because property can be damaged in other ways, and to meet this need, a number of extra perils (known as special perils) can be added on to the basic policy. These perils are:

- storm, tempest or flood;
- riot, civil commotion;
- burst pipes;
- malicious damage;
- earthquake;
- explosion;
- aircraft;
- impact.

It is important to remember that these additional perils must result in damage to the property, and it is as well to precede each by saying, 'damage to the property caused by ...'.

In most commercial policies the insured will require cover for buildings, machinery and plant, and stock. These are the three main headings under which property is insured and in some cases a list of such items can run to many pages, depending upon the size of the insured company.

In addition to these areas it may be necessary to arrange cover for property while it is still being built, that is buildings in course of erection, but this form of cover is gradually giving way to a policy known as 'contractors all risks' which will be referred to later.

Theft insurance

Theft policies have the same aim as the standard fire policy, in that they intend to provide compensation to the insured in the event of loss of the property insured.

The property to be insured, for a commercial venture, will be the same as under the fire policy except of course the buildings. The theft policy will, in addition, show a more detailed definition of the stock. The reason for this is that fire is indiscriminate, whereas a thief is not, so the insurers charge more for stock that is attractive to thieves.

The law relating to theft was brought up to date by the Theft Act 1968. This had an immediate impact on insurance companies, because it defined the term 'theft'. The legal definition was wider than that which the companies were prepared to offer, especially for business premises, because the definition did not mention any need for there to be force and violence in committing a theft. This meant that shoplifting, for example, was 'theft' and this kind of risk had traditionally been uninsurable. To remedy the problem, insurance companies included in their policies a phrase to the effect that theft, within the meaning of the policy, was to include force and violence either in breaking into or out of the premises of the insured.

All risks insurance

Uncertainty of loss is not restricted to events brought about by fire or theft, nor is it limited to events occurring on or about the insured's premises. This realization led, as we noted earlier, to the development of a wider form of cover known as all risks. However, the term 'all risks' is unfortunate because a number of risks are excluded, but it is an improvement on the scope of cover available.

Personal effects

All risks policies are very popular with individuals who seek a wider protection than that afforded by the policies available to cover household effects.

The all risks policy can be taken out on particularly expensive items such as jewellery, cameras and fur coats, and can also be arranged on unspecified goods for a lump sum. The twin objectives of such policies are to provide cover for the whole range of accidental loss or damage and to do so wherever the goods themselves happen to be at the time of loss.

Business all risks

The use of all risks policies in the commercial sector is becoming more popular, as expensive and sophisticated pieces of machinery are introduced to the factory and the office.

The advent of the microprocessor and the silicon chip mean that comparatively small machines, often desktop equipment, are replacing larger and bulkier apparatus. It would be quite easy for a small desktop computer to be accidentally dropped or otherwise damaged. Their small bulk conceals a high value and the owner may well consider an all risks policy to be worthwhile if it assists in removing some of the uncertainty.

Goods in transit

This form of cover provides compensation to the owner of goods if those goods are damaged or lost while in transit. Different policies can be taken out, depending upon whether the goods are carried by the owner's own vehicles or by a firm of carriers. In the same way the carrier can effect a policy because he is often responsible for the goods while they are in his custody.

We depend to a great extent on the carriage of goods by road and this form of cover is an important aspect of industrial activity.

Forms of goods in transit insurance are also available for those who send their goods by rail or by post. The compensation provided by British Rail or the Post Office is often far less than the value of the goods being carried, and in such cases it is a wise precaution to have arranged adequate insurance.

Contractors' all risks

This is one of the relatively newer forms of insurance that has been developed to meet the changing needs of industry. When new buildings or civil engineering projects such as motorways or bridges are being constructed, a great deal of money is invested before the work is finished. There is a risk that the particular building or bridge may sustain severe damage, prolonging the construction time and delaying the eventual completion date. The risk becomes more acute as the completion date draws near, and there are many examples of buildings and other projects sustaining severe damage, and even total destruction, only days before they were to be handed over to the new owners.

Should damage occur then the contractor would have to start building again, or at best repair the damage. The extra cost involved cannot be added on to the eventual charge the contractor will make to the owner for having carried out the building work. As a result, the need arose for some form of financial protection, and this came with the development of contractors' all risks insurance. The intention of the policy is to provide compensation to the contractor in the event of there being damage to the construction works from a wide range of perils.

Money insurance

The loss of money represents the final form of all risks cover that we shall consider. The policy provides compensation to the insured in the event of money being stolen either from his business premises, his own home, or while it is being carried to or from the bank. Even for the person running a medium-sized business, this is an extremely important form of cover because large sums of money are drawn from banks to meet wages and these can often be the target for robberies.

One important addition to this cover is often the provision of some compensation to employees who may be injured or have clothing damaged during a robbery.

Glass

Cover is also available against accidental breakage of plate glass in windows and doors. In the case of shops this is often extended to include damage done to shop window contents. It is generally rated on the area of glass, cost, type and location.

Engineering

As we saw earlier, the provision of engineering cover had its beginnings with boiler explosions, which still form a major part of the work done by engineering insurers. However, the increasing sophistication of industry has resulted in them moving on to cover other forms of engineering plant, particularly lifts, cranes, electrical equipment, engines and, more recently, computers.

The cover is intended to provide compensation to the insured in the event of the plant insured being damaged either by some extraneous cause or by its own breakdown.

Engineering insurers still continue to provide an inspection service on a wide range of engineering plant. This is a service much sought after by industry, not only because many forms of inspection are compulsory by law, but also because engineering insurers have built up a considerable expertise in this area.

Engineering cover can be summarized thus:

(a) damage to, or breakdown of, specific items of plant and machinery;

(b) an inspection service of those items;

(c) cost of repair of own surrounding property due to (a);

(d) legal liability for injury caused by (a);

(e) legal liability for damage to property of others caused by (a).

Liability Insurances

We have already dealt with the liability insurance arising under the specialist branches of motor, marine and aviation, and engineering insurances. It remains to look at brief details of what is sometimes termed 'general liability' and which comprises employers' liability, public liability, products liability and professional indemnity insurances.

Employers' liability insurance

When an employer is held legally liable to pay damages to an injured employee or to the representatives of someone fatally injured, he can claim against his employers' liability policy which will provide him with exactly the same amount he himself has had to pay out. The policy will also pay certain expenses such as lawyer's fees or doctor's charges where an injured person has been medically examined. The intention is to ensure that the employer does not suffer financially, but is compensated for any money he may have to pay in respect of a claim. The policy is restricted to damages payable in respect of injury and does not apply where property of an employee is damaged.

Insurance is compulsory for all but a few employers and this has resulted in employers' liability insurance forming a large part of the liability insurance transacted in Britain. With each policy an annual certificate is issued and this must be displayed at every place of business, as evidence of the fact that the employer has complied with the law and effected a policy.

Public liability insurance

Members of the public may suffer injury or damage to their property due to the activities of someone else, and public liability insurances have been designed to provide compensation for those who may have to pay damages and legal costs for such injuries, or for the damage to property. Particular types of policy are available for each type of risk:

Business risks policy

Every business organization is exposed to the risk of incurring legal liability due to its operations. The public may be in contact with the firm in its offices or the firm may be on the premises of others, in the street or on various sites. The policy will indemnify the insured for liabilities thus incurred. Cover provided is restricted to the insured's legal liability for sums payable in respect of third party death or personal injury or damage to third party property. It is usual for directly flowing 'consequential' losses to be included in the cover but it does not normally provide for pure financial loss. There is an indemnity limit which applies to any claim or series of claims arising out of any one event but unlimited in the period of insurance.

Products liability

An exception on most business public liability policies is liability arising out of goods sold. This is a very onerous liability and one that insurers prefer to deal with separately. If a person is injured by any product that he purchases (foodstuffs for example) and he can show that the seller, or in some cases the manufacturer, was to blame he could succeed in a claim for damages. Products covers tend to have a limit of indemnity for any one period of insurance.

Liability arising out of products which are likely to find their way into the construction of aircraft are dealt with by aviation insurance departments.

Professional liability

Another exception to the basic public liability policy is liability arising out of professional negligence. This can arise when lawyers, accountants, doctors, insurance brokers and a whole range of professional people do or say something that results in others suffering in some sense. For example, a lawyer may give advice carelessly that results in a client losing money. That client would then be able to sue the lawyer for an amount equal to what he had lost. The lawyer can effect professional liability insurance, often known as professional indemnity insurance, to meet the cost of any award against him. However, the cover offered will normally be limited to an overall total payment in any one period of insurance and premiums tend to be expensive for this form of cover. It is a very restricted market available for placing these risks, although schemes do exist for the major professions.

Personal public liability

Each individual owes a duty to his neighbour not to cause him injury or damage his property. Liability may arise out of the ownership of a house, a pet, out of sporting activities or just in the simple act of crossing the road without looking. The case of *Clark v. Shepstone* (1968) emphasizes the need for personal public liability cover. Mrs Shepstone stepped from the pavement without looking and caused a motorcyclist to swerve. The motorbike crashed and the pillion passenger, Mr Clark, suffered severe injury. He sued Mrs Shepstone and eventually accepted £28,500 in compensation. In the absence of a personal public liability policy, Mrs Shepstone would have been in serious financial difficulties.

Directors' and officers' liability

Over the past decade there has been an increasing tendency for courts to hold directors and officers personally responsible for their negligence in operating a company. Legislation has also made directors liable for the behaviour of a company so that shareholders, creditors, customers, employees and others can now take action against directors as individuals.

We have seen a number of such cases reach the national headlines when they have involved large, well-known companies.

The directors' and officers' policy provides cover for defence costs as well as the amount of compensation that a director may be liable to pay.

Credit Insurance

Traders can sustain heavy losses due to insolvency or protracted default on the part of buyers of their goods, and credit insurance can afford the requisite protection. For overseas trade, it may be impossible for customers to pay for goods because of the outbreak of war or government restrictions on remittances: this 'political risk' can be covered, along with the ordinary insolvency risk, with the Export Credits Guarantee Department. No private insurer could bear so heavy a risk; it is one essentially for a government department.

Suretyship or Fidelity Guarantee Insurances

The object of this class of business is to provide insurance against loss caused by the dishonesty of persons holding positions of trust. For some guarantees the protection goes beyond dishonesty to cover loss caused by mistake, for example, where a liquidator maladministers the affairs of a company being wound up by reason of a mistake in law. The main divisions are:

Commercial guarantees

These are effected by employers in respect of persons who have some post within the company where they may be in a position to perpetrate some form of fraud. There is a need for careful underwriting of these risks. Insurers normally require to know in great detail the checks on employees, the systems in operation and recruitment methods.

Local government bonds

These are the local government equivalent of the commercial guarantees described above.

Court bonds

Sometimes it is necessary for the courts to entrust the property or affairs of an individual to someone else. Before doing this they will require that 'administrator' to supply a bond or financial guarantee, which can be utilized to make good losses due to malpractice. Property that has to be looked after pending the result of litigation and the administration of the affairs of minors or those not mentally capable of administering their own affairs are examples of situations when bonds would be required.

Government bonds

Another common example is the Customs and Excise Bond. This guarantees that if dutiable goods, intended for export and on which no duty is payable, find their way into the home market or are stolen, the duty will be paid by the surety should the owner or manufacturer fail to pay.

General (or Other) Insurances

These will now be considered below.

Insurance of rent

When a building has been damaged to the extent that it cannot be used until repairs are carried out, the tenant may still be obliged contractually to pay rent to the owner. Alternatively the owner may lose rent where the tenant has been relieved of the obligation to pay it. In either case, this class of insurance covers the sum involved.

Interruption insurance

This form of insurance was originally called time loss, then loss of profits, consequential loss and, towards the end the 1970s, 'interruption insurance'. This last title is appropriate because the policies available deal with the loss of profits of a business, or the additional expenditure necessary, after some physical property has been damaged.

The fire, all risks and engineering policies, mentioned earlier in this unit, all deal with the value of the property damaged or destroyed, but not with the losses caused by reduced sales during the repair period and thereafter. These losses come about because:

- certain overhead costs will remain at their full level, even though sales are reduced;

- net profit will be reduced;

- there may be increased costs incurred, to keep the business going in a temporary manner.

The most common interruption policies are those that cover losses following:

- fire and special perils;

- engineering breakdown;

- computer damage and breakdown.

Special features of interruption policies are that the insured must claim an 'indemnity period' designed to be the maximum length of time from the outbreak of, say, a fire to the point at which full turnover can again be achieved. The sum insured is geared to this.

Legal expenses insurance

Cover is available to private individuals and organizations, both of whom now face an ever-increasing possibility of legal action. One growing area of cover is among trade unions and professional bodies that offer a legal service as one of the benefits of membership. With escalating costs it is very difficult for them to budget for this, but to ease the problem they can purchase legal expenses insurance and pay a fixed premium each year.

Miscellaneous insurances

Whenever there is a demand for a particular cover and the criteria for insurable risks (see section 3) have been met, the industry will usually provide the covers necessary.

Examples of such policies include livestock, weather (rain and sunshine deficiency), twins or multiple births, loss of licence, kidnap and ransom, strikes, and aquaculture (fish farms).

Combined and Comprehensive Policies

Many of the forms of cover already dealt with are required by the same individual or business. A householder who owns and occupies his own house will require fire, special perils, loss of rent, additional living costs if the house is damaged, theft, glass, money and liability insurances. The industrial purchaser may require the same with the possible addition of goods-in-transit, engineering, fidelity, credit and loss of profits insurance.

Combined insurances

The advantages of combining various forms of insurance into one policy form are:

- easier and cheaper administration;

- only one premium and one renewal date to deal with;

- less chance of overlooking one form of cover;

- easier to market as one product, rather than several independent policies.

These combined policies (sometimes known as 'traders' combined' or 'shopkeepers' combined') are very suitable for a large number of businesses; the larger the insured becomes, the greater the need to arrange insurances specifically for him.

Another example is the holiday and travel insurance policy where all risks cover is combined with personal accident, medical expenses, loss of deposits and delay covers on one policy.

Comprehensive insurances

A step on from issuing combined policies, which is only the combination of separate policies within the one folder, is the comprehensive policy. This form of insurance represents a widening in the scope of cover. For example, the household comprehensive policy covers the basic perils mentioned above and includes also cover against damage caused by collapse of television aerials, leakage of central heating oil, the breakage of underground water pipes, sanitary fittings and many more risks. This widening of scope of the perils insured has been accompanied by alterations in the basic method of providing cover, so that today it is possible to arrange a household comprehensive policy that provides cover against damage caused by almost any event and with the amount being paid representing what it will actually cost to replace the damaged property.

This widening in cover has not been without its problems and many insurers have experienced large losses on their household insurance business, as a result of which substantial increases in premiums have been introduced. We shall examine the area of household covers more fully in Unit 15.

Comprehensive policies are also available for offices and shops, where cover is provided as a package. This is an efficient and relatively inexpensive way to provide cover for small offices and shops.

Space Risks

One modern development is the provision of insurance to those who are involved with satellites. Ever since the first *Sputnik* was launched in October 1957, it was inevitable that the commercial use of space satellites would eventually follow. These satellites are now used for a wide range of telecommunications purposes; we have seen this most vividly in the proliferation of domestic satellite dishes for receiving television signals. A number of risks can now be covered in the marine market, the main ones being material damage during testing, launch or while in orbit, and loss of revenue.

Student Activity 2

Before reading the next section of the text, answer the following questions and then check your answers against the pages indicated.

1.   What is the difference between credit and suretyship insurances?

(page 43)

2.   What are the advantages of combined insurances?

(page 60)

If your answers are basically correct, then proceed to the Summary. If significant parts of your answers are wrong, then study the whole of the relevant sections again in detail. Note your areas of weakness, and be prepared for further questions on these areas in the self-assessment section at the end of this unit.

Summary

A number of important features have been introduced in this unit. The functions of insurance, the benefits to the individual and the economy, a brief account of the historical development of certain classes of insurance and a description of the main classes of insurance currently on offer today have all been covered. This is a lot of material to cover, but it is essential groundwork for anyone who intends to make a serious study of insurance.

Self-assessment Questions

Short Answer Questions

1.   What is the primary function of insurance?

2.   List the benefits of insurance.

3.   What special considerations apply to insurance of the motor trade?

4.   What is 'insurance for the masses'?

5.   List five 'special perils'.

6.   What cover is provided by directors' and officers' liability?

(Answers given in Appendix 1)

Specimen Examination Question

Explain the benefits of insurance to both the individual and the State.

(Answer given in Appendix 1)

3

THE INSURANCE MARKETPLACE

Objectives

After studying this unit, you should be able to:

- identify the main participants in the insurance market and define their role;

- state the size of the insurance market;

- describe the structure of Lloyd's and how its members transact business;

- explain the various forms of insurance company and their organizational structure;

- list the organizations representing the various sections of the insurance market.

3.1 The Place and Role of Insurance within the Financial Framework

The UK insurance industry is highly developed and its operations affect the country's economy in a variety of ways:

- a risk transfer mechanism;

- loss prevention and reduction;

- major institutional investment;

- major employer;

- contribution to invisible earnings and balance of trade.

Unit 2 covers these aspects in detail and you should re-read the sections on the functions and benefits of insurance, if necessary.

In the UK, the industry has two markets – direct insurance and reinsurance – and we shall look at each of these in detail.

The Insurance Market

Like any other market, the insurance market comprises:

- **sellers** – the insurance companies and Lloyd's underwriting members;

- **buyers** – the general public, industry and commerce;

- **middlemen** – the insurance brokers and agents.

In other markets the buyers, sellers and perhaps the middlemen can come together to examine the merchandise that is to be the subject of the sale. With insurance it is not possible to bring a house, factory or ship, etc. to a marketplace, and in any event what is being insured is the financial interest in that asset or a potential lawsuit.

The buying and selling of insurance takes place every hour of every working day and contracts are arranged as and when required, at a place convenient to the individual parties concerned. As was seen in Unit 2 when discussing the functions of insurance, the insurance market is providing a financial service. It is a service industry in that it is supportive to industry producing goods or services. The structure of the market is summarized in Figure 3.1 overleaf.

The Size of the Market

One way to measure the size of the market is to look at the number of participants in the marketplace.

Sellers

In 1994 there were 820 United Kingdom and foreign incorporated insurance companies authorized by the Department of Trade to transact business in the United Kingdom. Once those companies that are no longer writing new business and the subsidiaries of larger groups are deducted, we are left with about 500 independent outlets.

Intermediaries

The number of intermediaries is very much harder to estimate. This is mainly due to the range of different titles that apply, and the rules that regulate their application. One figure we can ascertain is the number of companies, partnerships and sole traders permitted to use the title 'broker'. They must register with the Insurance Brokers' Registration Council, and at the end of January 1995 that figure was 3,782.

Figure 3.1: The Structure of the Insurance Market

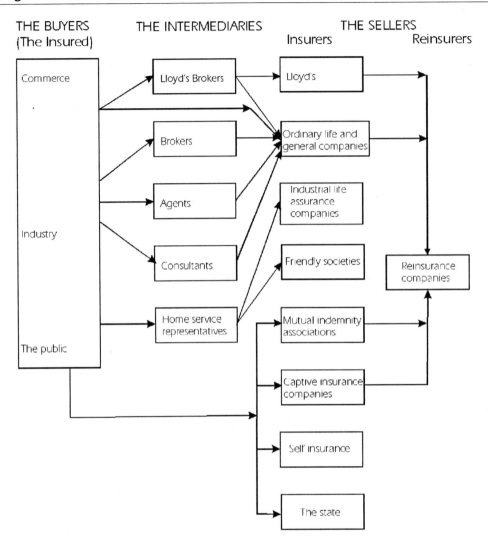

Buyers

It is impossible to say how many buyers of insurance there are. What we can say is that the *Family Expenditure Survey*, conducted by the Department of Employment, gave the following figures for 1993:

Table 3.1: Percentage of Households with Insurance Expenditure

Motor Insurance	64.5%
Medical Insurance	8.8%
Mortgage Protection	9.9%
Life Assurance	66.7%
Other Insurance	21.3%

This table gives only details of personal insurances and then for only certain types of cover. However, it is interesting to note the penetration of insurance.

We can only guess at the number of industrial and commercial organizations that insure. As we shall see later, some forms of insurance are compulsory, and when this is taken into account we could say that most firms in the country will have some form of insurance protection.

Another measure of size would be to look at the volume of business transacted in the marketplace. This can be done by looking at the money which passes through the marketplace and at the number of individual policies which are issued.

The total volume of premiums received is shown in Table 3.2. These figures are taken from the ABI Insurance Statistics booklet; we shall look at the role of the ABI later in this unit. The figures are for companies with their head office in the United Kingdom or for the United Kingdom operation of companies with their head office overseas. The ABI estimates that its figures cover 99% of total worldwide life assurance premiums and 93% of worldwide general insurance premiums.

Table 3.2: Worldwide Premium 1993 (£m)

	UK	Overseas	Total
Life	46,267	9,365	55,633
General	33,493	11,134	44,627

This gives some indication of the total volume of new money which passed through the market in 1993. The bulk of this premium relates to commercial insurances, but it is also interesting to consider household insurances.

We can now split this total into the two main forms of insurance:

Life Assurance

Total life assurance premiums in 1993 were £55,633m and this was made up from all forms of life business. The actual numbers of policies in force and issued during the year are shown in Table 3.3.

Table 3.3: Number of Life Policies 1993

	Number in force at end of 1993	New in 1993
Ordinary Individual Life	39,480	4,463
Individual Annuities	610	96
Industrial Life	44,451	1,213
Individual Pensions	17,932	1,838
Permanent Health Insurance	1,289	139

During 1993 the insurance industry paid out claims under life assurance policies of over £36,000m. This included payments on death and maturity and is a vast sum of money.

General Insurance

Looking at general insurance businesses we saw that total premiums were almost £45,000m. It is not possible to say how many policies this represents, but it is considerable. The claim payments give some indication of the magnitude of money flowing through the marketplace. For example, the total cost to the insurance industry of fire claims in Great Britain during 1993 was £647m. It is difficult to comprehend such a figure but it represents over £20 every single second of the year. Thefts of all kinds cost the industry £980m during the same year and estimated claims under employers' liability policies are £557m.

These figures give some idea of the magnitude of the insurance marketplace. They are not intended to be a complete or comprehensive analysis of the flow of funds associated with the insurance industry, nor is it recommended that readers memorize them. They serve only to underline the fact that this is an important marketplace, transacting business which can be measured in billions.

3.2   The Buyers

Most people without particular knowledge of insurance tend to think of insurance in terms of personal insurance. They recall the fact that they purchase private car insurance, household insurance, life assurance and that is the extent of their knowledge of insurance. There is of course no reason why they should have any broader knowledge; domestic or personal insurances do indeed form a large part of the buying market. However it is not personal insurances that occupy the most time in the insurance market. For most insurance companies it is commercial and industrial insurances that take up the time. When you consider that one single insured, one single company, could be spending many millions of pounds per year on insurance premiums you begin to get the market in perspective. Having said this, the schemes that exist for personal insurances are themselves multi-million pound schemes in some cases.

3.3   The Intermediaries (or Middlemen)

It is possible, as can be seen from Figure 3.1, to buy insurance direct. In the last ten years, a new style of direct insurer has emerged, and we shall comment upon this later in the unit. Many private individuals choose to do this. They decide what their insurance needs are, they may approach a number of insurance companies to obtain premium figures and then they decide with which company to insure. It is also possible for an individual to use the services of an intermediary. There are now many shop-type premises where individuals can call in and arrange insurances, or at least obtain quotations from an intermediary for a number of different insurers.

The commercial buyer of insurance is in a slightly different position. He may be faced with dozens of factory complexes spread throughout Britain, or the world, each one presenting many and varied forms of risk. He is in need of some expert advice to enable him to assess the risks he has and to match his needs to the best seller of insurance in the marketplace. The majority of commercial business is in fact handled by an intermediary of one form or another.

In legal terms an 'intermediary' is an agent who is authorized by a party, called the principal, to bring that principal into a contractual relationship with another, a third party. If the agent does not have prior authority to act in this way but purports to do so, and the principal later ratifies or confirms the agent's actions, then a contractual relationship will exist. (Agents can be appointed for other purposes, but these are beyond the scope of the present discussions, for example, employees can be agents of their employers.)

There are a number of different types of intermediary operating in the marketplace.

The Insurance Broker

A broker is an individual or firm whose full-time occupation is the placing of insurance with insurance companies. Legislation exists which governs the use of the word **broker**. It is not possible for a person or company simply to open an office and call themselves an insurance broker. We shall look at the registration procedure in a later unit.

The insured can obtain independent advice on a wide range of insurance matters from a broker, without direct cost to himself. For example, the broker will advise on insurance needs, best type of cover and its restrictions, best market, claims procedure, obligations placed on the insured by policy conditions, and he will up-date the information as time goes by to take account of market changes.

From the insurers' point of view, negotiations with brokers are easier and speedier because only the intricate points or special requirements require detailed discussion, thus saving time and money on routine matters.

The vast majority of commercial insurance is transacted through a registered broker. In large cases these brokers, often multinational companies in their own right, provide an invaluable service to large corporations. Premiums that can be measured in millions of pounds have to be managed and the service provided by the broker will extend far beyond the placing of insurance. The broker may also handle certain claims, draft policy wordings, carry out risk surveys, provide risk management services, and so on. Many industrial organizations have their own in-house brokers. These are subsidiaries formed by a company to act as that company's own broker.

Lloyd's brokers

A Lloyd's broker carries out the same functions as an ordinary insurance broker, but if one wishes to insure at Lloyd's the business must be placed there by a Lloyd's broker or other intermediary through a Lloyd's broker. Special direct dealing arrangements exist where a non-Lloyd's broker may deal direct with a syndicate. Managing Agents may set up service companies to deal direct with the public for personal lines and commercial motor business without any Lloyd's broker involvement.

The Council of Lloyd's registers brokering firms to act as Lloyd's brokers. They are required to satisfy the Council as to their expertise, integrity and financial standing. After being appointed, they can display the words 'and at Lloyd's' on their letter heading and name plates. The Lloyd's broker represents the insured in the transactions with the underwriter.

Although only registered brokers can enter 'The Room' and place business or place business electronically, the Lloyd's brokers are otherwise the same as other insurance brokers in their dealings with insurance companies.

Insurance Consultants

Another category of intermediary is the insurance consultant. We said earlier that regulations exist for those who wish to call themselves brokers. A person can act as an intermediary without registering under the relevant legislation, but cannot use the term broker. Many of these non-registered intermediaries refer to themselves as consultants.

Tied Agents

In law, an agent is one who acts on behalf of another. The 'Polarization' rules under the Financial Services Act require that all those giving advice on 'investment business' must be either completely independent, or tied to one particular company.

Such 'tied agents' can advise only on those products offered by their host company. There is a further distinction between Appointed Representatives and Company Representatives:

- **Appointed Representatives** are companies, firms or sole traders under a contract **for** services.
- **Company Representatives** may be salaried or self-employed, and are under a contract **of** service.

Home service representatives

Industrial life offices and friendly societies employ representatives to call at the homes of policyholders to collect premiums and pay claims. These home service representatives are company representatives of the industrial office or friendly society.

3.4   The Sellers or Suppliers of Insurance

We shall now look at each of these in turn.

Lloyd's

Lloyd's is quite unlike any of the other sellers of insurance. At the moment we shall consider the nature of Lloyd's as part of the overall insurance market and later (in section 5) we shall look at the way business is actually transacted there.

In Unit 2 we charted the brief history of Lloyd's from its beginnings in Edward Lloyd's coffee house. As the volume of business increased we saw that larger premises were found and a committee was formed. In 1871, the Lloyd's Act created the Corporation of Lloyd's. The Corporation did not transact insurance – this was still the province of individual underwriting members – but it did provide premises, services and assistance. It also, through the Council of Lloyd's, laid down the regulations and requirements that had to be met by anyone wishing to become a member.

Lloyd's Act 1982

The Lloyd's Act 1982 was the result of an enquiry under the chairmanship of Sir Henry Fisher into the constitution of, and self-regulation at, Lloyd's. Since then there have been a number of reports and enquiries into different aspects of the Lloyd's operation.

The 1982 Act created a new Council of Lloyd's. The Council has overall responsibility and control of affairs at Lloyd's, including rule-making and discipline. Up until 1992 the Council had 28 members, made up of working and external members of Lloyd's.

The Committee of Lloyd's comprises working members of the Council and is concerned more with the day-to-day running of affairs at Lloyd's, rather than any long-term planning or policy formulation.

Since 1982, there have been a number of reports and enquiries into different aspects of the Lloyd's operation, particularly following exceptionally heavy losses in the late 1980s. These include:

- The Neill Report 1987.
- The Morse Report 1992.
- The Sheldon Working Party Report 1994.

The Sheldon Report recommended that Council should not exceed 18 members, comprising six working, six external and six nominated members from 1 January 1995. The Council adopted these recommendations in August 1994.

Membership of Lloyd's

The capital behind the underwriting of insurances at Lloyd's is supplied by investors called 'Names'. Until 1994, Names had to be individuals investing in their personal capacity, but from January 1994, corporate members have also been admitted.

Names, or underwriting members, are usually not insurance professionals, and many come from the entertainment industry and the aristocracy. Those members who are 'Working Names' are engaged in insurance work but have to satisfy strict requirements as to knowledge of the market.

There are over 14,000 individual participating members of Lloyd's and over 120 corporate members, grouped into 180 syndicates. Names conduct their business through syndicates.

Each syndicate appoints a managing agent to manage its affairs and who appoints professional underwriters on behalf of the syndicate.

All premiums are paid into a trust fund, with payments allowed only to meet claims, reinsurance premiums and underwriting expenses. Profit is not distributed until three years have elapsed and the fund is subject to strict investment criteria.

Members are required to deposit assets, to be held in a trust fund, according to specified ratios. Individual members are required to deposit between 20% and 50% of the overall premium income limit, as well as showing a minimum level of personal wealth of £250,000. Corporate members must deposit 50%, with a minimum of £1.5 million capital. In addition, all members make an annual contribution into a central fund, available to meet claims in the event of a member being unable to meet his underwriting liabilities.

Individual Lloyd's Names have always been personally liable to the full extent of their means in respect of that share of the business underwritten on their behalf. Following exceptionally large losses in a minority of syndicates and the resultant financial ruin of Names associated with them, steps have been taken to reorganize the control and discipline of the market. These steps include:

- A special high-level stop loss scheme fund was introduced in January 1993 to protect members against such exceptional losses occurring again.

- Corporate investors were first admitted to Lloyd's in 1994 and this admission of limited liability capital was designed to attract new investment to Lloyd's. As at April 1995, the Business Plan Progress Report for Lloyd's reported that corporate members represented a 23% share of the market's overall capacity.

- A new reinsurance company was established to handle the 'old year' liabilities.

Insurance Companies

The majority of insurance sellers come under this heading and are limited liability companies with shareholders as proprietors.

Proprietary companies

Historically they have been created by Royal Charter, as in the case of The Royal Exchange Assurance; by act of parliament, as in the case of The Scottish Union and National (now part of the Norwich Union Group); and by Deed of Settlement (a form of partnership), but generally these companies have been reformed by registration under the Companies Acts.

The majority of insurance companies have been created by registration under the Companies Acts and it is almost certain that all new companies in the future will be created in this manner.

Proprietary companies have an authorized and issued share capital to which the original shareholders subscribed, and it is to the shareholders that any profits belong after provision for expenses, reserves and, in the case of life business, with-profit policyholders' bonuses. The shareholders' liability is limited to the nominal value of their shares (hence the term limited liability), but the company is liable for its debts and if the solvency margin cannot be met (see Unit 5) the company will go into liquidation. The public can deal direct with these companies but often an intermediary is involved. In most classes of business there is keen competition among proprietary companies and also between proprietary companies and other sectors of the market.

Mutual companies

Mutual companies have been formed by Deed of Settlement or registration under the Companies Acts. They are owned by the policyholders, who share any profits made. The shareholder in the proprietary company receives his share of the profit by way of dividends, but in the mutual company the policyholder owner may enjoy lower premiums or higher life assurance bonuses than would otherwise be the case.

Originally, the policyholders could be called upon to make further contributions to the fund if the original premiums were inadequate to meet the claims and expenses. Today most mutual insurers are limited by guarantee, with the policyholders' maximum liability limited to their premiums or an additional 50p or £1, at the most.

It is no longer possible to tell from the name of a company whether it is proprietary or mutual. Many companies which were originally formed as mutual organizations have now registered under the Companies Acts as proprietary companies, although they have retained the word mutual in their title. Others, registered as companies limited by guarantee and without the word mutual in their title, are actually owned by the policyholders.

The members or policyholders of mutual companies sometimes receive substantial benefits by way of lower premiums or higher bonuses, but this is by no means certain.

Mutuals may transact life or general business. A feature of mutual status is the difficulty in raising additional capital (unlike proprietary offices, they cannot issue additional shares). This has contributed to the failure of several prominent mutual general insurers in recent years.

Classification of insurance companies

In this unit we have classified companies according to their form of ownership, but companies can also be classified in other ways:

- **Specialist companies** are those that underwrite one type of insurance business only, for example, life companies and engineering insurance companies.

- **Composite companies** are those that underwrite several types of business. Composite companies form the bulk of the market, and in fact the ten largest composite groups account for over 50% of general premium income and about 40% of life income written by British insurers.

Insurance has been affected significantly in the past 15 years by the activities of banks, building societies and other financial institutions. The deregulation of the financial services marketplace has led to many banks and building societies setting up their own life and general insurance companies and diversifying into non-traditional areas of business. The involvement of banks and other financial institutions in the traditional insurance market is known as 'bancassurance'.

One major bank subsidiary has developed the successful selling of private motor, household and mortgage products by telephone using the latest telecommunications technology, and this has been copied by many traditional composite insurers. Composite insurers now often have direct writing subsidiaries which accept business from the public direct and bypass the intermediary. This growth in direct writing has had a major effect on personal lines business.

Insurers have themselves set up joint venture companies with several banks and building societies. They have also diversified into areas such as estate agency. The trend towards a 'one stop financial supermarket' gathered pace during the late 1980s, but some institutions have since pulled back from this approach more recently because of escalating costs and general effects of the recession, particularly on the housing market.

Industrial Life Assurance Companies

Many of these companies are proprietary companies whose activities are controlled by the Industrial Assurance and Friendly Societies Acts.

Premiums are collected weekly or monthly on industrial business, but such companies often also transact ordinary branch life business. We saw earlier that there has been a reducing trend in the numbers of industrial life assurance policies sold. The attractiveness of the one-stop shop for financial services which we commented on above may well have contributed to the decline in popularity of industrial life assurance. However, there are deeper sociological issues involved.

Collecting Friendly Societies

These societies are run on a mutual basis and are formed by registration under the Friendly Societies Acts. They transact industrial life assurance and, in some cases, personal accident and sickness covers. Although some of these societies are nationally known names, most operate within the area of their registered office.

Their growth arose out of the Industrial Revolution, when industrial workers required funeral benefits (at least). These societies provided small policies with the premiums being collected weekly and therefore at a cost the worker could afford, for example, 1d. per week. Levels of cover and premiums have now risen to keep pace with the needs of society and the large home service insurers of today grew from these small beginnings. The Friendly Societies Act 1992 modernized laws relating to friendly societies dating back over 150 years. It increased protection for members' funds and allowed societies to offer policies similar to their modern competitors, such as the former Peps and Tessas.

Captive Insurance Companies

Captive insurance is a method of transacting risk transfer that has become more common in recent years among the large national and international companies. The parent company forms a subsidiary company to underwrite certain of its insurable risks. The main incentives are to obtain the full benefit of the group's risk control techniques by paying premiums based on its own experience, avoidance of the direct insurers' overheads and obtaining a lower overall risk premium level by purchasing reinsurance at lower cost than that required by the conventional or direct insurer.

All direct insurers retain only a portion of many risks and reinsure or insure again the portion that is above their financial ability to retain. Because the direct or commercial market insurer has all the procuration and survey costs to bear, the net cost of reinsurance is substantially less than the cost of direct insurance. Hence, the captive company can have access to the lower cost reinsurance market and, through the proportion of the risk retained, still have the advantages to the group of self-insurance for that amount of risk. The premiums paid to the captive company are allowable against Corporation Tax, although in the USA the Internal Revenue Service (the US equivalent of our Inland Revenue) has disallowed such premiums where the captive transacts no business from risks created outside the parent company. The general rule is that the captive must be dealt with at arm's length and be charging reasonable premiums in relation to what is available in the general market.

The captive concept has grown considerably over the past decade and now very many of the country's large, and not-so-large, companies operate their own insurance company. Many captives are operated from offshore locations such as Bermuda, Guernsey and the Isle of Man. This does give the captive certain fiscal advantages, but it also reduces the volume of paperwork associated with registering as an insurer and, because so many captives are offshore, allows the captive to tap into all the necessary ancillary services such as investment management, banking, accounting, and so on.

Reinsurance Companies

We saw earlier that the principal function of insurance was to accept the transfer of risk from the public. In a similar way, the insurers may find some of the risks transferred to them too onerous, and they in turn reinsure the amount above the limit of retention that they can afford to carry.

A very large international market has developed and many companies and groups (the reinsurers) specialize in accepting the transfer of this surplus or excess insurance from the companies who initially accepted the transfer from the public.

Reinsurance furthers the principle of spreading the risk, and offers the insurer stability and protection against catastrophe, as well as a wide range of technical services.

Mutual Indemnity Associations

Mutual indemnity associations differ from mutual companies in that the companies will accept business from the public at large, whereas an indemnity association originally would accept business only from members of a particular trade. However, over the years many of the associations have had to accept business from members of the public in order to have greater financial stability and spread of risk, and have been reformed as mutual or proprietary companies.

The true mutual indemnity associations grew out of trade associations and are common pools into which members of a particular trade contribute, and from which they can make a claim when necessary. The associations were formed because members of a particular trade felt that the cost of commercial insurance was too high relative to their particular claims experience, or that they had an insurance need that was not being met by the commercial market at that time.

Examples of trades with such associations at one time were pharmacists, farmers, furniture manufacturers and shipowners. Sometimes there were a number of associations within a trade, with each one underwriting business from a fairly local area, e.g. farmers within one county or part of a county.

Contributions were made to the fund on the basis of tonnage or value and, in bad years, the members would be called upon to make additional contributions to keep the fund solvent.

Most of these associations have now been taken over by the normal insurance market, but there is still a very healthy marine market in this area. Their survival is probably due to the fact that they are the largest and longest established and were thus not under the same financial strain as other trade mutuals.

In recent years, some associations have been set up to meet the professional indemnity insurance needs of certain trades and professions.

An organization along similar lines to a mutual indemnity association is the NHS Clinical Negligence Scheme for Trusts, which created a central fund to meet a member Trust's potential liability for larger clinical negligence claims.

Protection and Indemnity Associations

The best known form of mutual indemnity associations are the Protection and Indemnity Associations (P and I Clubs). These marine associations (clubs) insure liabilities for cargo, liabilities to crew, to passengers, and to third parties, including one-quarter of the shipowner's liability for damage done to another ship in collision, because the shipowner's hull policy covers only three-quarters of such liability.

Self-insurance

As an alternative to purchasing insurance in the market, or as an adjunct to it where the first layer or proportion of a claim is not insured in the commercial market, some public bodies and large industrial concerns set aside funds to meet insurable losses. Because the risk is retained within the organization, there is no market transaction of buying and selling, but such arrangements have an overall effect on the funds of the market in general and on premium levels where the organization is carrying the first layer.

These organizations have made decisions to self-insure because they feel they are large enough financially to carry such losses and because the cost to them, by way of transfers to the fund, is lower than commercial premium levels because they are not paying the insurer's administration costs and profit. This could happen where an organization decides that it has an exposure to loss involving a large number of incidents, all of which are of fairly low severity. This high frequency and low severity profile implies that the losses are predictable. If the organization considers them to be predictable then the insurer, with its much larger pool to draw on, would certainly find the losses predictable. Were the organization to insure such losses, there would be a kind of pound swapping exercise with the organization paying a pound to an insurer only to get it back when the losses, which both parties knew would occur, actually take place. The problem for the insuring company is that it also have to recover its costs and so the amount paid in premiums would probably exceed the cost of the predictable claims.

In such cases a fund could be created, out of which the losses will eventually be met. The reader should note the difference between 'self-insurance' where a conscious decision is made to create a fund and 'non-insurance' where either no conscious decision is made at all, or where no fund is created.

Self-insurance schemes, while having certain advantages, also have some serious disadvantages.

Advantages of self-insurance

The advantages of such a scheme may be summarized as follows:

- Premiums should be lower because there are no costs in respect of broker's commission, insurers' administration and profit margins.

- Interest on the investment of the fund belongs to the insured and can be used to increase the fund or to reduce future premium contributions.

- The insured's premium costs are not increased because of the adverse claims experience of other firms.

- There is a direct incentive to reduce and control the risk of loss.

- No disputes can arise with insurers over claims.

- As the decision to self-insure is likely to be limited to large organizations, they will already have qualified insurance personnel on their staff to administer the fund.

- The profits from the fund accrue to the insured.

Disadvantages of self-insurance

The disadvantages of self-insurance arrangements are as follows:

- Although unlikely, a catastrophic loss could occur, wiping out the fund and perhaps forcing the organization into liquidation.

- Although the organization may be able to pay for any individual loss, the aggregate effect of several losses in one year could have the same effect as one catastrophic loss, particularly in the early years after formation of the fund.

- Capital has to be tied up in short-term, easily realizable investments which may not provide as good a yield as the wider spread of investments available to an insurance company.

- It may be necessary to increase the number of insurance staff employed, at an extra cost.

- The technical advice of insurers on risk prevention would not be available and, because the insurers' surveyors would have a wider experience over many firms and different trades, this knowledge could be advantageous to the insured.

- The claims statistics of the organization will be derived from too narrow a base for predictions to be made with confidence as to future claims costs.

- There may be criticism from shareholders and other departments:

    – at the transfer of large amounts of capital to create the fund and at the cost to dividends that year, and

    - at the low yield on the investment of the fund compared with the yield obtainable if that amount of capital were invested in the production side of the organization.

- In times of financial pressure there may be a temptation to borrow from the fund, thus defeating the security it had created.

- Pressure may be brought to bear on the managers of the fund to pay losses that are outside the cover (make ex gratia payments), with the resultant depletion of the fund for its legitimate purposes and thus making statistical analysis more difficult.

- The basic principle of insurance, that of spreading the risk, is defeated.

- The contributions made to the fund do not qualify as a charge against Corporation Tax, whereas premium payments are allowable. However, losses incurred by the fund are allowed as a business expense.

The State

The state is the final supplier of insurance we shall mention. The actual cover provided will be examined in Unit 4 when we look at the whole role of government in relation to insurance.

We move on now to look at the more operational aspects of the marketplace including transaction of business at Lloyd's, the structure of insurance companies and the trade and professional bodies associated with insurance.

Student Activity 1

Before reading the next section of the text, answer the following questions and then check your answers against the pages indicated.

1.   Distinguish between a composite and a specialist insurer.   *(page 73)*

2.   Identify the benefits of self-insurance.   *(page 77)*

If your answers are basically correct, then proceed to the next section. If significant parts of your answers are wrong, then study the whole of the relevant sections again in detail. Note your areas of weakness, and be prepared for further questions on these areas in the self-assessment section at the end of this unit.

3.5   Transaction of Business at Lloyd's

The procedures and practices within the Lloyd's market are quite different from those of any other insurer. They are built on years of tradition, as we shall see, and still rely to a large extent on personal contact between those wishing to place insurance and those willing to carry the risk.

The Room

Lloyd's is housed in a modern, purpose-built building in the centre of the City of London. Underwriters and their staff sit at **boxes**, each with a number, and the Lloyd's brokers negotiate their contracts there. The Room at Lloyd's is the only place in the country where there is a recognized insurance marketplace.

Transaction of Business

It was mentioned previously, and shown in the diagram of the insurance market, that only Lloyd's brokers may place insurance at Lloyd's. When requested to place insurance at Lloyd's, the Lloyd's broker prepares a **slip**.

From 1996, an electronic placing support system was in operation and electronic versions of contracts for all business placed at Lloyd's are now required.

The slip

This is a sheet of paper containing details of the risk to be insured. It shows:

● details of insured;

● period of cover required;

- inception date of cover;

- perils or type of cover required;

- property to be insured;

- sums insured or limits of liability;

- special conditions to be incorporated;

- expected premium.

Underwriting

The broker takes the slip to an underwriter who specializes in this class of business, with a view to his accepting the **lead** or first proportion of the risk. Discussions on other aspects of the risk such as the claims experience, take place and the underwriter may feel obliged to amend some of the terms on the slip before he can accept, for example, the rate of premium or the conditions. Once agreement on terms has been reached, the underwriter stamps and initials the slip for the proportion he is prepared to accept for his syndicate. This proportion may be very low, say 5%, and the broker will proceed to other underwriters until 100% is underwritten. If the broker establishes a good 'lead', other underwriters will accept the terms of the leading underwriter, otherwise the broker has to start again on the new terms.

Each underwriter records details of the risk underwritten for his own records.

Policy Signing Office

When the slip is complete, the broker returns to his office and has the policy prepared in accordance with the slip. The policy and slip are then submitted to Lloyd's Policy Signing Office (LPSO), where the policy is checked with the slip and signed on behalf of all syndicates.

From 1 January 1996, all risks had to be closed electronically through LPSO and policy/ slip information was already contained in the LPSO system. Accounts are prepared from the date recorded.

Claims

The Lloyd's broker also provides a service to his client in the settlement of claims. He negotiates with the staff of a central office called the Lloyd's Claims Office. Motor claims are handled by motor syndicates at their own offices.

Other Functions of Lloyd's

Lloyd's fulfils a number of functions other than writing insurance business; these are considered below.

Lloyd's intelligence and other services

It will be recalled from Unit 2 that Edward Lloyd started to give shipping news in his coffee house some 300 years ago. This service has been increased many fold, so that today Lloyd's is the leading source of shipping information in the world. Information is received daily from all over the world by the Intelligence Department which distributes the information through various publications:

- *Lloyd's List* is a daily newspaper dealing with matters of general interest to shipowners and others with maritime interests. It also reports marine and aviation accidents, arrivals and departures of merchant shipping throughout the world, together with details of ships due to arrive, or in dock, at selected UK ports.

- *Lloyd's Shipping Index* is published Monday to Friday inclusive and lists ocean going ships alphabetically showing type of vessel, owner, flag, classification society, year of build, gross and net tonnage, current voyage and last reported position.

- *Lloyd's Loading List* is published weekly, and its monthly supplement *Cargo by Air* provides exporters with a valuable guide to cargo carrying services.

- *Lloyd's Law Reports* specialize in shipping, insurance, aviation and commercial cases heard in the English, Scottish, Commonwealth, and United States courts.

Other publications are *Lloyd's Nautical Year Book*, *Lloyd's Survey Handbook*, *Lloyd's Weekly Casualty Reports*, *Lloyd's Voyage Records*, *Lloyd's Maritime Atlas* and *Lloyd's Shipping Economist*.

Casualty Reports are prepared daily for all sections of the market and displayed on notice boards in 'The Room'.

Lloyd's Register of Shipping, which is a detailed register of survey details of ships, is not published by Lloyd's although members of the Council of Lloyd's serve on the Committee of *Lloyd's Register of Shipping*.

Lloyd's agents

Lloyd's agents are situated in the leading ports and areas of the world and are the source of much of the information published. They also conduct surveys and arrange for surveys to be carried out in connection with losses and, if appointed as claims-settling agents, they can settle claims abroad. At present there are in the region of 900 Lloyd's agents and sub-agents throughout the world.

3.6 Organizational Structure of Insurance Companies

In order to appreciate how an insurance company operates, it is helpful to look at the organization from two particular aspects, the personnel and the geographical organization.

The Personnel

There is no uniformity of practice or of titles from one company to another, so that the terminology and structure of an individual company may not coincide with Figure 3.2, but all of these functions will be performed under some title or other. The diagram shows the structure of a typical composite insurer.

Board of directors

The function of the Board is to formulate the overall plan of operation for the company, in the best interests of the owners (the shareholders) taking into account the interests of policyholders, staff, the public and the effect of market competition.

Figure 3.2: Organization Structure

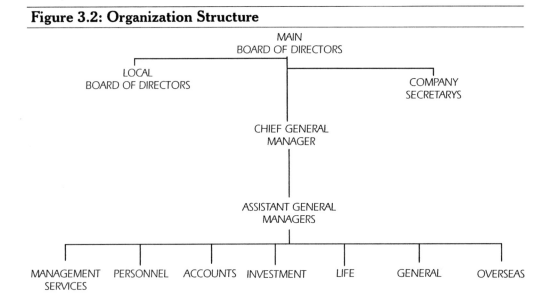

Boards comprise both executive and non-executive directors. The former are involved in the day-to-day operation of the company and are members of its senior management. Non-executive directors come from many other areas and could include some titled persons who may add prestige to the company and give the benefit of their experience in other business pursuits. Prominent people from the industrial, commercial and academic world are often involved as non-executive directors, providing the benefit of their expertise.

Local boards of directors

Some companies have boards of directors attached to leading branch offices. These are non-executive directors and are appointed to promote the interests of the company locally and to give advice on local affairs to the branch manager.

General managers

The chief general manager is the chief executive of the company, and he is assisted by a deputy and several assistants, depending upon the size of the company. The chief general manager is charged with the responsibility of implementing the policy laid down by the Board. He is of course a member of the main Board.

Each assistant general manager has a particular area of responsibility. There may well be a general manager or assistant general manager responsible for many of the areas we have identified in Figure 3.2.

Company secretary

The responsibilities of the company secretary are those of the administration of the organization as a registered company and ensuring that the company complies with company and insurance company law.

Management services

The activities and costs of a large insurance company are now so vast that many of them have set up departments of specialists, for example organization and methods of staff, statisticians and economists, to advise on any changes in plan which may be necessary in the future. In this way it is hoped that the company can cope with change, and progress smoothly in a rapidly changing world.

Under this heading is also the use of information technology. Reading through the Annual Reports of the major composites one cannot escape the conclusion that the use of all forms of modern information technology is very much on the increase.

Personnel

It is essential that any large organization has a steady flow of new recruits of the correct type and that those already employed by the company are well trained, remunerated and motivated. These functions fall within the remit of the personnel department. In current times, when there are likely to be fewer school leavers available for work, the role of the personnel department has become even more crucial.

Accounts

With such large sums of money flowing through an insurance company, there is a need for a very sophisticated form of accounting. The accounts function is an important part of any corporate structure in insurance. We shall see later that stringent regulations are in force governing the reporting of insurance accounts and the accounts department works closely with the office of the company secretary to ensure compliance with the law.

Investment

In any large insurance company, the reserves amount to several millions of pounds and this vast fund must be invested for security and income. In Unit 2 the investment portfolios of British companies were summarized. If long-term business is transacted, the company must have an actuary to meet the legal requirements and he may be the investment manager or the life manager, perhaps with assistant general manager status.

Figure 3.2 also shows life, general and overseas functions at the same level as we have for the others already mentioned. There may be general or assistant general managers responsible for particular branches of insurance and there may be a senior manager responsible for the branch network itself.

Geographical Organization

The geographical organization of a typical company is shown in Figure 3.3.

Figure 3.3: Organization of a Typical Composite Company

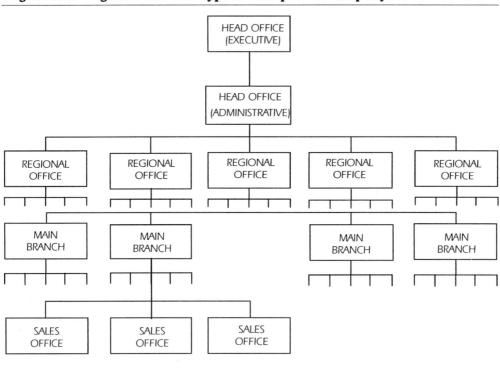

Not all companies operate with regional offices and this is discussed below.

Executive head office

This is usually situated in London although there are head offices in Norwich, Liverpool, Kendal, Perth, Glasgow and Edinburgh. Some companies maintain complete head offices in London, but because of the high cost of office space and salaries in London and difficulties in communication, many companies have moved the general administrative and underwriting work to a second head office in the provinces. These companies maintain only departments essential to London and small underwriting sections in the city.

Administrative head office

The main burden of management and underwriting is carried out here, usually in the provinces where costs are lower. The computer centre is likely to be outside London for better telecommunications.

Regional offices

Some companies operate on a partly decentralized system (see later) where certain zonal or regional offices have underwriting authority for branches within their region.

Main branches

These branches are responsible for initial underwriting within their area and that of their sub-branches. They are also responsible for claims handling (unless taken over by a regional office) and mainly for sales promotion.

Sub-branches

The prime purpose of a sub-branch is sales promotion in its area.

Decentralization of Authority

The operational organization of an insurance company can range from complete centralization of all decision making at head office, to complete decentralization with branches having wide-ranging powers within broad guidelines. Between these two extremes is the regional system, whereby certain main centres are given substantial authority on underwriting and claims for the branches within the region.

Centralization

When a company is centralized all underwriting, claims, policy drafting, renewals and accounts work is handled from head office, with the branches being merely sales outlets.

Some advantages of centralization are:

- uniformity of policy, practice and routine;

- most economic use of mechanized methods;

- fewer experts required, with a resultant saving in salaries;

- branches relieved of routine work and can then concentrate on selling;

Some disadvantages are:

- the system is often run from an area of high salary, building and rating costs, for example London;

- poor service can result from the administration being remote from the customer;

- excessive power in a few hands, dictatorial attitudes can develop in underwriting to the detriment of the company;

- lack of promotion prospects for most of the staff.

Decentralization

Under this system each main branch is responsible for its own underwriting, policy drafting and claims.

Some advantages of decentralization are:

- local officials best understand local conditions;

- good local service is possible;

- branch staff become more knowledgeable by having to make decisions;

- brings democracy to the underwriting policy of the company;

- creates better staff morale by providing more chances of promotion to the higher grades of post required at the branches.

Some disadvantages are:

- many experts are required, resulting in a higher salary bill;

- branches inundated with routine work, instead of concentrating on selling, which is their main function;

- wasted effort in trying to make each branch expert in everything;

- divergence of practice is likely to develop between branches and this can be embarrassing if it becomes known to the public. It can also lead to misleading statistics for the company nationally.

Few companies are either completely centralized or completely decentralized and in the 1960s there was a general shift to the mid-point of a regional system.

Regional system

Under this system the country was divided into, say, ten regions and the principal branch became the regional office. It took over the underwriting, policy drafting and claims work from head office or the branches depending upon the system previously in force. In this way an attempt was made to remove most of the disadvantages of both systems, while retaining many of their advantages.

In the latter part of the 1970s, the tendency appeared to be to remove some of the authority from main branches to regional offices and from regional offices to head office. While this may appear to be a backward step, it must be seen in the light of technological change and the greater capabilities of the computer as a labour-saving device along with the need to increase sales volume in order to achieve the best of use of those facilities where costs cannot be reduced.

The present scene appears to indicate the closure of some sub-offices; withdrawal of routine work from some main branches to make them sales offices only; and removal of routine work on underwriting, endorsements and claims to the central computer, often by means of modems and visual display units (VDUs) at regional offices.

Direct insurers

Use of the latest technology in telecommunications and telesales techniques means that the new direct writers do not require extensive branch networks to service their business. Their administration and underwriting centres can be located anywhere in the country and contact with customers is simply subject to the cost of a telephone call and postage of documentation. Cost of office accommodation and proximity of a suitable workforce are the most important considerations in the choice of location.

3.7   Reinsurance

Reinsurance can be defined as 'insuring the insurer'. Just as an individual will want to spread the risk of loss, an insurer will need similar protection and will seek reinsurance for the largest and most difficult risks, or will seek to cover his whole account to protect himself against unexpected losses and catastrophes.

For this course it is only necessary to have an awareness of reinsurance and how it fits into the overall marketplace.

Why Reinsure?

The main reasons why an insurance company will seek reinsurance are summarized below :

- Spread of risk
  An insurer will wish to relieve itself from uncertainty of loss and by spreading the risk of loss the insurer will have security and peace of mind.

- Stability
  Reinsurance helps to avoid fluctuations in claims from year to year.

- Capacity
  Every insurer will have a financial limit on the size of loss it will be prepared to accept. By purchasing reinsurance, the insurer can accept all sizes of risk in the knowledge that it can reinsure any part of the loss which it feels is too large.

- Catastrophe
  The possibility of complete catastrophe and many claims from one event such as an earthquake can be protected against by special catastrophe agreements with a reinsurer.

- Statute
  The Department of Trade and Industry (DTI) will want to ensure that adequate reinsurance arrangements exist under the Insurance Companies Act 1982.

- Technical services
  Reinsurers have experience in dealing with the largest and most difficult risks. They can provide information to insurers and often become involved in researching new areas of the market on behalf of a number of their clients.

The Market

The business of reinsurance is international. However, the marketplace for reinsurance, wherever it is bought or sold, is the same.

- Buyers: direct insurers, captive insurers, Lloyd's syndicates, reinsurers.

- Intermediaries: reinsurance brokers.

- Sellers: specialist reinsurers, direct insurers, captive insurers, Lloyd's syndicates, pools.

It should be noted that the insured has no involvement in the contract for reinsurance. The reinsurance agreement is between the insurer and the reinsurer. The insured has a claim only against the insurer and will be unaware of the existence of any reinsurance arrangement.

Transacting reinsurance

There are two main ways of transacting reinsurance: facultative and treaty.

Facultative involves the 'ceding' of each risk individually to the reinsurer by the direct office, and the reinsurer decides in each case whether to accept the risk.

Treaty is now the most popular form of reinsurance and involves an agreement between the direct office and reinsurer that all risks within certain parameters will be ceded and the reinsurer must accept such risks. This arrangement has obvious benefits to both parties.

Treaty reinsurance can be further divided into proportional and non-proportional.

There are two types of proportional treaty: quota share is a reinsurance of a fixed proportion of each and every risk (usually expressed as a percentage); surplus treaties are based on ceding the excess over a predetermined retention amount.

Non-proportional treaties include excess of loss and stop-loss arrangements. In each case reinsurance is based on the losses which may be incurred rather than the sums insured. Excess of loss occurs where the reinsurer covers any loss in excess of a predetermined figure, up to a maximum amount. Stop-loss provides protection for an entire portfolio of risk rather than individual losses, the reinsurer paying out only if the ratio of losses to premium income exceeds a predetermined percentage.

The area of reinsurance is complex and it should be noted that only an outline knowledge of the subject is necessary to provide a full picture of the insurance market.

Student Activity 2

Before reading the next section of the text, answer the following questions and then check your answers against the pages indicated.

1.   What is the role of the LPSO?   *(page 80)*

2.   Why do insurance companies reinsure?   *(page 87)*

If your answers are basically correct, then proceed to the next section. If significant parts of your answers are wrong, then study the whole of the relevant sections again in detail. Note your areas of weakness, and be prepared for further questions on these areas in the self-assessment section at the end of this unit.

3.8   The International Insurance Market

Although much insurance business is domestic, a significant proportion is worldwide. The crucial part that marine insurance plays in financing world trade is a good example of the international importance of insurance to all countries throughout the world. In the UK, insurance represented £4,623 million of invisible earnings in 1993 and was the biggest single earner.

Insurance can be described as 'international' in any of the following situations:

- **Cross-frontier Business**
  The insured buys a policy from an insurer established in another country, either because cover cannot be placed locally or because it is cheaper to buy cover elsewhere.

- **Establishment Business**
  The insured purchases from an insurer established in the same country, but its head office is in another country and its shareholders reside abroad. The reason for such a purchase could be that cross-frontier business is not permitted or is not profitable, or that the local market provides an opportunity for growth.

- **International Movement of Goods and People**
  The insured and the insurer are in the same country but the insurance relates to the international movement of goods or people. Common examples are marine and aviation insurances.

There has been significant progress in the liberalization of trade in goods through the General Agreement on Tariffs and Trade (GATT) set up in 1948. Services, including insurance, have been included in the activities of GATT, but many countries still operate protectionist policies for either economic and/or political reasons and progress is slow. These protectionist policies include the setting up of state insurance and reinsurance companies with suitable restrictive legislation, restricted access to overseas markets, exchange controls and discriminatory tax rules.

Insurance and the Single European Market

The most ambitious plans for liberalizing insurance trade have been those of the European Union. A single European market in insurance was initially timetabled for 1969 with the aim of encouraging growth across borders. However, difficulties in harmonizing the diverse systems of regulation and supervision mean that the task of achieving a single European insurance market in practice is still some way off.

The Treaty of Rome defines an internal market as 'an area without internal frontiers, in which the free movement of goods, persons, services and capital is ensured'.

The creation of a single market in insurance means that the insurance market is without internal barriers. Insurance companies and intermediaries should be able to carry out their business activities without restriction in all the member states. The goals are freedom of establishment, freedom of services and a single licence.

The **First Non-life Directive 1973** and **First Life Directive 1979** had the aim of freedom of establishment. This means allowing any European Union (EU) insurer to set up branches in other countries. Their main provisions included:

- standard authorization procedure;
- harmonized definitions for classes of business;
- right to authorization in other member states provided supervisory requirements satisfied;
- solvency margins harmonized across the community;
- restrictions on combining life and non-life insurance in the same 'composite' company.

The **Second Non-life Directive 1988** and **Second Life Directive 1990** had the aim of freedom of services, allowing any EU insurer to sell business throughout the Community without having to set up a branch in each country. Their main provisions included:

- Freedom of services for 'large risks' introduced only by Non-life Directive.

  Large risks are policyholders that are companies with 250 or more employees.
- Freedom of services for cases where the policyholder sought a cross-border policy 'at his own initiative'. For those cases where the initiative came from an insurance company or intermediary, freedom of services would not apply and local control and supervision would be the norm.

The Second Directives were significant in that they introduced freedom of services for some insurance business, despite difficulties in obtaining agreement for such harmonization. However, the provisions of the Second Directives have now been superseded by the Third Directives.

The **Third Non-life Directive (1992)** and **Third Life Directive (1992)** had the purpose of extending the principle of freedom of services, allowing all insurance to be sold throughout the Union, and ignoring the distinctions introduced under the Second Directives.

Their main provisions included :

- **Single licence**: an EU company needs only one authorization to operate throughout the Community.

- **Home country control**: operations throughout the Community are supervised by one set of supervisors in the country where the company has its head office. This includes operations through local branches (freedom of establishment) and cross-border operations (freedom of services).

- **Mutual recognition of supervisory authorities**: the supervisor in each member state recognizes that the control exercised by supervisors in other member states is sufficient.

- **Abolition of monopoly insurers** (especially Germany).

- **Harmonization of rules** on technical reserves, permitted assets, solvency requirements.

These Directives were a significant move towards a single European market in insurance and the development of cross-border business **but** in practice they have had little effect on the UK market. Significant barriers, particularly in life and personal business, still exist.

Agreement was quickly reached on reinsurance mainly because these transactions were already relatively free. The **Reinsurance Directive** issued in 1964 abolished all laws restricting the ability of reinsurers to become established in, or provide reinsurance in, other member states. The Directive was a liberalizing one: it did not co-ordinate or harmonize the laws of member states, or lay down minimum standards or conditions of supervision.

There is no single licence regime for reinsurance. However, a few member states subject reinsurers and retrocessionaires to authorization and supervision. The UK is an exception: a reinsurer or retrocessionnaire must secure authorization from the DTI to transact business and thereafter the DTI supervises the business. This rule has been allowed to continue because the UK is not discriminating against other member states; the requirement applies to both UK and Community reinsurers. A Community reinsurer must therefore obtain authorization from the DTI before establishing in the UK.

The UK government is currently pressing the European Commission to introduce a requirement that all reinsurers and retrocessionaires in the Community are subject to common conditions of authorization and control.

Other important directives in the insurance area include:

Legal Expenses Directive

Member states must allow insurers to transact both legal expenses and other classes of insurance (removing the previous German specialization requirement). However, there are certain provisions to maintain the independence of handling claims where the same company is dealing with two claims from different classes of insurance.

Tourist Assistance Directive

Tourist Assistance is to be regarded as insurance under the First Non-life Directive. Providers therefore have the right to become established in other member states.

Co-insurance Directive

This permitted co-insurers to provide co-insurance of major risks on a services basis throughout the Community. Therefore, a co-insurer established and authorized in one member state could cover a risk located in another member state without having to be established and authorized in that state.

Insurance Accounts Directive

This introduced common accounting rules specifically for insurance business. Information in accounts must give a 'true and fair view' of the insurer's assets, liabilities, profit, loss and financial position; there is a specified format for the balance sheet and profit/loss accounts; non-life business must show underwriting and investment income separately; prescribed minimum information; disclosure of acquisition costs for new business. There are separate rules for the Lloyd's market.

Insurance Intermediaries Directive

The aim of this Directive was to facilitate freedom of establishment and freedom of services for insurance agents and brokers. Community conditions and standards for professional competence, conduct, and financial standing are available to assist in the mutual recognition of an intermediary's status. The Directive is only a transitional measure and is limited in its success. It will be replaced at a later date by further directives.

Unfair Contract Terms Directive

This applies to all consumer contracts including insurance. Terms in writing must be in 'plain intelligible language' and if there is any doubt as to the meaning of a term, the interpretation most favourable to the policyholder will prevail. An unfair contract term will not be binding upon a policyholder.

Conclusion

The extent to which a single market for insurance actually exists in Europe is not clear at present. Although the Single European Act 1987 ensured that the Community formally became a single-frontier, free market from 1 January 1993, so that in principle goods, persons, services and capital are free to move as in a single state, in practice the insurance market still has a long way to go.

The First, Second and Third Life and Non-life Directives have provided a right of establishment and freedom of services throughout Europe in theory. However in practice, the various insurance directives have had a greater effect on changing business within individual national markets and so far the actual level of cross-border business has been relatively small. This is mainly due to practical reasons: it is difficult to market, distribute and sell the same products in more than one country.

The alternative methods of transacting insurance business in the EU are therefore:

- Set up a subsidiary company under the freedom of establishment measures.
- Set up a branch under the freedom of establishment measures.
- Write cross-border business without creating any local branch or subsidiary under the freedom of services measures.

The choice of method will depend on a variety of factors. However, it is worth noting the following points:

- There are still formidable barriers to the development of cross-border business, especially in life and personal non-life business. Lack of access to distribution is a major barrier because in most of the major European markets there is relatively little independent distribution and it is controlled by existing local companies.

- Many companies have therefore chosen to acquire existing companies and their established distribution methods.

- The development of pan-European groups is a common way of avoiding some of the difficulties mentioned, with many companies choosing to acquire existing companies with established distribution methods. In personal lines business, a pan-European group usually involves each company operating as a domestic company in its own national market rather than operating as a single European insurance company. This is not the case in commercial business.

- British companies have taken little part to date in the moves to create pan-European groups. However, Commercial Union has acquired companies in The Netherlands and France.

3.9   Market Associations

We turn now to a range of organizations that represent the various sections of the insurance marketplace.

Association of British Insurers

The largest and arguably the most important of the market associations is the Association of British Insurers (ABI). This association was formed in 1985 as the principal body representing insurers carrying on business in the United Kingdom. We have already referred to the ABI several times when quoting figures for premium income, losses, policies in force, and so on. Before 1985 there was a body known as the British Insurance Association and several other specialist associations dealing with particular aspects of the marketplace. In 1985, all of these were grouped together under the ABI.

The Association states as its objectives:

● To protect and promote the interests of members in respect of all classes of insurance business and in their related activities.

● To take concerted measures whenever the interests of members may be affected by the action of any government, body or agency.

● To cooperate with other any association having similar objectives.

The ABI operates with a staff of over 180 and is engaged in a wide variety of work associated with the practice of insurance. This work falls under the remit of two councils, the General Insurance Council and the Life Insurance Council. Work on fire prevention, liability, fraud, motor accidents, life underwriting, framing of codes of conduct and the gathering of relevant market statistics is all included. The ABI represents around 430 insurance companies, which account for over 90% of the UK insurance company business.

In addition the ABI plays a major role in public relations, endeavouring to create a greater awareness of the role of insurance.

The British Insurance and Investment Brokers Association

Before 1977 there were four organizations representing insurance brokers: the Corporation, the Association, the Federation and the Lloyd's Insurance Brokers' Association. In 1977 these interests joined, to be represented by one body known as the British Insurance Brokers Association (BIBA).

With the growth in financial services and the passing of the Financial Services Act 1986 it became clear that BIBA would have to alter its scope if it was to remain the main representative body of both general and life brokers. In 1987 it changed its name to the British Insurance and Investment Brokers Association (BIIBA); thus it continued to attract registered brokers and also welcomed those who were registered with the Financial Intermediaries Managers and Brokers Regulatory Association (Fimbra) as authorized to carry on any kind of investment business.

BIIBA is a national body with local representation in many parts of the country. It stands in roughly the same relationship to brokers as the ABI does to insurers.

AIRMIC

The Association of Risk and Insurance Managers in Industry and Commerce (AIRMIC) is slightly different from the others we have mentioned. It is concerned with the interests of the buyers of insurance, rather than the suppliers. It has over 500 members who are engaged in industry, commerce or the public sector and have a responsibility for the purchase of insurance.

We could continue to provide a long list of organizations associated with different aspects of the insurance marketplace. There would be no great merit in this; suffice to say that almost every aspect of the market is represented by some form of association.

IRM

The Institute of Risk Management provides professional education for those wishing to obtain a qualification in risk management.

3.10   Specialist Consultants

A wide range of specialist services is now available to help insurance companies and risk managers which they can buy as and when needed. The trend is currently to 'outsource' services wherever costs can be saved. The range of specialists include:

- risk management consultants;
- computer software houses;
- claims management consultants;
- disaster recovery services;
- credit rating specialists;
- management consultants;
- specialist brokers.

Summary

We have looked at the general structure of the marketplace, its participants and how some of them are organized. We also introduced some of the market associations, which are mentioned again in Unit 11.

Self-assessment Questions

Short Answer Questions

1. Who are the buyers of insurance?

2. What is a home service representative?

3. Who can be a name at Lloyds?

4. Where an insurance company has NO shareholders, what type of company will it be: proprietary or mutual?

5. What is a P and I Club ?

6. What does a slip at Lloyd's contain?

7. List three publications issued by Lloyd's.

8. What does IRM stand for?

(Answers given in Appendix 1)

Specimen Examination Question

Direct writing has become an increasingly common method of offering insurance. Comment on the types of insurance that can successfully be marketed on a direct basis and discuss the advantages of this method of distribution.

(Answer given in Appendix 1)

4

GOVERNMENT SUPERVISION

Objectives

After studying this unit, you should be able to:

● outline the history of government supervision of the insurance industry;

● state the main provisions of the Insurance Companies Act 1982 and the Financial Services Act 1986;

● justify the state regulation of insurance activities;

● describe the means of supervision of intermediaries;

● identify the main forms of compulsory insurance, and why they exist;

● provide the arguments both for and against the nationalization of the insurance industry.

4.1   The Role of Government Supervision

Government has always taken an interest in insurance activities over the years. On occasions this supervision has amounted to direct intervention and the state provision of insurance, such as with the National Insurance scheme, which is considered later. More often the supervision has taken the form of statutes governing aspects of the transaction of insurance. In more recent years, in relation to the long history of insurance, governments have legislated to make certain forms of insurance compulsory.

Before going on to suggest why there should be any element of government supervision, let us look back and trace the historical growth of supervision.

Historical Development of Supervision

Some would say that the earliest record of government intervention in the practice of insurance was possibly the Chamber of Assurances founded in 1575, whereby marine policies had to be registered.

Life Assurance Companies Act 1870

However, the pattern of modern supervision could be said to have started in 1870 with the

Life Assurance Companies Act, which made it obligatory for life assurance companies to make a deposit of £20,000 with the High Court before they could transact business. In addition, detailed accounting and actuarial returns had to be made to the Board of Trade in order that the solvency – the extent to which assets exceeded liabilities – could be monitored. Similar controls were also imposed on companies transacting employers' liability insurance by the Employers' Liability Insurance Companies Act 1907.

Assurance Companies Act 1909

By this act, the supervision of insurance business was extended beyond life assurance to fire, personal accident and bond investment. Lloyd's underwriters were exempted from the provisions of the act, provided that they complied with specified requirements. This act was the framework upon which supervision of insurance was built for half a century.

Industrial Assurance Act 1923

The act provided that industrial assurance was to be treated as a separate class of business (it has since been incorporated in later legislation) and limited its transaction to certain specified organizations. One major innovation was the establishment of an Industrial Assurance Commissioner, who was to exercise the statutory powers of the Board of Trade in relation to industrial life assurance.

Assurance Companies Act 1946

Since the passing of the 1909 Act, several new classes of business had been introduced and their regulation was incorporated in this 1946 act. Motor, aviation and transit insurances were brought within the scope of the act, as was the more established marine business. The main reason for noting this act is, however, the fact that it abolished the need for deposits and replaced them with a new system.

Several insurance companies had found their liabilities exceeding their assets; that is, the sums which they had to pay, or were to pay in the future, had exceeded the amount of money they had to meet these payments.

In the main this was attributable to the substantial growth in motor insurance business, with not all companies who offered insurance being in a financially sound position to do so. The Assurance Companies (Winding Up) Acts 1933-35 are evidence that there was a need for some tightening up of insurers' financial reserves.

In place of the deposits, in the case of non-life business, companies were required to satisfy certain solvency requirements measured in terms of **solvency margins**. The margin related to the amount by which assets were to exceed liabilities. In brief, this meant that each company had to maintain a balance between how much it had in terms of assets and how much it knew it had to pay or would be likely to pay in liabilities. The exact requirement under the 1946 act was that each company should have:

● a minimum paid-up share capital of £50,000; and

- assets exceeding liabilities by £50,000 or 10% of the previous year's premium income, whichever was the greater.

The present position regarding solvency margins is discussed later.

Companies Act 1967

Part II of the Companies Act 1967 met the need for stronger powers that had arisen during the early 1960s. A number of motor insurers had failed during this period, despite the solvency requirement, and fresh margins for non-life business were set at (a) a minimum paid-up share capital of £100,000; (b) in the first year of trading assets had to exceed liabilities by £50,000; (c) in subsequent trading periods assets were to exceed liabilities by £50,000, where the premium income in the previous year was not greater than £250,000, but where the premium income exceeded £250,000, the margin was to be at least 20% on the first £2,500,000 plus 10% on the balance of that income.

Regulations relating to authorization of insurers, reinsurance requirements, management of companies, initial conduct of business, actuarial valuation of life funds and insolvency and winding up were also made.

Following the collapse of the Vehicle and General Insurance Company in 1971 and the report of the Scott Committee on Property Bonds and Equity Linked Life Assurance in 1973 came the Insurance Companies Amendment Act 1973, which introduced additional regulatory powers.

Current position

In 1974, the Insurance Companies Act consolidated the 1958, 1967 and 1973 provisions in one statute. During the latter part of the 1970s, a large volume of legislation and regulations was passed concerning various aspects of supervision.

This increase in legislation during the 1970s, particularly the latter half of the decade, was probably due to two quite different factors.

Firstly, there were a number of failures of insurance companies and this prompted many to suggest that the then current legislation lacked power in certain directions. The lack of effective supervision of insurance company operations was demonstrated in 1965 when Emil Savundra's Fire Auto and Marine Insurance Company failed. A tightening of legislation followed, but in 1971 the Vehicle and General Insurance Company failed, leaving hundreds of thousands of motor policyholders uninsured. Further legislation ensued, but it was not sufficient to prevent another failure in 1974, this time in the life assurance sector of Nation Life. These three insurance company failures, linked with the growing move towards increased consumer protection, played a major part in encouraging parliament to take action to increase its powers.

The second factor that prompted the growth of insurance company legislation was the UK entry into the EEC. Under the Insurance Companies Act 1974, some 22 statutory instruments were passed, many of which were made to implement the terms of the EEC

Non-Life Establishment Directive 73/239/EEC. These instruments, intended to bring about some harmonization of European insurance legislation, dealt with matters such as solvency margins, defining new classes of business, authorization of insurance companies, and so on. In 1979 the EEC Life Establishment Directive 79/267/EEC was introduced and was followed closely by the Insurance Companies Act 1981, which consolidated much of the European legislation then in existence.

One can easily see how complicated the whole area became, because of the desire to respond to the consumer-orientated problems in Britain and the need to conform with the European directives. Fortunately, the position was greatly clarified by the passing of the Insurance Companies Act 1982, which came into effect on 28 January 1983. This act, supplemented by other legislation, now represents the regulatory powers as they currently apply. The particular agency of government that is concerned with the implementation of the terms of the act is the Insurance Division of the Department of Trade and Industry, under the direction of the Secretary of State for Trade and Industry.

4.2 The Insurance Companies Act 1982

Although there is a plethora of statutes relating to insurance and the transaction of insurance, by far the most significant in setting out the ways in which solvency requirements, authorization procedures and conduct of business rules are to apply is the Insurance Companies Act 1982.

This act, in 100 sections, consolidates without change to previous law the provisions of the Insurance Companies Act 1981. All statutory instruments made under preceding legislation continue in being and are interpreted as if they had been made under the corresponding sections of the 1982 Act. It would not be totally accurate to say that all regulatory issues are now contained within the 1982 Act because, for example, the Insurance Companies Regulations 1981 (SI 1981 No. 1654) are still current.

However, we must decide what it is necessary to know in order to gain some appreciation of the current legislative position. We shall therefore outline the main provisions of the 1982 act, making reference, where it is felt necessary, to other regulations.

The 100 sections of the act fall into five main parts:

(1) **Restriction on Carrying on Insurance Business.** This part is concerned with defining the various classes of business and with the requirements to be met by those wishing to carry on the business of insurance.

(2) **Regulation of Insurance Companies.** Part Two of the act is by far the largest, with 57 individual sections. Primarily it is concerned with financial matters such as annual accounts, actuarial investigation, winding up and other matters.

(3) **Conduct of Insurance Business.** Insurance advertisements, 'cooling-off' notices for life assurance and the disclosure by intermediaries of connections with an

insurance company are some of the items dealt within the ten sections of Part Three.

(4) **Special Classes of Insurers.** These sections are concerned chiefly with Lloyd's, industrial life assurance and companies established outside the United Kingdom.

(5) **Supplementary.** Much of this final part is concerned with the criminal proceedings that would follow any breach of the act. It also provides for the Secretary of State for Trade to make an annual report on the operation of the act.

For our purposes we shall concentrate on six main areas: authorization, solvency, monitoring, intervention, conduct of business, and winding up.

Authorization

The general result of the regulations concerning authorization is that any company wishing to transact insurance must be authorized to do so by the Department of Trade and Industry. To gain this authorization, the Department must be satisfied that the applicant complies with a number of conditions, as laid down in the act and the 1981 Insurance Company Regulations. The objective is that only companies operated by 'fit and proper' persons should transact business.

In short the Secretary of State has the power to authorize a company to transact long-term business or general business, including reinsurance. He can also restrict authorization to specific types of business. No new authorizations will now be given to carry on both long-term and short-term business.

Classes of business

When a company decides that it wishes to transact insurance in the United Kingdom, lengthy forms have to be completed and submitted to the Department of Trade and Industry. One of the key items covered by these forms is the exact nature of the class of insurance that the company wishes to offer.

The 1974 Insurance Companies Act originally designated eight classes of business, in addition to ordinary and industrial life assurance. In 1977 the Insurance Companies (Classes of Business) Regulations came into effect and introduced into UK legislation the 17 classes used in the EEC Directive 73/239/EEC, which we mentioned above.

The 1982 Act maintained these classes, and an additional general class has since been added. It also divided all insurance business in the United Kingdom into two groups, long-term and general, with the various individual classes as follows:

Long-term

Class I	Life and annuity
Class II	Marriage and birth
Class III	Linked long-term

Class IV	Permanent health
Class V	Tontines
Class VI	Capital redemption
Class VII	Pension fund management

General

Class 1	Accident
Class 2	Sickness
Class 3	Land vehicles
Class 4	Railway rolling stock
Class 5	Aircraft
Class 6	Ships
Class 7	Goods in transit
Class 8	Fire and natural forces
Class 9	Damage to property
Class 10	Motor vehicle liability
Class 11	Aircraft liability
Class 12	Liability for ships
Class 13	General liability
Class 14	Credit
Class 15	Suretyship
Class 16	Miscellaneous financial loss
Class 17	Legal expenses
Class 18	Assistance

It can be seen that these classes indicate forms of risk rather than forms of insurance business. For example, classes 10, 11, 12 and 13 are all different types of liability risk but are shown separately rather than as a type of insurance (liability insurance).

In order that those who transact general business can identify which classes relate to which forms of business, the following schedule shows the eight old classes (with which many people were familiar) and against each indicates which of the new classes apply.

Table 4.1: The Eight Old Classes with their New Equivalents

Number	Designation	New Classes
1	Accident and Health	1 and 2
2	Motor	3, 7, 10 and part of 1
3	Marine and Transport	4, 6, 7, 12 and part of 1
4	Aviation	5, 7, 11 and part of 1
5	Fire and other damage to property	8 and 9
6	Liability	10, 11, 12 and 13
7	Credit and Suretyship	14 and 15
8	General	All

Most of the classes of insurance will be familiar, but perhaps something should be said about class V of long-term business. The **Tontine** is now almost extinct as far as can be traced. It was a concept developed in the late 17th century and was a form of annuity. A group of people formed a Tontine and paid in a principal sum, in return for an annuity for life.

The difference between the Tontine and any ordinary annuity was that, as members of the group died, their income from the Tontine was distributed among the survivors. The Tontine itself ended with the death of the last subscriber.

Types of company seeking authorization

There are three basic forms of company described by the 1982 Act: UK companies, Community companies and External companies. Separate authorization requirements apply to each type. We shall look only at the general nature of the questioning of applicants, rather than at the detail of any differences between the three basic forms of company. Firstly, however, let us distinguish, as the act does, between the three types.

United Kingdom companies

These are firms that have their head office in the UK and are formed under the Companies Acts 1948 to 1985, or are registered societies or are established by Royal Charter or act of parliament.

Community companies

A Community company is one that has its head office in one of the member states of the EU, other than the UK, but nevertheless has a branch or some underwriting agency in the UK.

External company

This is a company having its headquarters outside the EU but having a branch or underwriting agency in the UK.

Questions about authorization

The Secretary of State will not issue authorization to transact business unless, under the terms of the 1982 Act, he is satisfied by all the information supplied to him by the applicant. This information is given on an application form, a different one being required for long-term and general business; a different form is also required for each of UK, Community and External companies.

The application forms are detailed and there would be little point in expecting readers to memorize the kind of information requested. In broad terms, the forms ask for information concerning:

- the company itself – including date of formation, objects, auditors, bankers, names of key personnel;

- scheme of operations – the source of business, premium tariffs, reinsurance arrangements, assets, costs of installing administrative services;

- projections – estimates over the first three financial years of management expenses, premiums, claims, balance sheet;

- other information – nature of investments, copies of reinsurance treaties, copies of agreements that the company will have with brokers or agents.

Solvency Margins

The intention of a solvency margin, along with solvency margin regulations, was stated earlier when we looked at the Assurance Companies Act 1946 and the first introduction of margins of solvency. A relationship is established between assets and liabilities in such a way as to satisfy the regulatory body that the company is in a position to meet its liabilities. If the minimum solvency margin is not maintained the Secretary of State has the power to intervene.

The regulations concerning solvency are contained in the Insurance Companies Act 1982 and the Insurance Company Regulations 1981. The actual value of the solvency margin, in monetary terms, varies from company to company. Obviously it would not be sensible to lay down one figure by which assets should exceed liabilities, because there are vast differences in the volume of business transacted by insurance companies. What the act does set out are certain formulae, which produce given ratios. The actual formula depends upon the type of company, that is UK, Community or External.

We shall concentrate on UK companies, looking at the margins required for general business and long-term business respectively.

As a result of harmonization of solvency margins throughout the EU, it is not possible for each member state to express its solvency margin regulations in terms of its own currency. This is a problem encountered in many other aspects of the Community's work and, to overcome it, the Community created the **European Currency Unit (ECU)** which is a form of artificial currency, to which all currencies of member states are fixed.

The ECU changes with movements in the currency of the member state itself and the conversion rate is fixed by the European Commission. For solvency margin purposes, the conversion rate used is the one published in the *Official Journal of the European Communities*. For any 12 months commencing 31 December, the actual figure to be used is the value of the ECU on the last day of business of the preceding October.

As an example of the value of an ECU, the exchange rate at July 1995 was in the order of £0.85.

General business

The margin is determined by taking the greater of two sums resulting from the application of two sets of calculations called respectively the **Premium Basis** and **Claims Basis**.

Premium basis

Gross premiums received are transferred into European Currency Units (ECU) at the appropriate conversion rate. The company calculates 18% of the first 10 million ECU and 16% of any balance over and above 10 million. For example, if a company had gross premiums equivalent to 15m ECU the calculation would be as follows:

Gross premiums =	15m ECU	
10m x 18%	=	1.8m
5m x 16%	=	0.8m
		2.6m

The figure of 2.6m ECU is then modified, to take account of the level of reinsurance operated by the company. Clearly, an insurer who arranges a very high level of reinsurance will not have as great a potential liability to pay claims as one with very little reinsurance protection. Therefore, the 2.6m is reduced by a fraction that represents this level of reinsurance: the ratio of net claims paid to gross claims paid. For example, an insurer has gross claims of 8m ECU in the year, but was able to recover 2m ECU from its reinsurers, then the fraction would be 6/8ths or 75%.

The required solvency margin is:

Net claims paid	=	6m
Gross claims paid	=	8m
	=	$^6/_8$ x 2.6m
	=	1.95m ECU

The maximum reduction for reinsurances is 50%. In the above example, if the insurer had recovered 5m ECU from reinsurers, the reduction would have been limited to 50% and the solvency margin would have been:

50% x 2.6m   = 1.3m ECU.

Claims basis

The second method is based on claims. The total of all gross claims paid during the preceding three years is found, converted into ECU and the average taken. 26% is calculated of the first 7m ECU and 23% of any excess over 7m. The resultant figure is then multiplied by the same ratio as in the premium basis, to reflect reinsurances arranged. Using the figures from the above example we have:

Average claims paid	=	8m ECU
7m x 26%	=	1.82m
1m x 23%	=	0.23m
		2.05m
Net claims paid	=	6m
Gross claims paid	=	8m
	=	$^6/_8$ x 2.05m
	=	1.5375m ECU

In the majority of cases, the higher figure will be the one derived from the Premium Basis. The Claims Basis would produce a higher figure where the insurer was experiencing an exceptionally high claims ratio and low premium growth figures. It would also apply to those insurers who are no longer writing new business in a class, but still have claims coming in.

We can see this if we alter the claims figures in the above example. Let us say that the insurer still has gross premiums of 15m, but the gross claims are now 12m with a net claims figure of 10m. The claims ratio is now 12/15 rather than the 8/15 which was the case in the example. The result on the two methods can be seen as follows:

Premium basis

Gross premiums	=	15m ECU
10m x 18%	=	1.8m
5m x 16%	=	0.8m
		2.6m
Net claims paid	=	10m
Gross claims paid	=	12m
	=	$^{10}/_{12}$ x 2.6m = 2.17m ECU

Claims basis

Average claims paid	=	12m ECU
7m x 26%	=	1.82m

$$5m \times 23\% \quad = \quad \underline{1.15m}$$
$$2.97m$$

Net claims paid $\quad = \quad 10m$

Gross claims paid $\quad = \quad 12m$

$$= \quad {}^{10}/_{12} \times 2.97m = 2.48m \text{ ECU}$$

The Claims Basis is now the higher of the two and this does seem correct, because the insurer is experiencing a much higher claims ratio and is therefore required to maintain a higher margin of solvency.

Guarantee funds

A further regulation provides that a minimum benchmark figure must be maintained at all times. This is referred to as the **Minimum Guarantee Fund**. This fund must be maintained at the greater of either a specified amount, depending on the classes of business written, or one third of the solvency margin, derived from the higher of the Premium or Claims Bases.

Long-term business

One major effect of implementing the EEC Life Establishment Directive, mentioned earlier, has been the introduction of prescribed solvency margins for life assurances. These solvency margins applied to newly authorized companies from 1 January 1982 and to existing assurance companies from 15 March 1984.

The basic framework of solvency margins for life business is the same as that explained for general business. There is a ratio that is calculated and must be maintained, subject to a minimum fund which varies according to the type of company, that is mutual reinsurer or proprietary.

The calculations are based on actuarial liabilities and this is the main difference between life solvency and general solvency. In general business, the solvency margin was determined by examining premiums and claims. On life business, the claims are long-term and their actuarial value is calculated. In this way the life assurer is compelled to retain an adequate level of funds to meet these actuarially calculated liabilities.

A different set of calculations is required for Classes I and II, III and VII, IV and VI, and V. The required solvency margin for the company is then the aggregate of these different margins.

It may seem that rather a long time has been spent on this one aspect of government supervision, but there can be few things more important than ensuring that an insurer has the assets to meet all its potential liabilities.

Monitoring

Having established a system of authorization for intending insurers and of determining solvency margins, it is essential that there be some means by which the regulatory body can ensure that the standards are being maintained. Regular monitoring of companies is therefore an important aspect of the 1982 Act.

This continual monitoring of companies, while they are in the business of transacting insurance, should help to identify those companies where trouble can be anticipated.

Intervention

The whole process of monitoring the performance of companies will be of value only if the regulatory body can take some action when difficulties are detected. Sections 37 to 46 of the 1982 Act set out the circumstances in which the Department of Trade and Industry may intervene and the powers it can exercise.

Clearly, if a company fails to comply with any of the requirements laid down in the act, such as the submission of accounts or the maintaining of solvency margins, then the Department can and would intervene. The Department can also intervene where, for example, a company has departed significantly from the business plan as set out in the original application, or when a person has been appointed to a key post who is considered unsuitable to hold such a position.

In these and other cases, the Department has the power of intervention and can require the company, for example:

- to restrict its premium income;

- to submit accounts at more frequent intervals than every year;

- to supply any additional information over and above the accounts;

- to allow a full actuarial investigation of any life funds;

- to restrict the categories of investment it makes.

These powers are far-reaching and could, effectively, bring a business to a standstill. They are not, however, used unwisely and there would have to be a real likelihood of policyholders suffering, before drastic action would be taken.

Conduct of Business

The ten sections of Part III of the 1982 Act fall under the general heading of 'Conduct of Business'. These sections are concerned with the more day-to-day aspects of the company's business, rather than with the broader financial aspects we have dealt with so far.

The aspects of the business with which this part is concerned fall into a number of distinct areas including:

Advertisements

Regulations concerning insurance advertisements are made in the Insurance Companies

(Advertisements (Amendment) (No.2)) Regulations 1983 SI 1983 No. 396. The chief aim of these regulations is to ensure that the public is adequately protected against possible misleading advertisements placed by life assurance companies not having head offices in the UK. Without going into too much detail, we can say that the company placing the advertisement must state, if it is not an 'authorized insurer', that policyholders will not be protected by the Policyholders' Protection Act 1975.

Misleading statements

This part of the act makes it an offence to induce a person to effect insurance by knowingly making a misleading statement; for example, if a whole-life contract with premiums ceasing at age 65 was knowingly misrepresented as a policy maturing at age 65.

Connected intermediaries

Where an insurer has some connection with an intermediary, as in the case of an insurer that owns or has a controlling interest in a broker, this relationship must be disclosed to potential personal policyholders. This arose following the Vehicle and General collapse, where that company owned a broker (Andrew and Booth Limited) and received a large volume of business from it. The current legislation would mean that the relationship would have to be revealed to clients of Andrew and Booth Limited.

Winding up

In the end, if an insurance company has failed to meet the terms of the act, it can be wound up. This is the formal cessation of the life of the company and must be regarded as the final step, after all other paths have been explored. This winding up may be a voluntary act on the part of the company itself, or compulsory by the Department of Trade or by ten or more policyholders who have policies with an aggregate value of not less than £10,000.

4.3 The Financial Services Act 1986

This piece of legislation was introduced following the publication of the Gower Report in 1984 with the aim of ensuring that investors in the UK can invest their money with confidence, knowing that they can rely on certain basic standards of conduct and integrity from both suppliers and intermediaries.

The act applies only to 'investment business', which is strictly defined. This includes gilts, shares, debentures, unit trusts, investment trusts, options, futures and long-term insurance business. It does not include mortgages or general insurance business. The powers of intervention and control under the act is vested in the Treasury department, but the day-to-day responsibility for the policing of the act has been delegated to the Securities and Investments Board (SIB).

Full details of the act, its main provisions and its effect on both intermediaries and insurance companies are covered in Unit 14.

4.4   Supervision of Intermediaries

For many years anyone could describe himself as an insurance broker, whether he had any insurance knowledge or not, and it was difficult for the public to distinguish the genuine professional expert from the amateur. By the end of the 1970s, 9,000 firms called themselves brokers (compared with many tens of thousands of part-time agents) and there were four organizations of brokers which sought to maintain varying standards of conduct for their members.

These organizations were Lloyd's Insurance Brokers' Association (LIBA), the Corporation of Insurance Brokers (CIB), the Association of Insurance Brokers (AIB) and the Federation of Insurance Brokers (FIB). However, it was felt desirable within the insurance broking industry that there should be just one body to represent the profession and to supervise the standing and operations of those permitted to call themselves insurance brokers.

In January 1976 the four associations established the British Insurance Brokers' Council (BIBC), which prepared proposals with the approval of the Secretary of State for Trade for the registration and regulation of insurance brokers. It proposed the creation of a Registration Council which would satisfy itself as to the experience, qualifications and financial status of applicants for registration as brokers. The proposals of the Brokers' Council were the basis of a Private Member's Bill which became the Insurance Brokers (Registration) Act on 29 July 1977.

Following this, the British Insurance Brokers' Council and the four independent associations were disbanded in 1977 and the British Insurance Brokers' Association (BIBA) was formed. As we saw in Unit 3, this is now the British Insurance and Investment Brokers Association.

Insurance Brokers (Registration) Act 1977

From 1 December 1981 it has been illegal for anyone to describe himself as an insurance broker if he is not registered under the act. A person who does not qualify for registration or does not seek registration can refer to himself as a **consultant** or **adviser** but not a **broker**. This does give some kind of guidance to the insuring public, because registered brokers have to comply with a set of strict operating conditions.

In addition the Financial Services Act 1986 laid down regulations as to who could transact **investment business** and an **ABI Code of Practice** provides guidelines for the practice of brokers involved in general insurances. We shall mention both of these later, but in the meantime let us look at the role of the Registration Council.

Insurance Brokers' Registration Council

Under the 1977 Act, the Insurance Brokers' Registration Council (IBRC) was established to govern the registration and regulation of insurance brokers. The IBRC is a legally created, separate, independent body from the BIIBA, which is a voluntary trade association. It is made up of 12 individuals who are representative of, and elected by, registered brokers. In addition there are five people nominated by the Secretary of State.

The register was opened for applications at the end of 1978 and it is maintained and up-dated by the Council. The Council has also drawn up a code of conduct for registered members, rules concerning professional indemnity, accounting procedures, discipline, and so on.

Registration of individuals

For an individual to be registered he must:

(a)   hold an approved qualification;

(b)   have carried on business as, or have been employed by, an insurance broker or full-time agent for at least two companies, or been employed by an insurance company, for at least five years;

(c)   hold a recognized qualification and have carried on business, or been employed as in (b) above, for at least three years.

(At present the only qualifications recognized for the purposes of registration are the Associateship or Fellowship of the Chartered Insurance Institute, but the Council has power to accept others.)

The individual must satisfy the Council that he has had suitable work experience.

Registration of companies

Sole traders, partnerships and limited companies must comply with further conditions regarding solvency, accounting practices and professional indemnity insurance cover. In the case of limited companies, at least half the directors must be registered insurance brokers and the code of conduct requires that all work shall be under the day-to-day supervision of registered persons.

Investment Business

In the case of life assurance, the Financial Services Act stated that intermediaries who deal with investment business must be defined as either company representatives or independent intermediaries. The act defines what forms of life assurance are classified as investment business. **Company representatives** are people who deal with only one life assurer and that company accepts responsibility for their actions. The **independent intermediary** must deal with many companies, be independent of them and seek authorization to transact investment business. This authorization must come from the Securities and Investment Board direct, PIA or one of the Recognized Professional Bodies. It is this last point which is relevant to the insurance broker. The IBRC is a Recognized Professional Body as far as the SIB is concerned, provided that the broker's income from investment business does not exceed 49% of the firm's total income.

The ABI Code of Practice

After consultation with the government, the ABI produced two Codes of Practice, one for intermediaries involved in life assurance but who fall outside the rules we have mentioned above and another for intermediaries involved in general insurance but who are not registered insurance brokers.

Member insurance companies of the ABI have undertaken to enforce the code. Remember that the intermediaries are not themselves members of the ABI, it is the insurers who are members and are trying to enforce a code of practice on the intermediaries.

In conclusion, we can say that there has been a real effort to ensure that the public know who they are dealing with when they consult an intermediary. It may be that the number of different titles in use by intermediaries has been reduced, but the number of definitions has increased and one is left to question whether the public is better off or not!

Student Activity 1

Before reading the next section of the text, answer the following questions and then check your answers against the pages indicated.

1.   What is a solvency margin?   *(page 104)*

2.   When can the DTI exercise its power to wind an insurance company up?

                                                                          (page 109)

3.   What type of business is covered by the Financial Services Act 1986?

                                                                          (page 109)

If your answers are basically correct, then proceed to the next section. If significant parts of your answers are wrong, then study the whole of the relevant sections again in detail. Note your areas of weakness, and be prepared for further questions on these areas in the self-assessment section at the end of this unit.

4.5   Reasons for State Regulation

The words control, regulation, supervision and intervention are being looked upon as interchangeable, although some writers have attached separate meanings to each. For our purposes, we can say that governments have taken more than a passing interest in the transaction of insurance and whether we describe this interest as intervention, control, regulation or supervision is incidental to the question: 'Why have state regulation?'

Having looked at both the development and current status of governmental intervention in insurance activities, we can suggest some reasons why such supervision is necessary.

The main justification for state control is to protect the public, but this aim is also accompanied by one relating to socially desirable measures. In the following list, items (a) to (c) relate to protection and (d) to (f) to social measures:

(a) **Maintain solvency**. Perhaps the greatest step taken by legislation was to introduce solvency margins that were related to premium income. In this way, a ratio was established between the margin and the amount of business undertaken. This prevented certain people with fraudulent aims from providing insurance, and acted as a continual monitor on those already transacting it.

(b) **Equity**. The term equity has been used, but equally suitable would have been morality, fairness or reasonableness, because each implies the fact that an element of fairness must exist between companies and policyholders. The insurance contract is one of considerable complexity and it is essential that controls exist for the protection of policyholders.

(c) **Competence**. The buying and selling of insurance is unlike many other forms of product purchasing. A tangible product is not being purchased; a promise to provide indemnity, an exact compensation, is what is being bought and sold. Those who deal in such promises must be competent persons and able to fulfil their pledges when the need arises. Therefore, regulations are necessary in the management of insurance and investment business.

(d) **Insurable interest**. Insurable interest is one of the basic doctrines of insurance. Governments have found it necessary to introduce legislation in order to eradicate any element of gambling. It was not acceptable that unscrupulous persons could benefit by effecting policies of insurances where they had no financial interest in the potential loss, other than the profit they would make if it occurred.

(e) **Provision of certain forms of insurance**. An element of intervention has been in evidence where forms of cover have been made compulsory, as in the case of employers' liability and third party motor accident injuries. The intervention is not in the provision of cover by government, but in establishing the nature of the cover to be granted.

(f) **National Insurance**. For some areas of social risk, the Government's intervention has been total and it has assumed the responsibility for providing certain covers. This has been the case in areas such as unemployment, sickness and widows' benefits; the State carries the risk under the National scheme.

4.6 The Impact of Regulation and Deregulation

Regulation of the financial services sector can be classified broadly into three areas:

● **Structural Regulation** of the type and form of business activities carried out.

- **Prudential Supervision** in terms of solvency, liquidity and capital adequacy.

- **Investor Protection**, which overlaps with both of the above, and covers the manner in which business is carried out.

In recent years, structural regulatory provisions have been relaxed. This has allowed different types of financial institutions to offer new and extended services. This deregulation has involved the freeing up of financial markets and removal of traditional barriers between traditional classes of financial institutions. Examples include the 'Big Bang' in October 1986 and the Building Societies Act 1986.

A direct effect of measures such as the Building Societies Act is to increase the potential for institutions to enter into non-traditional and non-core markets. 'Bancassurance' is the term given to banks and building societies selling non-banking products such as life assurance and pensions to their customers. The term originated in France, where around 40% of new life assurance premiums were generated by retail banks.

Although some building societies made a conscious decision to concentrate on core business areas following the Building Societies Act 1986, others enthusiastically entered into new markets such as estate agency and pensions. The aim was to diversify so that less reliance was placed on, for example, the housing market and provision of mortgages, but, at the same time, to take full advantage of the potential profit opportunities offered in new areas of business. Building societies were particularly keen to capitalize on existing good relationships with customers and the opportunities of cross-selling and direct marketing alongside their core business of mortgages and savings.

Increased competition, the loss of market share in some areas and leaner margins on lending, coupled with the lure of large potential profits, enticed the banks to enter into similar new areas of business. They, too, have the advantage of a High Street branch network and large databases of customer information, plus established life and pension subsidiaries.

The idea of the one-stop financial supermarket seemed ever closer. Deregulation provided the opportunity for both diversification and conglomeration.

At the same time as the relaxation of structural rules, investor protection measures have been tightened. Before the Financial Services Act, investor protection was fragmented and Professor Gower's *Investor Protection* Report in 1984 highlighted the need for a single, more precise system of regulation for investment business. Since 1986, this has been reviewed and extended through the MacDonald and Clucas Reports. These measures are discussed in detail in Unit 14.

This complex system of self-regulatory organizations responsible to the Securities and Investments Board involves new layers of costly regulation. These are designed to protect the investor by ensuring that only those who are authorized can give advice on or provide investment products.

As a result of the Financial Services Act and its detailed rules, the client is now told in clear terms the exact status of the person who is giving him advice, details of the benefits, charges and potential disadvantages of the product he is buying, as well as the amount the adviser is being paid for his services. Authorization also means that should the adviser or company subsequently become insolvent, a compensation scheme is available to the client.

In addition, stricter disclosure requirements introduced in 1995 have meant all life and pensions offices now have to disclose the **exact** effect their charges have on the potential yield a contract will bring. Unfortunately, these protection measures are proving to be expensive, with the cost being passed on ultimately to the client.

While compliance with the authorization, record keeping and product disclosure rules are adding to the office's costs, the requirements to disclose charges to the client so that he can compare products across the market is exerting a downward pressure on these costs.

Furthermore, new entrants into the life and pensions market, such as Marks & Spencer Financial Services, Virgin Direct and Direct Line, are able to capitalize on these problems by selling on the basis of simple products, no salespersons and low charges.

In order to compete, many life offices are having to rationalize their product ranges and reduce staff numbers. Mergers and acquisitions are also common to achieve economies of scale and to enable institutions to compete in UK, European and international markets.

4.7   Compulsory Insurance

One important aspect of government involvement in insurance is where it has made certain classes of insurance compulsory. This is the case for certain types of injury and damage following road accidents, certain injuries at work, riding establishments, nuclear risks, oil pollution, solicitors professional indemnity and certain other, smaller cases. We shall look at the two most common forms of compulsory insurance first – motor and employers' liability – and then briefly summarize the regulations applicable to the other areas.

Motor Insurance

The Road Traffic Act 1988 consolidated a great deal of previous legislation. Section 143 of the act states:

> *it shall not be lawful for a person to use, or cause or permit another person to use, a motor vehicle on a road unless there is in force in relation to the use of the vehicle by that person or that other person, as the case may be, such a policy of insurance or such a security in respect of third party risks as complies with the requirement of this Part of this Act ...*

In brief, we can say that:

- The third party risks referred to are death of, or bodily injury to, any person and damage to third party property. This includes pedestrians, passengers in other cars, passengers in the policyholder's car, other third party cars or property. Until

December 1988 the legislation referred only to third party bodily injury.

- The security, in place of insurance, is a deposit of £500,000 with the Accountant General of the Supreme Court and this removes the need to insure only when the car is driven under the control of the insured.

- A certificate of insurance has to be issued and a policy is not effective in the terms of the Road Traffic Act unless one is. Note that a certificate of insurance is one of the documents required before a person can obtain a road fund licence.

- It is the user of the car, not the driver, who must be covered by insurance and a person is deemed to have the use of a car if he retains an element of control, management or operation of the vehicle at the relevant time.

- The policy of insurance has to be issued by an 'authorized' insurer – that is, an insurer carrying on motor insurance in Great Britain and who has satisfied the requirement of the Insurance Companies Act 1982. Such an insurer must also be a member of the Motor Insurers' Bureau.

Employers' Liability Insurance

The Employers' Liability (Compulsory Insurance) Act 1969 came into effect on 1 January 1972 and from that date every employer carrying on business in Scotland, England or Wales has had to insure against liability for bodily injury or disease sustained by employees and arising from their employment. Note the following points (separate statutes apply to other parts of the UK):

- The act refers only to bodily injury and disease and, while it therefore covers a whole range of problems, it does not include any element of property damage.

- The policy must be effected with an 'authorized' insurer, and in this connection the points above regarding an 'authorized' motor insurer apply here also.

- A certificate of insurance has to be issued and must be displayed at every place of business.

- The person injured must be employed by the policyholder and the injury or disease must arise out of that employment.

- Certain employers need not insure, such as local government councils and industries under national ownership or control.

- Insurance must be maintained for an amount of £2million in respect of claims relating to any one or more employees arising out of a single occurrence.

Other Compulsory Insurances

- The Riding Establishment Act 1970 makes it compulsory for anyone holding a licence to run a riding establishment to have public liability insurance.

- The Nuclear Installations Act 1965 requires operators of any nuclear plant to purchase insurance for liability for third party injury and property damage.

- The Solicitors Act 1974 requires solicitors to have professional indemnity insurance.

- The Insurance Brokers (Registration) Act 1977 requires insurance brokers to have professional indemnity insurance. Lloyd's brokers are excepted from this requirement.

- The Merchant Shipping (Oil Pollution) Act 1971 requires ships carrying in excess of 2,000 tons of oil to have appropriate insurance cover.

- The Dangerous Animals Act 1971 requires any owner of a wild and dangerous animal to have public liability insurance.

Why Have Compulsory Insurance?

There are one or two additional areas where insurance is required, but is not compulsory. For example, contractors who want a tax exemption certificate from the Inland Revenue have to hold public liability insurance and mortgagors buying a house are required by the building society to have buildings insurance.

The provision of funds

There would be no point in awarding damages to someone if there were no money to meet the award. Notice that the insurance is for liability against injury, except in the case of nuclear sites when damage is also included, thus emphasizing the importance placed upon injury in the eyes of the law. The enactment of compulsory insurance ensures, as far as possible, that funds will be available when damages are awarded. An interesting point for discussion is the extent to which this fact influences the eventual size of the award, if in fact it influences it at all.

Ease the state's burden

It is unlikely that the state would allow people injured at work, or in similar accidents, to go without compensation entirely. If the responsible party did not have sufficient funds to provide this, the likelihood is that the state would come forward with some money. The existence of insurance eliminates this possibility.

The response to national concern

Apart from riding establishments, the areas where insurance has been made compulsory represent areas of national concern. When we traced the development of motor and employers' liability insurance, we saw how public attitudes changed over the years until concern over accidents was so high that legislation was introduced to ensure the provision of insurance. Nuclear risks is a far more recent area of concern and it may be pertinent to note that it is the only risk where insurance is required for injury or damage. This may be due partly to the grave concern voiced by many and to the difficulties that could be involved in trying to separate injury and damage claims when radioactive material leaked from some installation.

Protection

It is not suggested that by making a person effect insurance, you also make him more careful, thus assisting in the protection of the potential injured persons. This may or may not be true, but what can be said with more certainty is that, because insurance is involved, the insured will have access to all the expertise available from insurers, which may improve the risk and thus assist in protecting people.

An example from the employers' liability field is the case where a liability surveyor from an insurance company insists on special guards on machines, to minimize the risk of injury. The insured may not have contemplated doing this himself, but is forced to by the insurers.

4.8   Nationalization

The ultimate step in government supervision would be complete nationalization.

In 1976, the Labour Party accepted proposals at its annual conference for the nationalization of Britain's seven largest insurance companies, and in 1978 the insurance industry completed its evidence to the Wilson Committee, which had been set up to review the functioning of insurance institutions. As yet no companies have been nationalized, but this does not mean that the issue is dead and we should certainly acquaint ourselves with the arguments for and against. The topic is one that arouses deep feelings with certain people and it is often difficult to put forward a balanced, objective portrayal of the situation. The following represent certain of the basic points on each side.

For Nationalization

- Governmental control of funds would be to the benefit of society at large.
- It would be possible to introduce uniformity in wordings and practice.
- Statistics could be pooled.
- Premium rates could be reduced in the absence of the profit motive.
- The cost exercise of making the statutory returns would be eliminated.
- There would not be so great a reliance on reinsurance, with a commensurate saving in costs.
- It may be better if those forms of insurance made compulsory by government were provided by the state.

Against Nationalization

- It is difficult to 'nationalize the international'. It could be that some overseas countries would not trade with a government-owned insurance industry.

- Insurance has grown and developed in private hands for many centuries and there is no reason to think that any better service would result from state ownership.

- Experience of certain nationalized industries is one of overloaded bureaucracy.

- Competition encourages efficiency and innovation.

- The present tax revenue from insurance companies would be lost.

- The large-scale nature of any state insurance organization may lead to a strictness in practice and interpretation that would not benefit the public.

- The government has no experience in underwriting insurable risks.

Summary

This unit may seem to have covered a great deal of ground but the quantity of information only reflects the level of interest that governments have had in the transaction of insurance. This serves to underline the importance and value insurance has both at the macro and micro level.

We have considered a brief history of government regulation in the insurance industry, along with more detailed study of current legislation. This has included the Insurance Companies Act 1982 and current arrangements for the supervision of intermediaries. We have ended by considering compulsory insurances, why they exist and the likely consequences of nationalization for the insurance industry.

Self-assessment Questions

Short Answer Questions

1. What currency is used in determining solvency margins?

2. What is the minimum guarantee fund?

3. What is the IBRC?

4. Identify the purpose of a cooling off notice?

5. List three examples of compulsory insurance.

6. What is the ultimate State intervention for insurance?

(Answers given in Appendix 1)

Specimen Examination Question

Discuss the reasons for State regulation of insurance.

(Answer given in Appendix 1)

5

SPECIAL PRINCIPLES OF INSURANCE CONTRACTS I

Objectives

After studying this unit, you should be able to:

● define the doctrine of insurable interest;

● outline ways in which the doctrine has been modified;

● apply the doctrine to the main classes of insurance;

● explain what is meant by 'utmost good faith';

● list facts that do and do not have to be disclosed;

● relate the doctrine of utmost good faith to the use of agents.

5.1   Insurable Interest

Insurable interest is a basic requirement of any contract of insurance unless it can be, and is, lawfully waived. The party to the insurance contract who is the insured or policyholder must have a particular relationship with the subject matter of the insurance, whether it is a life or property or a liability to which he is exposed. The absence of the required relationship renders the contract illegal, void or simply unenforceable, depending on the type of insurance.

The **subject matter of insurance** can be any form of property, or an event that may result in the loss of a legal right or the creation of a legal liability. Thus the subject matter of insurance under a fire policy can be buildings, stock or machinery; under a liability policy it can be a person's legal liability for injury or damage; with a life assurance policy the subject matter of insurance is the life being assured; in marine insurance it can be the ship, its cargo or the shipowner's legal liability to third parties for injury or damage.

It is extremely important however to grasp one fundamental fact. It is not the house, ship, machinery, potential liability or life that is insured, but the **pecuniary interest** of the insured in that item.

The **subject matter of contract** is the name given to this financial interest that a person has in the subject matter of the insurance. This concept is at the root of the doctrine of insurable interest and was expounded very clearly in the case of *Castellain v. Preston* (1883) in these words:

> *What is it that is insured in a fire policy? Not the bricks and materials used in building the house but the interest of the insured in the subject matter of insurance.*

Insurable Interest Defined

Insurable interest can be defined as **the legal right to insure arising out of a financial relationship, recognized at law, between the insured and the subject matter of insurance.**

Essentials of Insurable Interest

There are at least four features essential to insurable interest:

- There must be some property, right, interest, life, limb or potential liability capable of being insured.

- Such property, right, interest etc. must be the subject matter of insurance.

- The insured must stand in a relationship with the subject matter of insurance whereby he benefits from its safety, well-being or freedom from liability and would be prejudiced by its damage or the existence of liability.

- The relationship between the insured and the subject matter of insurance must be recognized at law.

The case of *Macaura v. Northern Assurance Company* (1925) illustrates the need for the relationship between insured and subject matter of insurance to be recognized at law. Mr Macaura effected a fire policy on an amount of cut timber on his estate. He had sold the timber to a one-man company of which he was the only shareholder. A great deal of the timber was destroyed in a fire and the insurers refused to meet the claim on the basis that Mr Macaura had no insurable interest in the assets of the company of which he was the principal shareholder. A company is a separate legal entity from its shareholders and what was established by the case was that the relationship between the timber and Mr Macaura, whereby he stood to lose by its destruction, had to be one recognized or enforceable at law. In this case such a relationship did not exist, because his financial interest in the company as a shareholder was limited to the value of his shares and he had no insurable interest in any assets of the company.

Another example of the circumstances in which a person does not have insurable interest arises out of divorce. A divorced person cannot insure or claim for his/her erstwhile partner's goods if they have not been made part of the divorce settlement. Before divorce he or she could have done so.

History

A contract of life insurance was enforceable at common law despite the absence of any relationship between the insured and the life insured, and even in the face of judicial reluctance. The reason for this was that wagers in general were legally enforceable and thus the courts had no option but to enforce wagers in the form of life insurance contracts.

An increase in these practices, which were clearly distasteful and which indeed could serve as an inducement to murder, led to growing concern and, ultimately, legislative action in the form of the Life Assurance Act 1774. As far as other types of insurance were concerned, there was abundant authority recognizing as valid marine policies without interest, which were the other common form of insurance at the time. However, statute, in the form of the Marine Insurance Act 1745, put a stop to this practice.

The legislature intervened further with a series of statutes, finally rendering all contracts by way of gaming or wagering void under the Gaming Act 1845, S18. The details of the relevant provisions will be examined shortly, but it is useful at this stage briefly to summarize how the various statutory provisions apply to the various types of insurance:

- Marine policies are now governed by the Marine Insurance Act 1906, by S4 of which such policies without interests are void.

- Life policies are governed by the 1774 Act, and a failure to show interest renders a policy illegal.

- All other policies except those on 'goods and merchandises' may also be covered by the Life Assurance Act, despite the misleading short title.

- In respect of policies on goods, there is no statutory requirement of insurable interest *per se*. However, the Gaming Act 1845 will strike down any goods policy which is really a wager, and it seems that the Marine Insurance Act 1788 still technically requires that every goods policy must contain the name of a person interested in it.

Marine Insurance Act 1745

This act forbade the issuing of policies of assurance which were made by:

> *any person or persons, bodies corporate or politic on any ship or ships belonging to his Majesty or any of his subjects or on any goods, merchandise or effects, laden or to be laden, on board of any ship, or ships, interest or no interest, or without further proof of interest, or by way of gaming or wagering, or without benefit of salvage to the assurer.*

Every such assurance was, to all intents and purposes, null and void.

The reference to 'interest or no interest or without further proof of interest' relates to the practice that had developed of attaching a clause to marine policies which stated that the holding of the policy was the only proof of interest required.

Thereafter, any policies issued 'policy proof of interest' (p.p.i.) where the nature or extent of the interest could not be defined with certainty were 'honour' contracts only, because the parties could not sue upon them in the courts.

Life Assurance Act 1774

The 1745 Act related only to marine insurance and it was still possible to gamble on lives and other events. The Life Assurance Act 1774, sometimes referred to as the Gambling Act, forbade the making of any policy:

> *on the life or lives of any person or persons, or on any other event or events whatsoever, wherein the person or persons for whose use, benefit, or on whose account such policy or policies shall be made, shall have no interest, or by way of gaming or wagering.*

The essential features of the act are as follows:

● Insurances on the lives of persons or on any other event whatsoever whereby the person benefiting from the insurance has no interest are null and void.

● No policies on lives or other events shall be lawful, unless the name of the person for whose benefit the policy is being effected is inserted in the policy.

● No greater sum may be recovered than the amount of the interest of the insured.

● The act did not extend to insurances on ships, goods or merchandises.

With regard to the second category listed above, the Insurance Companies Amendment Act 1973 permits unnamed persons to benefit, provided they fall within a certain class or description stated in the policy. Essentially, it must be possible at any given time to establish the identity of any person who is entitled to benefit under the policy.

Marine Insurance Act 1788

By 1788 it was illegal to make policies on British ships and goods laden on them, and other insurances except ships, goods and merchandises, where no insurable interest existed. The loophole appeared to be policies effected on goods unconnected with a ship. The Act of 1788 remedied this position and insisted on insurable interest for policies on any ship or 'any goods, merchandises, effects or other property whatsoever'.

The act also required the name of one person interested or concerned to be inserted on the policy document.

The legislation up to this date had been restricted to insurance contracts, and the Gaming Act 1845 was therefore introduced to render all contracts of gambling or wagering null and void. One effect of this, as far as insurers were concerned, was that insurance contracts where no insurable interest existed were rendered null and void, because such contracts were nothing more than wagers.

Marine Insurance Act 1906

This Act repealed the 1745 Act and those parts of the 1788 Act relating to marine insurance. The Act codified these previous statutes and declared void any marine insurance contract where no insurable interest existed at the time of any loss. The Act defines insurable interest in the following terms:

> *In particular a person is interested in a marine adventure where he stands in any legal or equitable relation to the adventure or to any insurable property at risk therein, in consequence of which he may benefit by the safety or due arrival of insurable property, or may be prejudiced by its loss, or by damage thereto, or by the detention thereof, or may incur liability in respect thereof.*

Marine Insurance (Gambling Policies) Act 1909

Although gaming or wagering contracts were unenforceable, nothing had been done to make them illegal until the passing of this act. It now became a criminal offence to effect a marine policy where no insurable interest existed or where there was no bona fide expectation of there being an interest.

The following table compares insurance contracts and wagering contracts.

Insurance contract	Wagering contract
insurable interest in the subject matter is essential	the interests are limited to the stake to be won or lost and, as such, they are not recognized at law
the insured is immune from loss and his identity is known before the event	either party may win or lose and the loser cannot be identified until after the event
full disclosure (*uberrima fides*) is required by both parties to the contract	full disclosure is not required by either party
in most cases an indemnity only is secured	the stakes are not paid by way of indemnity. Payment is made without suffering loss beforehand
the contract is enforceable at law	neither party has any legal remedy

- We have mentioned seven acts as important in the development of the concept of insurable interest. Before going on, be sure that you can name them and that you have a reasonable idea of their significance.

Creation of Insurable Interest

Insurable interest may arise at common law: for example, the ownership of property, or the potential liability a negligent car driver has for a claim by a pedestrian injured by his negligence.

In some **contracts** a person agrees to be liable for something for which he or she would not be liable in the absence of the contractual condition. A landlord, rather than his tenant, is normally liable for the maintenance of property he owns. Many modern leases, however, contain a condition that makes the tenant responsible for the maintenance or repair of the building. Similarly, in building contracts, the contractor may be responsible for the negligence of subcontractors or of the employer.

Clearly, such contracts place the tenant or the contractor in a legally recognized relationship to the building or the potential liability, and thus give them an insurable interest which would not be present in the absence of the contracts.

Some **statutes** place responsibilities on people similar to the contracts mentioned above, for example:

- Married Women's Policies of Assurance (Scotland) Act 1880 (as amended by the Married Women's Policies of Assurance (Amendment) Act 1980).
- Married Women's Property Act 1882.

These acts provided married women with an insurable interest in their own lives and in policies on their husbands' lives for their (the wives') own benefit.

- Industrial Assurance and Friendly Societies Act 1948 and Amendment Act 1958.

These acts allow a person to effect an industrial life assurance policy on the life of a parent, step-parent or grandparent for an amount up to £30. The original intention was to allow cover to be provided for funeral costs, because the parent/child relationship does not normally support insurable interest.

Statutes Modifying Insurable Interest

Over the years the liability of certain people was considered to be too onerous, and statutes were passed to modify this liability. When the responsibility was modified it followed that the insurable interest was correspondingly reduced. However, although the statutes modified liability in certain instances, in others they left a full liability with the person who was originally liable. As a result the practical position relating to insurable interest may be unaltered.

- Carriers' Act 1830. A common carrier is exempted from liability for certain valuable articles of greater value than £10 each, except where the value of the item has been declared and any extra charge paid.

- Carriage of Goods by Sea Act 1971. Liability of the carrier in this case is limited to 10,000 gold francs per package or unit, or 30 gold francs per kilo gross weight of the goods lost or damaged, whichever is the higher.

Note: various contracts relating to the carriage of goods and passengers may extend or limit liability, and there are many other statutes relating to carriage of goods by road, rail, air and sea which apply in specific cases. The two statutes mentioned are sufficient for present purposes to establish the role that statutes may play in the modification of liability at common law.

- Hotel Proprietors' Act 1956. Where people have booked sleeping accommodation at a hotel, and provided the hotelier displays a copy of the schedule of the act in a prominent position, his liability for loss of or damage to the property of guests is limited to £50 on any one article and £100 on any one guest. These limits do not apply where the loss or damage was brought about by the negligence of the proprietor or his staff, or in the case of goods deposited or offered for safe keeping.

- Trustee Act 1925. Trustees can effect fire insurance on trust property up to three quarters of the value, paying the premium out of trust income. This act does not alter the fact that in his own right the trustee can insure the property for its full value.

Application of Insurable Interest to Main Forms of Insurance

We shall look at each of these in turn.

Life assurance

Everyone has unlimited insurable interest in his or her own life and, theoretically, is entitled to effect a policy for any sum assured. In practice the cost of the policy often limits a person's ability to insure his or her own life. In addition to having insurable interest in one's own life, a person who is married also has an interest in the life of his or her spouse: wives can effect policies on the lives of their husbands and vice versa. This idea of mutual insurable interest is founded in common law, but statutory authority for a wife to assure her own life was provided by the Married Women's Property Act 1882.

A blood relationship does not imply an automatic insurable interest, the only exception to this being noted above in the case of industrial life assurance, as mentioned earlier in this unit.

In addition, certain people can insure the life of another person to whom they bear a relationship, recognized at law, to the extent of a possible financial loss. Accordingly, business partners can insure each others' lives up to the limit of their financial involvement, because they would stand to lose on the death of any one of them. In the same way a creditor stands to lose money if a debtor dies before repaying the loan, and therefore has insurable interest to the extent of the loan plus interest.

Property insurance

In property insurances, insurable interest normally arises out of ownership where the insured is the owner of the subject matter of insurance, as in the case of a houseowner insuring his house, a sportsman insuring his golf clubs or a shopkeeper insuring his stock. There are, however, cases involving legal relationships and financial interests other than full ownership, and these include:

Part or joint owners

A person having a part interest in some property is entitled to insure to the full value of that property rather than just to the extent of his actual interest. This does not mean that he will benefit in any way should the property be destroyed completely, because he is looked upon as a **trustee** for the other owner or owners. When he receives any claim money that exceeds his own financial interest he does so as an agent for the others, holding such money in trust for them.

Mortgagees and mortgagors

Mortgages are most common in the area of house purchase, where they involve a building society or other financial institution (the mortgagee) and the purchaser (the mortgagor). Both parties have insurable interest, the purchaser as owner of the house and the building society as a creditor. The interest of the mortgagee is limited to the extent of the loan. The normal practice in house purchase is for the building society to insist, as a term of the mortgage contract, on the house being insured by the mortgagor in the joint names of mortgagor and mortgagee.

Executors and trustees

Executors and trustees often need to effect insurance on property over which they assume control. They are legally responsible for the property under their charge, and this gives rise to their insurable interest in it.

Bailees

A bailee is a person legally holding the goods of another either for payment or gratuitously. Pawnbrokers, launderers and watch repairers are examples of bailees: each has a responsibility to take reasonable care of the goods and to look after them as if they were his own.

Agents

Where a principal has insurable interest, his agent can effect insurance on his behalf.

Husband and wife

Each spouse has an insurable interest in the property of the other in much the same way as they have mutual insurable interest in each other's lives.

Liability insurance

A person has insurable interest to the extent of any potential legal liability he may incur by way of damages and other costs. It is not possible to predetermine what the extent of that interest is, because it is not known in what way and how often liability may be incurred. It could be said that the extent of a person's interest in liability insurance is without limit. In fact, while this is so in a theoretical sense, in a practical situation liability to pay damages is based largely on legal precedents. This means that whether a case is settled in or out of court the damages awarded against the insured will have been calculated bearing in mind similar claims in the past. As far as insurable interest is concerned the insured still has no exact figure representing his interest but must wait until the case has been settled. This is different from a person insuring a large factory complex. He does know the maximum loss sustainable but not the size of any one loss. The same point, however, underlines both cases. The insured has insurable interest up to the limit of his potential liability, whatever it may be, or up to the extent of his financial interest as owner in the complex.

When Insurable Interest Must Exist

The Marine Insurance Act 1906 S6 states that the assured must be interested in the subject matter insured at the time of the loss, although he need not be interested when the insurance is effected. This follows from the customs of maritime trading: cargo may change ownership while in transit. The marine insurance policy is one of the essential documents in the transfer of title in such cases, and the buyer of goods is thus permitted to have a legitimate insurable interest in the goods from the time of transfer even though he did not have an interest when the policy was effected.

In life assurance, insurable interest is required only at inception. In 1854, the case of *Dalby v. The India and London Life Assurance Company* set down the principle that the interest need be valued only at inception and so there is no requirement for insurable interest at the time of a claim.

Other insurances, being contracts of indemnity, require the insured to have suffered a loss before there is liability, so that the insured must have insurable interest at the time of loss. The Gaming Act 1845 in effect requires insurable interest at inception, because contracts without it would be wagers.

Common Features of Insurable Interest

There are five common features of insurable interest:

Insurers' insurable interest

Insurance companies have their insurable interest in the liability to pay claims to insureds. This interest gives them the right to seek reinsurance, and still satisfy the doctrine of insurable interest.

Enforceable at law

The mere expectation of acquiring insurable interest in the future, however certain that expectation is, may not be enough to create insurable interest.

... suppose the case of the heir-at-law of a man who has an estate worth £20,000 a year, who is ninety years of age, upon his deathbed intestate, and incapable from incurable lunacy of making a will, there is no man who will deny that such an heir-at-law has a moral certainty of succeeding to the estate, yet the law will not allow that he has any interest, or anything more than a mere expectation.

Lucena v. Craufurd (1806)

Two apparent exceptions to the general rule should be mentioned:

- It is possible for a legal right to be created which is based upon an expectancy. For example, if someone has an expectancy under a will, they may prefer to raise some money on the potential security of that expectancy. Let us say that A expects to inherit under a will, and contracts to sell his expectancy to B for £2,000 now. A condition of the contract is that in the event of A being disinherited, he will repay the £2,000 to B. B runs the risk that A will predecease the creator of the will. He can insure A's life to protect his interest. B's interest arises out of the contract, not out of the expectancy: *Cook v. Field* (1850).

- Some people have certain legal rights, but only an expectancy that those rights will materialize. If a trader owns some property or goods and sells them, he has a legal right to any profits the price may allow. He expects to make a profit if the property or goods remain undamaged. If the property or goods are destroyed, the expectancy to that legal right is defeated. This expectancy to profit is insurable: *Barclay v. Cousins* (1802). The crucial difference between *Lucena v. Craufurd* and *Barclay v. Cousins* is that, in the former case, the beneficiary has no legal right to the benefits of the will until two things are certain:

    - the individual dies; and

    - the deceased had not previously changed his will.

In the latter case, there is a legal right to the profits through the ownership of the goods. The second expectancy (to profits) supports insurable interest, whereas the former does not.

Equitable interest

Equitable interest may arise in a number of ways. For example, where a formal mortgage deed has not been drawn up, the lender will have an equitable interest in the property; such an equitable interest is enough to create insurable interest.

Possession

Lawful possession of property normally supports insurable interest, provided that such possession is accompanied by responsibility.

Interest need not be specified.

It is not necessary to state the exact nature of the insurable interest in the policy.

Criminal acts

A person cannot recover under a policy in respect of his own criminal acts, *Beresford v. Royal Insurance* (1938), although it is quite in order to arrange insurance to meet the **civil** consequences of some breach of the criminal code. This happens regularly when drivers are found guilty of some road traffic offence and at the same time receive indemnity from insurers for damage to their own or another's property. No insurance is available in respect of any fine.

The *Beresford* case concerned a suicide under a life assurance policy, but the statement by the judge had a wider application:

> *the absolute rule is that the courts will not recognize a benefit accruing to a criminal from his crime ...*

This means that a person who, for example, deliberately sets fire to his own premises will gain no benefit from his fire policy if his criminal act is discovered.

An insured is allowed to receive an indemnity for civil liabilities arising out of a breach of the criminal code because the benefit is not retained by him but is passed on to the third party who has suffered loss arising out of the criminal act.

Financial Valuation

In general, the amount of insurable interest must be capable of financial valuation. This is relatively straightforward in the case of insurance of property, liability and rights interests. Valuation is difficult in the case of one's own life or the life of a spouse, where it is taken that there is unlimited interest.

With regard to other policies on the life of another, certain interests are capable of valuation: the creditor's interest on the life of a debtor for the amount of the debt, plus interest and insurance premium. In other cases, for example an employer in an employee's life, the interest must be in a reasonable sense capable of valuation in money: *Simcock v. Scottish Imperial* (1902). It would appear from the more recent cases of *Green v. Russell* (1959) and *Marcel Beller Ltd v. Hayden* (1978) that, provided an insurable interest is established, the courts are not too concerned about the amount so long as it appears to be reasonable.

Assignment of Personal Contracts

In general, assignment of personal contracts is valid only with the consent of the insurers. Thus policies covering property, liability and pecuniary (or rights) interests are not freely assignable. **When the insurer consents to the assignment of a policy, a new**

contract is in fact created. The process of entering such a new contract is termed **novation.**

The process of asking for the insurer's approval can create difficulties in some circumstances. For example, when a person dies his contract lapses and the property or other risk is uninsured; the beneficiary or trustee has no cover until he is aware of the death and has time to arrange cover.

Transfer of Interest by Operation of Law

Insurers frequently seek to alleviate such hardships by giving their consent by a policy condition, so that, in the event of a transfer of an interest in the subject matter of insurance by will or operation of law, they will automatically transfer the insurance as well. At first renewal there would be a duty to disclose the new interest if such disclosure had not been made before then.

Assignment of Marine Policies

The Marine Insurance Act 1906 S50 allows for the free assignment of marine policies. This clause is an enactment of the custom of maritime trading where the marine insurance policy is an essential document in the transfer of title to cargo. Since cargo is not within the custody or control of the owner for most of the time, the marine insurer is not prejudiced by a change in ownership.

In the case of hull insurance, however, the shipowner has control of the management of the ship and therefore of the likelihood of loss. For this reason insurers usually treat hull policies as **personal** contracts and a policy condition prohibits transfer of the insurance without agreement.

Assignment of Life Policies

The assured under a life policy has a reversionary interest in that his or her enjoyment is deferred until the policy matures or death occurs. In view of the reversionary interest, life policies are freely assignable. In addition, in the majority of cases the conduct of the assured does not have the same effect in relation to the likelihood of a claim arising, as it would with fire or motor insurance.

Absolute assignments

Life policies may be assigned to anyone whether or not he has an insurable interest in the life assured. As with **personal** contracts the assignee acquires all the rights and liabilities of the original assured.

Conditional assignments

In many cases, the assignment of a life policy is not given absolutely and is by way of a conditional assignment for the purpose of giving security to a mortgagee for a loan given. On repayment of the loan and interest, the original assured has the right to have the policy reassigned to him. This is termed a legal mortgage.

Sometimes, the policy may simply be deposited with the lender. The legal interest does not pass to the mortgagee who acquires an equitable interest in the property mortgaged. In this case, there is not a legal assignment of the policy and in the event of a claim the mortgagee would have to prove his right in equity.

Policies of Assurance Act 1867

This act allows for an assignee to sue in his or her own name on the life policy provided he or she has served notice of the assignment on the assurer, and received an acknowledgement of such notice having been received.

Assignment of Policy Proceeds

Apart from the assignment of rights under a policy, another less complex form of assignment is where the proceeds of a policy are assigned, as in the case of a houseowner assigning the proceeds of the household insurance policy to a roof repairer. There is generally no objection to assignment of policy proceeds in this way because the insured is still in a contractual relationship with the insurers and must comply with all terms and conditions of the policy. All that is done is that the insurer is directed to make any claim money payable to some person other than the insured, e.g. the roof repairer. Insurers can protect themselves when making such payment by asking the person receiving the money to sign a form discharging the insurer from any further liability.

The Married Women's Property Act 1882, the Married Women's Policies of Assurance (Scotland) Act 1880 and the Friendly Societies Act 1955 allow for nominations under life policies. This involves the assured in nominating a person to whom the policy proceeds should be paid and really constitutes assignment of the proceeds of the policy.

Student Activity 1

Before reading the next section of the text, answer the following questions and then check your answers against the pages indicated.

1. Distinguish between the subject matter of insurance and the subject matter of contract. *(page 121)*

2. When must insurable interest exist:
    -   for marine insurance?
    -   for permanent health insurance?
    -   for fire insurance?
    -   for life assurance? *(page 129)*

If your answers are basically correct, then proceed to the next section. If significant parts of your answers are wrong, then study the whole of the relevant sections again in detail. Note your areas of weakness, and be prepared for further questions on these areas in the self-assessment section at the end of this unit.

5.2   Utmost Good Faith

This is a crucial concept in relation to insurance. We shall now look more closely at its significance.

Non-insurance Contracts

Most commercial contracts are subject to the doctrine of *caveat emptor* (let the buyer beware). These contracts are subject to the Sale of Goods Act 1979, the Misrepresentation Act 1967, the Supply of Goods (Implied Terms) Act 1973 and the Unfair Contract Terms Act 1977, but basically it is the responsibility of each party to the contract to ensure that he makes a good or reasonable bargain. In most of these contracts each party can examine the item or service that is the subject matter. So long as one does not mislead the other party and answers questions truthfully, there is no question of the other party avoiding the contract. There is no need to disclose information that is not asked for.

Insurance Contracts

Although the proposer can examine a specimen of the policy before accepting its terms, the insurer is at a disadvantage because he cannot examine all aspects of the proposed insurance that are material to him. Only the proposer knows, or should know, all the relevant facts about the risk being proposed. The underwriter can have a survey carried out but he must rely on information given by the insured in order to assess those aspects of the risk that are not apparent at the time of a survey. In order to make the situation more equitable the law imposes a duty of *uberrima fides* or 'utmost good faith' on the parties to an insurance contract. The contract is deemed to be one of faith or trust, and most contracts of a fiduciary nature are subject to the same doctrine.

This has been summed up by Scrutton L J, as follows:

> *As the underwriter knows nothing and the man who comes to him to ask him to insure knows everything, it is the duty of the assured ... to make a full disclosure to the underwriter without being asked of all the material circumstances. This is expressed by saying it is a contract of the utmost good faith.*
>
> Rozanes v. Bowen (1928)

Reciprocal Duty

The duty of full disclosure also rests on the underwriters: *Carter v. Boehm* (1766). They must not withhold information from the proposer, so as to lead him into a less favourable contract.

Examples of this duty are:

- not to withhold from a proposer that the sprinkler system in his premises entitles him to a substantial discount on his fire insurance premium;

- not to accept an insurance which they know is unenforceable at law, or which they are not registered to underwrite;

- not to make untrue statements during negotiations for a contract.

This principle is well illustrated by the case of *Banque Financière de la Cité S.A. v. Westgate Insurance Co. Ltd* (1990). In this case, banks agreed to lend money to someone provided that appropriate credit insurance policies guaranteeing the loans were obtained. The broker involved wrongly told the banks that full insurance cover had been obtained when in fact at the time it had not been; this fact later came to the knowledge of the insurers, but they failed to tell the insured banks which made further loans. It was held that the insurers were in breach of a duty of disclosure imposed on them by reason of the principle of *uberrima fides*. The banks were able to avoid the policy and recover their premium and, in addition, were entitled to damages.

Definition

The duty of utmost good faith can be defined as **'a positive duty to voluntarily disclose, accurately and fully, all facts material to the risk being proposed, whether asked for them or not'**.

Material fact

The current legal definition of a material fact is contained in the Marine Insurance Act 1906 S18(2).

Every circumstance is material that would influence the judgement of a prudent insurer in fixing the premium, or determining whether he will take the risk.

This statement has been reaffirmed in the Road Traffic Act 1972 and in *Lambert v. CIS* (1975) in similar terms. Over the years there has been some criticism of the use of the term 'prudent underwriter' and there has been a tendency to substitute 'reasonable underwriter', in applying the rule: *March Cabaret v. London Assurance* (1975).

In many cases it has been suggested that the view of a 'reasonable insured' rather than a reasonable underwriter should be the test of whether a fact is material or not, and the rule may be changed in the future.

At the present time it is irrelevant whether the proposer or, indeed, the individual insurer, regards a fact as material, the test being the view of a prudent or reasonable underwriter.

Facts that must be disclosed

Any fact that would influence the insurer, in accepting or declining a risk or in fixing the premium or terms and conditions of the contract, is material and must be disclosed. The fact must be material at the date at which it should be communicated to the insurer. A fact that was immaterial when the contract was made, but later become material, need not be disclosed in the absence of a policy condition requiring continuous disclosure. It is not for a particular insured or for a particular insurer to decide what view is material, but ultimately for the courts to decide what a prudent or reasonable insurer would take to be material.

Facts that must be disclosed are:
- facts that show that the particular risk being proposed is greater because of individual, internal factors than would be expected from its nature or class;
- similarly if external factors make the risk greater than normal;
- facts that would make the likely amount of loss greater than that normally expected;
- previous losses and claims under other policies;
- previous refusal to insure or adverse terms imposed on previous proposals by other insurers;
- facts restricting subrogation rights due to the insured relieving third parties of liabilities they would otherwise have;
- existence of other non-indemnity policies such as life and accident;
- full facts relating to and descriptions of the subject matter of insurance.

Examples of facts requiring disclosure:
- **fire insurance:** the form of construction of the building and the nature of its use;
- **theft insurance:** nature of stock and its value;
- **motor insurance:** the fact that a vehicle will be driven regularly by someone other than the insured;
- **marine insurance:** in cargo insurance, the fact that a particular consignment will be carried on deck;
- **life assurance:** previous medical history;
- **personal accident insurance:** previous history that might make an accident more likely, the results more severe, or the recovery slower than normal;
- **in all classes of insurance:** previous loss experience and all facts that the proposer could be reasonably expected to know; for example a landlord should know the nature of occupancy of his property by a tenant.

Facts that need not be disclosed

It was stated above that everything is material that could influence the terms offered. It follows that in addition to the detrimental facts outlined in the previous paragraph, there could be facts that improve the risk. If the proposer does not disclose these facts he is not putting the underwriter at a disadvantage. There are other circumstances when the insurer may be assumed to be in possession of the full facts. Facts, even if material, need not be disclosed if coming within the following headings:

- **Facts of law**: everyone is deemed to know the law.

- **Facts that an insurer is deemed to know**: facts of common knowledge such as the strife in Northern Ireland, or the usual or normal processes within a particular trade.

- **Facts that lessen the risk**: the existence of an alarm system in a theft risk or sprinklers in a fire risk.

- **Facts about which the insurer has been put on enquiry**: the most common example is where the proposer has referred the insurer to the claims record under a previous policy or with a previous insurer, and the insurer does not follow up this line of enquiry. The insurer will be regarded as having waived his right to the full information.

- **Facts that the insurer's survey should have noted**: material facts that are clearly visible, or which any reasonable surveyor would enquire about. On the other hand the proposer is not permitted to conceal material matters from the surveyor.

- **Facts covered by policy conditions**: a fact that it is superfluous to disclose by reason of any expressed or implied warranty, for example that burglar alarms are regularly maintained.

- **Facts that the proposer does not know**: one cannot be expected to disclose what is outside one's knowledge, but if it should have been within that knowledge there is a duty to disclose it.

- **Facts (convictions) that are 'spent' under the Rehabilitation of Offenders Act 1974.** (In this context, spent means 'no longer deemed to exist'.)

Duration of the Duty of Disclosure

At common law

The duty at common law starts at the commencement of negotiations for a contract and terminates when the contract is formed: when there is offer and acceptance. During the currency of the contract the duty is one of good faith, not of utmost good faith, in that at common law there is no need to disclose changes while the contract is running.

Contractual duty

Sometimes the conditions of a policy extend the common law position by requiring full disclosure during the currency of the contract, and giving the insurer the right to refuse to underwrite the change. In other cases the policy condition may require disclosure of certain types of fact only.

Position at renewal

The duty of disclosure at time of renewal depends on the type of contract.

Long-term business

For life assurance and permanent health insurance contracts, the duration of the duty to disclose material facts lasts only until completion of the contract, that is until payment of the first premium. This is because these are 'long-term' contracts and the insurance company assesses the risk at commencement. It is therefore obliged to continue with the policy and accept 'renewal' premiums if the assured wishes to continue the contract. However, it is usual for a continuous disclosure clause to be included in PHI contracts, requiring the insured to disclose any change in occupation **wherever** it occurs. This clause modifies the usual rule.

Other business

In other cases renewal requires the assent or agreement of the insurer, and in such cases the original duty of disclosure is revived. The facts as applying at the time of negotiating the renewal must be disclosed: *Pim v. Reid* (1843).

Alterations to the contract

If during the currency of the contract it is necessary to alter the terms of it, perhaps to increase the sum insured or alter the description of property insured, then there is a duty to disclose all material facts relating to the alteration. This applies to both long-term and other business.

Representations and Warranties

There are important differences between representations and warranties. It is useful to compare the two.

Representations

Written or oral statements made during the negotiations for a contract are termed 'representations'. Some of these statements will be about material facts and others will not. Those that are material must be substantially true, or true to the best knowledge or belief of the proposer.

Warranties

Warranties in insurance contracts, on the other hand, are fundamental conditions which go to the root of the contract and allow the aggrieved party to avoid it.

A warranty is an undertaking by the insured that something shall or something shall not be done, or that a certain state of fact does or does not exist.

These warranties are imposed usually for the following reasons:

- to ensure that some aspect of 'good housekeeping' or good management is observed: this may be in fire insurance that rubbish is cleared up each night, or in theft insurance that an intruder alarm system is kept in good order under a contract of maintenance;

- to ensure that certain features of higher risk are not introduced without the insurer's knowledge, because the premium charged has been based on the fact that they are not present. An example of this would be where no oils are stored, and are therefore not charged for, in fire insurance. It would be warranted that no oils are kept.

Express warranty

Warranties are usually expressed in or written into insurance contracts and must be strictly accurate; even slight deviations from the facts contained in the warranty will allow the aggrieved party the right to avoid the contract in law.

Frequently warranties are incorporated into the contract by a statement in the policy that the proposal form is the basis of the contract, and on the proposal form there is a declaration by the insured that the answers given are true to the best of his knowledge and belief.

Implied warranty

Normally, warranties must be written conditions of the contract. However, in marine insurance there are implied warranties or undertakings that the vessel is seaworthy and that the adventure is lawful: Marine Insurance Act 1906, S39 and S41.

It is generally held that implied warranties do not exist in other classes of insurance.

Comparison of representations and warranties

Representations:

- need only be substantially correct;

- allow repudiation only if a breach (misrepresentation) is material;

- do not normally appear on the policy.

Warranties:

- must be strictly and literally complied with;

- give the right to repudiate on any breach;

● are written into the policy, except for implied warranties. However, there is no legal requirement to do this directly, because the proposer may be asked to sign a warranty on the proposal form, the policy stating that the proposal is the basis of the contract.

Disclosure and the Use of Agents

A very high proportion of insurance business is brought about by the services of insurance intermediaries.

For some of these, the bringing together of proposer and insurer is their full-time business. These include insurance brokers and insurance consultants.

In other cases, the arrangement of insurance contracts is brought about by intermediaries whose main business is in another field; garages, solicitors, accountants, estate agents, building societies and banks. In the case of banks, many of them have set up separate insurance broking companies, although the initial contact by a member of the public may be to the local bank manager.

In law, all intermediaries are agents of the principal whom they represent. Insurance practice generally refers to the part-time intermediary as an 'agent', whereas the full-time specialist is called a broker or a consultant. Here we shall use the word 'agent' to apply to any intermediary. The law of agency is dealt with in more detail in the Law and Practice subject; what follows here is a brief summary to give you an idea of how utmost good faith is affected by the use of agents.

Where a principal engages another person to act for him in negotiating a contract, the principal is liable for the fraud, concealment or misrepresentation of the agent, where that agent is apparently acting in the course of the principal's business as authorized. Where an agent, acting for an insurer, accepted a premium for a risk even though he knew that the insured had broken a policy condition, the insurer was prevented from avoiding the policy: *Wing v. Harvey* (1854). This is an example of the doctrine of **estoppel**.

This concept arises out of the principle of equity. Sometimes one party makes a concession which he or she is under no obligation to make and for which he or she receives no consideration. If the other party relies on this concession it would be unjust if he were to suffer loss by the concession being withdrawn retrospectively.

In *Wing v. Harvey*, the agent, by accepting the premium, was waiving his principal's rights of refuting the policy on the grounds of breach of condition. Having relied on that principal's waiver by assuming that he was insured, it would have been unjust to the policyholder if liability had been denied.

A similar position arises in the case of *Murfitt v. Royal* (1922). Here the agent had no authority to issue cover but the company had ratified his *ultra vires* action on two previous occasions. This led the insured to think that the agent had authority to issue cover and he (the insured) would have been prejudiced if this in fact was not the case.

The insured, intermediary and insurer

Where the insured uses an intermediary, the knowledge of the agent is imputed to the principal and vice versa, and this knowledge, where material, must be communicated to the insurer.

Difficulties sometimes arise as to whether an agent is an agent of the proposer or of the company. In the one transaction he can be an agent of both, but the individual actions within that transaction will decide on whose behalf he is acting at a particular time.

The following distinctions can be made:

The agent is agent of the proposer:

- if the only recognition he receives from the insurers is the payment of commission: *Bancroft v. Heath* (1900);

- if he and the proposer are in collusion over fraud against the insurers;

- if he fills in, alters, or adds to the answers in a proposal form, and the proposer knew or ought to have known of this: *Newsholme Bros v. Road Transport & General* (1929);

- if he completes a form on the proposer's behalf and the form incorporates a wording to the effect that if the form is completed by someone other than the proposer, that person is deemed to be the agent of the proposer: *Facer v. Vehicle & General Ins. Co. Ltd* (1964) (but see *Stone v. Reliance Mutual* below);

- if an agent gives advice to the proposer as to the cover he requires and the market in which he should place his business;

- if the agent gives the insured advice about how to formulate his claim.

The agent is agent of the insurance company:

- if he has express authority from it to receive and handle proposal forms;

- if he handles the forms according to a previous course of business with the insurers and within an implied authority that has arisen;

- if he surveys and describes the property on the insurer's behalf;

- if he acted without express authority, where the company either ratifies his action or has ratified such action in the past: *Murfitt v. Royal*;

- if he expressly or impliedly has authority to collect premiums;

- if he is instructed by the insurer to ask questions and fill in the answers on a proposal form; he is then the insurer's agent even when the proposal contains a declaration to the contrary: Stone v. *Reliance Mutual Ins. Soc. Ltd* (1972).

The fact that a broker can act for both parties in the one transaction can, at present, lead to some disquieting situations. In *North & South Trust Co. v. Berkeley; Berkeley v. North &*

South Trust Co. (1970), a broker negotiating in a claims settlement on behalf of the insured was held in the Court of Appeal to be the agent of the insurer when he was shown documents which were the basis of the repudiation of liability, and so was not at liberty to disclose their contents to the insured.

Duties of agent to principal

- He must act with due care and skill for that class of agent. For example, there is a higher duty of skill resting on an insurance broker, because he is holding himself out to be an insurance expert, than on a solicitor or accountant acting as an agent whose expertise lies in other areas.

- He must act in accordance with the terms of his agency contract, which may be oral, written or implied from actions, and he must carry out all legal instructions.

- He must act in perfect good faith with his principal, disclosing to him all material facts relating to the contract. He must not accept secret commissions. It will be assumed through custom of the trade that insurance intermediaries are paid commission by the insurers. In the event of the insured appearing to be unaware of this fact, it must be disclosed to him.

- He must account to the principal for all moneys received on his behalf.

- He must perform his duties in person to comply with the rule *delegatus non potest delegare* (an agent can not delegate his duties to another). There are, however certain important exceptions to this rule:

  - where custom sanctions delegation;

  - where delegation is necessary to the proper performance of the agent's duties;

  - where there is an express or implied agreement to allow delegation.

Delegation of duties by a broker to his staff would probably fall within the exceptions, but in the case of other agents the right to delegate may be restricted.

Duties of principal to agent

- He must pay the agreed remuneration.

- He must indemnify the agent against all losses, liabilities, and expenses incurred in the normal course of the agency work. The expenses of running an insurance agency/brokerage are generally held to be paid by the agent out of his commissions. On the other hand, brokers frequently pay premiums on behalf of clients, and for this they are entitled to be repaid.

Liabilities of agent

- He is liable for breach of warranty of authority. If an agent purports to act as an agent when he has not been given that authority, he is liable to compensate the party with whom he contracts.

● He is liable to his principal if he commits a tort which lays his principal open to a loss. There are many cases where agents/brokers have failed to carry out instructions regarding arrangement of cover and have had to compensate the insured for uninsured losses.

● He is liable for breach of contract.

Student Activity 2

Before reading the next section of the text, answer the following questions and then check your answers against the pages indicated.

1. Distinguish between a representation and a warranty. *(page 138)*

2. Who does utmost good faith apply to? *(page 134)*

3. How can the conditions of a policy extend the usual common law duty of utmost good faith? *(page 137)*

If your answers are basically correct, then proceed to the next section. If significant parts of your answers are wrong, then study the whole of the relevant sections again in detail. Note your areas of weakness, and be prepared for further questions on these areas in the self-assessment section at the end of this unit.

Breach of the Doctrine of Utmost Good Faith

Breaches of utmost good faith arise under one or both of the following grounds:

● **misrepresentation**, which can be either innocent or fraudulent;

● **non-disclosure**, which can be innocent or fraudulent. In the latter case it is often called 'concealment'.

Misrepresentation

Whether innocent or fraudulent a misrepresentation must:

● be substantially false;

● concern facts that are material to the assessment of the risk, or material to the benefits obtained by the proposer;

● have induced the recipient to enter into a contract of insurance.

Misrepresentation and the Financial Services Act 1986

Section 133 of this act makes it a criminal offence with a maximum penalty of seven years' imprisonment knowingly or recklessly to make misleading or false statements to induce someone to enter most long-term insurance contracts.

Non-disclosure

Non-disclosure will arise, and give grounds for avoidance by the second party, where:

- a fact is within the knowledge of the first party (either in actual fact or as presumed by law);

- a fact is not known to, or not deemed to be known to, the second party; and

- a fact is calculated, if disclosed, to induce the second party either not to enter the contract at all, or else to enter it only at better terms (to the second party).

Remedies for breach of utmost good faith

The aggrieved party has the following options:

- to avoid the contract by either:

    - repudiating the contract *ab initio*; or

    - avoiding liability for an individual claim;

- to sue for damages as well, if concealment or fraudulent misrepresentation is involved;

- to waive these rights and allow the contract to carry on unhindered.

The aggrieved party must exercise his option within a reasonable time of discovery of the breach, or it will be assumed that he has decided to waive his rights.

Compulsory Insurances

Certain insurances, for example motor (third party injuries and third party property damage), are required by statute. The purpose of these statutes is to try to ensure that insurance money will be available to the employer or driver/user to enable him to meet injury or property damage claims from third parties.

The Road Traffic Act 1972 prohibited the insurer from avoiding liability on the grounds of certain breaches of utmost good faith. The 1972 Act has now been consolidated with other Road Traffic Acts in the Road Traffic Act 1988.

Insurers do, however, endorse their policies to the effect that amounts paid in claims that would not have been paid in the absence of statutory limitations may be recovered from the insured.

The practical difficulties of recovering from an insured are so great that often insurers do not enforce this right.

Self-assessment Questions

Short Answer Questions

1. Define insurable interest.

2. What is the significance of the Hotel Proprietor's Act 1956?

3. Distinguish between *caveat emptor* and *uberrima fides*.

4. What is concealment?

5. Give two examples of warranties in insurance contracts.

(Answers given in Appendix 1)

Specimen Examination Questions

1. Mr Smith is lending £10,000 to Mr James, to be repaid over five years. Mr Smith would like to effect a policy on Mr James's life to cover the loan should Mr James die. Mr James would like to insure Mr Smith's life just in case he dies and the beneficiaries of his will insist that the loan be repaid early.

    What is the extent of insurable interest in each case?

    Consider any necessary action if the loan was later repaid earlier than anticipated.

2. Mrs Bates submitted a proposal for a combined household policy to your office. In reply to the question about previous claims experience, she writes 'see your records'. The policy is accepted at normal rates of premium but six months later she claims for a burst pipe. On investigation the claims department find that the underwriter did not investigate the insurance company's records and that Mrs Bates had in fact claimed for fire damage two years ago. What will be the insurer's liability?

(Answers given in Appendix 1)

6

SPECIAL PRINCIPLES OF INSURANCE CONTRACTS II

Objectives

After studying this unit, you should be able to:

- explain what is meant by 'proximate cause';

- apply the doctrine to individual situations;

- show how the doctrine may be modified or excluded;

- give examples of the application of proximate cause to different classes of insurance;

- outline the steps that must be taken to show that a loss is insured;

- explain the importance of the concept of indemnity;

- outline different ways in which indemnity may be provided;

- apply the concept of indemnity to different classes of insurance;

- explain the link between indemnity, subrogation and contribution;

- explain how subrogation and contribution rights arise;

- determine in which situations subrogation and contribution apply.

6.1   Proximate Cause

The following section covers the principle of proximate cause.

Introduction

In an insurance contract it is necessary to state the perils against which cover is given, so that the intention of the parties is clearly defined. It would appear to be a simple matter to understand what is meant by an insurance against fire, or accident, or maritime perils; but where does the operation of these perils start and when does their effect end?

All contracts are subject to conditions. Frequently, conditions in insurance contracts state that certain causes of loss are excluded or that certain results of an otherwise insured peril are excluded. The reasons for this are simple, in that the additional cover may warrant an additional charge which has not been agreed in the premium for the policy, or the peril may be one which insurers regard as a fundamental risk and so more properly dealt with by the state (for example, war risks or nuclear explosive devices).

The relationship between insurance cover and proximate cause will be explained in three distinct steps:

● the meaning of proximate cause;

● a simple policy wording, and the effect of the operation of the doctrine of proximate cause on cover under the policy;

● modification, or non-application, of the doctrine because of the cover given in less straightforward policy wordings.

Definition of Proximate Cause

The standard legal case on the topic is that of *Pawsey v. Scottish Union and National* (1908), where the doctrine was defined as follows:

> *Proximate cause means the active, efficient cause that sets in motion a train of events which brings about a result, without the intervention of any force started and working actively from a new and independent source.*

The proximate cause is not necessarily the first cause, nor the last cause: it is the **dominant, efficient or operative** cause.

In general, causation is to be viewed by applying commonsense standards. For example, 'explosion' is to be understood in its everyday meaning and not as an extremely rapid fire, as a chemist might view it. In a similar way, centrifugal disintegration is not an explosion even though those nearby may hear a loud 'bang' and doors may be displaced.

Stating that a cause is active and efficient means that there is a direct link between the cause and the result, and that the cause is strong enough that in each stage of the events one can logically predict what the next event in the series will be, until the result under consideration takes place. If there are several causes operating, the proximate one will be the dominant or most forceful one operating to bring about the result.

Train of Events

Seldom does a single event take place and cause a loss in isolation. Something caused the loss-making event to happen, and perhaps something else caused that cause, and so on.

For example, think of six dominoes standing on their ends so that the space between each is only about half the height of each domino. If the top edge of domino 1 is tapped this will cause it to fall against domino 2, which in turn will fall against domino 3 and so on, until domino 6 falls down. Here there is a train (or chain) of events bringing about a result (the fall of domino 6); and the active, efficient cause which set it all in motion was the act of knocking over domino 1.

If an observer of this experiment had stopped domino 3 from touching domino 4, and then changed his mind and knocked over domino 4 himself, the proximate cause of domino 6 falling would have been that observer. There would have been an intervention in the chain started by domino 1 falling, and so it was no longer the proximate cause of the fall of domino 6.

Causation

In practical situations, it is sometimes difficult to determine the efficient cause of a loss, as the volume of case law on the subject illustrates.

Frequently, it is fairly obvious what the initial event and the last event were. The difficulty arises in deciding if there is a direct chain of causation between them, or whether some new force has intervened to supersede the initial cause as the event bringing about the ultimate loss. One way of coming to a decision is to start with the first event in the chain and ask oneself what is logically likely to happen next. If the answer leads one to the second event and this process is repeated until one reaches the final event, then the first event is the proximate cause of the last.

If, at some stage in the process, there is no obvious connection between one link in the chain and the next, then there is a break in the chain and something else must be the cause of the loss.

Another method is to start at the loss and work backwards along the chain, asking oneself, at each stage, why did this happen? In an unbroken chain, one arrives back at the initial event.

Example 1

- A storm blew down the gable wall of a timber building;
- this falling wall broke electrical wiring;
- the broken wiring short-circuited and sparked;
- the sparks caused a fire in the timber building;
- the fire brigade was called;
- they used water hoses to put out the fire and to cool neighbouring buildings;
- the water caused damage to the unburnt contents of the timber building and to the neighbouring buildings.

Using either of the methods described above, we see a direct line of causation between the storm, the collapse of the gable, the fire damage and the water damage.

Example 2

- An earthquake overturned an oil stove;

- the spilt oil caught fire from the burning wick;

- the burning oil set fire to the building;

- the first building, by radiated heat, set fire to a second building;

- sparks and burning embers blown in a breeze set fire to a third building;

- several more buildings caught fire in the same ways;

- eventually, 500 yards away from the first fire, a building caught fire from its neighbouring building.

The fire in this last building was held to be proximately caused by the earthquake: *Tootal Broadhurst Lee Co. v. London and Lancashire Fire Insurance Co.* (1908).

Example 3

- A dropped match set fire to rags in a garage;

- fire developed and overheated some acetylene gas cylinders;

- the cylinders exploded;

- a wall of the garage was blown out and burning materials were blown onto a neighbouring office;

- the office caught fire.

Example 4

- Lightning damaged a building and weakened a wall;

- shortly afterwards, the wall was blown down by high winds.

Lightning was the proximate cause of all the damage.

Example 5

- Fire damaged a wall and left it weakened;

- several days later a gale blew the wall down.

In this case the fire was not the proximate cause of the wall falling down.

Remote causes

These examples are real cases determined by the courts. The differences between Examples 4 and 5 is that in 5 it was felt that the fire was the **remote** cause, whereas we are concerned with **proximate** cause.

In Example 4 the wind occurred shortly after the lightning damage, whereas in Example 5 several days passed between the fire and the storm.

In cases like this, where damage has occurred but there is no imminent likelihood of further loss, then the original cause becomes weaker and weaker as the prime cause as time goes by. In practical terms, the possibility of effecting repairs or securing the property from further loss is the important point. If time was too short, as in Example 4, the initial cause is usually held to be the proximate cause. If there was time but nothing had been done, the original cause is deemed to be too remote.

It should be noted in this context, however, that where the damage is serious and further loss is almost inevitable, the initial cause will be the proximate one while attempts at removing the danger are being made and until the danger is removed. Examples 6 and 7 below illustrate this.

Example 6
- It was wartime;
- a ship was hit by an enemy torpedo;
- it was badly holed and in danger of sinking;
- the master managed to reach port;
- repair work was started;
- a storm blew up;
- the ship was still in danger of sinking, this risk aggravated by the storm;
- to save the harbour from being blocked by the sunken ship, the harbour master ordered it out of port;
- it succumbed to the storm outside the port.

Since the danger of sinking had never been removed, the war is the proximate cause.

Example 7
- Fire seriously damaged a building;
- a wall was in danger of collapsing onto the building next door;
- for safety reasons, the local authority ordered demolition;
- during demolition the wall fell on the neighbouring premises.

Once again, the danger of collapse had not been removed and fire (or its cause) was the proximate cause of damage to the neighbouring building: *Johnston v. West of Scotland Insurance* (1828).

In these examples, the storm and the demolition respectively were deemed to be remote or contributory causes but not the active efficient causes.

Concurrent causes

Occasionally, two causes that are independent of each other may occur at the same time, and each contributes to the loss. For example, a fire may break out during a storm but not be caused by the storm, and there may be some burning damage and some wind damage. Similarly, a fire could break out during a riot but independently of it. Ultimately, damage is done both by the original fire and by a fire started by rioters.

Such situations are relatively rare, and their effect on insurance contracts will be considered later.

Nature of the Perils Relevant to Proximate Cause

The perils relevant to an insurance claim can be classified under three headings:

- **insured perils:** those named in the policy as insured;

- **excepted or excluded perils**: those stated in the policy as excluded, either as causes of insured perils, or as a result of insured perils;

- **uninsured or other perils**: those not mentioned at all in the policy.

Indirect Causes

Policy wordings dealing with exclusions sometimes exclude a peril if it is caused directly, **or indirectly,** by another one: for example, exclude death directly or indirectly caused by war.

In the case of *Coxe v. Employers' Liability Insurance Corporation Ltd* (1916), the policy excluded death caused directly or indirectly due to war. During wartime, sentries were posted along a railway line, and an officer who was inspecting these sentries was knocked down and killed by a train. His death was directly or proximately due to an accident and not to war. However, if there had been no war, he would not have been on the line, so that war was an indirect cause of his death.

Under the terms of that policy, war, even as an indirect cause, prevented a claim being paid.

Concurrent Causes and Insurance

Let us assume that a policy covers damage by fire but specifically excludes damage caused by riot.

Figure 6.1: Concurrent Causes

Events A		Events B
Fire————————————DAMAGE————————— Fire		
Storm ——————————————————————Riot		

If events 'A' occur concurrently but independently of each other, and it is not possible to distinguish which part of the damage was caused by the fire and which part by the storm, all the damage is deemed to be insured since **no excepted peril** is involved. If the damage can be separated out, only that part caused by the fire will be insured.

In the case of events 'B', if the damage cannot be separated, none of it is covered since **an excepted peril** is involved. If it can be separated out, only that part caused by the fire is covered by insurance.

Summary of Proximate Cause

- The insured peril need not be the initial cause.

- The insured peril must not be a direct result of the operation of an excepted peril (unless the policy wording specifically overrules this, as above).

- Damage as the direct result of an insured peril is covered even though the immediate peril causing that damage is not mentioned in the policy (unless the policy specifically excludes the result, as shown above); thus water or smoke damage after fire are covered.

- Property can be covered even though the named peril does not actually cause damage to the insured property, so long as the named peril does operate and its results cause loss to the insured. For example, if the building next door to the insured catches fire and the only damage the insured suffers is by water or smoke, his fire policy will operate (provided the original fire was not caused by a peril named as excluded in the insured's policy).

- The risk insured against must actually take place. The fear of losing goods by an insured peril does not constitute loss by that peril.

- Further damage to the subject matter, due to attempts to minimize a loss already taking place, is covered. Therefore water damage from sprinklers or firemen's hoses is covered.

- *Novus actus interveniens*: 'a new act intervening'. It has been seen in the definition from the *Pawsey* case that the intervention of a new act is outside the doctrine. Thus, if during a fire onlookers cause damage to surrounding property, the cause of such damage is the misdemeanour of the crowd, and not the fire.

- 'Last straw' cases. In instances where the original peril has meant that loss was more or less inevitable, the original peril will be the proximate cause even though the last straw comes from another source.

Summary of examples by class of business

The following are brief details of the most important features of establishing proximate cause. They will help you to understand the principles explained in this unit.

Marine

Leyland Shipping Co. v. Norwich Union (1918): see Example 6 above.

Ionides v. Universal Marine Insurance Co. (1863). A captain lost his course and took his ship inshore to try and pick out a lighthouse. Due to hostilities, the light was extinguished and the ship ran aground. The hostilities and loss of the light were deemed to be too remote to be the proximate cause.

Fire

Harris v Poland (1941). It is the intention of insurance to cover risks which are accidental or fortuitous to the insured. In fire insurance there must also be something on fire which should not be on fire. The insured hid money and jewellery in his fireplace and later inadvertently lit a fire. The judge likened the loss to something accidentally falling into the fire, and allowed the claim.

Everett v. London Assurance Co. (1865). Premises were damaged by an explosion half a mile away, this explosion being caused by a fire. It was held that the fire was too remote and that the damage was caused by explosion.

Gasgarth v. Law Union Insurance Co. (1876): see Example 5 above.

Roth v. South Easthope Farmers (1918): see Example 4 above.

The crucial factor seems to be whether the original peril was still operating and was the dominant cause of loss. In the first case it was evidently felt that the wall was secure after the fire, whereas in the second case this was not so and the gale operated before remedial action could be taken.

Johnston v. West of Scotland Insurance Co. (1828): see Example 7 above. Because the building was in a dangerous state following fire, the risk from the fire was still operating until the danger was removed. The demolition contractors were attempting to minimize that risk by a planned demolition but were unsuccessful.

Other property

Winikofsky v. Army and Navy General (1919). Where thieves took advantage of a blackout during an air raid it was held that war was not the proximate cause.

Shiells v. Scottish Assurance Corporation Ltd (1889). Where a livestock policy provides differing benefits following injury and death, the death benefits are payable where an injury requires the animal to be slaughtered on humane grounds.

Marsden v. City and County Assurance Co. (1865). Where a mob tore down shutters and broke a window while a fire raged in nearby premises, this was held not to be a loss proximately caused by fire, but a glass claim.

Personal accident

Etherington v. Lancashire and Yorkshire Accident Ins. Co. (1909). The insured fell from his horse and suffered injuries which forced him to lie in cold and damp conditions whereby he contracted pneumonia and died. It was held that he died of an 'accident' which was insured and not a disease which was excluded.

Liability policies

Vandyke v. Fender (1970). Where an employee was injured while a passenger in a car provided by his employer to take him to and from work, he was not injured in the course of his employment because there was no obligation on him to use that method of transport.

Gray v. Barr (1971). Gray had an affair with Mrs Barr. Mr Barr thought one evening that his wife had gone to Gray's house, and he went there with a loaded shotgun. Barr did not believe Gray when he said that Mrs Barr was not there, and went upstairs to see for himself, firing a shot into the ceiling to frighten Gray. A scuffle broke out during which the gun went off and Gray was killed. Barr was acquitted of murder and manslaughter, and attempted to claim an indemnity under his public liability insurance for a claim against him by Mrs Gray.

It was held that the proximate cause of Gray's death was his liaison with Mrs Barr. The judges could not all agree on whether the first or second shot was the proximate cause of Barr's loss, nor on whether the cause was accidental or not. However, all four judges agreed that it would be against public policy for him to be indemnified, and so his claim failed.

The use of a gun is the crucial point here, since it is well established in law that one is entitled to an indemnity under the third party section of a motor policy for culpable manslaughter.

The various cases quoted are examples of the operation of the rules of proximate cause. In applying these rules to other circumstances, the student can be guided by these decisions, but since it is likely that many losses will have a unique set of circumstances surrounding them, the establishment of the proximate cause will arise from the application of common sense to the facts of the case.

Proof of Loss

When a loss has occurred it is important that certain conditions are observed. These are discussed below.

Conditions as to time

It is the practice of insurers to incorporate into their policies provisions to the effect that particulars of proof of loss are to be delivered in a certain way or within a certain time. In *Welch v. Royal Exchange Assurance* (1939), the policy provided that no claim was to be payable unless the required particulars were given within a reasonable time. It was held by the Court of Appeal that production of the particulars within a reasonable time was a **condition precedent to recovery.**

If the stipulation as to time is a condition precedent, a failure to furnish particulars puts an end to the insurer's liability and the assured cannot revive his rights by delivering particulars at a later time.

The benefit of any such clause can be waived by the insurer, although a mere failure to mention the clause as a defence to a claim at an early stage will not amount to a waiver.

The insurer may grant an extension of time, but any conditions attached to such an extension must be strictly followed.

Sufficient particulars must be given by the insured. It is a question of fact whether particulars are sufficient, which must depend on all the circumstances of the case, such as the means of information open to the insured and, no doubt, the time within which particulars must be delivered. The phrase 'full particulars' has been said to mean 'the best particulars the assured can reasonably give', and if the insured has failed to give a detailed account of his loss when he could have done so, he will be unable to recover.

The form of proof

When the insured is under obligation to produce proofs of his loss, for example by verifying the particulars by documentary evidence as required by the insurer, the same principles apply as for the furnishing of particulars.

It is usually stipulated that proof is to be satisfactory to the insurer, which means that reasonably satisfactory proof is sufficient. What is reasonable must depend on the circumstances and, in life insurance cases, the insurer is not compelled to be satisfied by a legal presumption against suicide or even necessarily by an order presuming death made by the court. On the other hand, it has been held that the insurer is entitled to call for vouchers, accounts, invoices, and a builder's certificate of the value of a house. The proof must be reasonably detailed. A mere notice that an accident has happened and that an injury has resulted is not proof, nor is a mere affidavit sworn by the insured of the value of the goods which he claims to have lost.

The ordinary rules of evidence apply to insurance claims. The insured must prove his loss but the parties may agree to reverse the burden of proof or to dispense with proof of any particular fact or requirement for recovery.

Certain injuries are themselves *prima facie* evidence of accidental death and, in the absence of other evidence, a court will presume that violence was accidental and not intentionally self-inflicted. But if the facts point to suicide as the only reasonable conclusion or even as a justifiable conclusion, a court should not be influenced by presumptions in favour of accidental death but should decide the cause of death on the balance of probabilities. Where the issue is between death by accident and death from natural causes, there is no presumption in favour of accidental death; once again, the court must decide the question on the balance of probabilities.

The policy may provide that the claimant shall furnish all such information and evidence as the insurers may from time to time require. Under this clause the insurers can ask for evidence and information which may not be absolutely necessary to prove the claimant's case. Any such evidence or information must not, however, be asked for unreasonably.

Student Activity 1

Before reading the next section of the text, answer the following questions and then check your answers against the pages indicated.

1.   Why is it important to determine the proximate cause of loss?

(page 146)

2.   How can a policy wording modify the usual principle of proximate cause?

(page 151)

If your answers are basically correct, then proceed to the next section. If significant parts of your answers are wrong, then study the whole of the relevant sections again in detail. Note your areas of weakness, and be prepared for further questions on these areas in the self-assessment section at the end of this unit.

6.2   The Concept of Indemnity

Lord Justice Brett, in the case of *Castellain v. Preston* (1883), said that indemnity was the 'controlling principle in insurance law'. The centrality of indemnity to the operation of insurance has brought with it a number of problems. There are difficulties in defining the concept, how it is to be applied to the various classes of insurance and how, if at all, it is to be modified to cope with changing needs.

The essence of the problem is really in deciding how much an insured is to receive when the event insured against occurs. Take a factory owner who bought a machine for £25,000 five years ago but knows that it would cost £30,000 to replace today. How much should he receive if there is a valid claim under a policy of insurance?

Definition

> *The very foundation, in my opinion, of every rule which has been applied to insurance law is this, namely, that the contract of insurance contained in a marine or fire policy is a contract of indemnity and of indemnity only, ... and if ever a proposition is brought forward which is at variance with it, that is to say, which either will prevent the assured from obtaining a full indemnity or which gives the assured more than a full indemnity, that proposition must certainly be wrong.*
>
> (*Castellain v. Preston* (1883))

Indemnity, for the purposes of insurance contracts, can be looked upon as **exact financial compensation,** sufficient to place the insured in the same financial position after a loss as he enjoyed immediately before it occurred.

Link with Insurable Interest

There is a link between indemnity and insurable interest, because it is the insured's interest in the subject matter of insurance that is in fact insured. In the event of any claim, the payment made to an insured cannot therefore exceed the extent of his interest and, as will be seen later, there often are cases where insureds receive less than the value of their interest.

As with insurable interest, the principle of indemnity relies heavily on financial evaluation so we must consider the position of those policies where such valuation is difficult. In life assurance and personal accident insurance there is generally an unlimited interest, and in these cases indemnity is not possible. Another way of putting this is to say that life and personal accident policies are not contracts of indemnity, because the value of a person's life or limb cannot be measured by money.

Whereas life and personal accident contracts are not generally regarded as being contracts of indemnity, that is not to imply that care is not exercised in arranging cover. Rather than caution being exercised at the time of a claim, as is the case in indemnity contracts, caution is exercised when the contract is entered into. In life assurance, the amount for which a person may be insured is limited by his own ability to meet premiums. In personal accident policies offering weekly benefits, it is limited to an amount that will not provide an unreasonably high benefit in relation to a person's normal earnings. Similarly, in life assurance, the underwriter would ensure that the sum assured on the life of a debtor or partner was a reasonable estimate of the amount of interest, to comply with the Life Assurance Act 1774.

How Indemnity Is Provided

When the claim occurs the insured is invariably suffering from some degree of shock, and insurers with their experience of claims do all they can to smooth the claims process. The vast majority of claims are settled to the satisfaction of insureds, with very few resulting in any real degree of dispute.

When a valid claim does arise there are at least four methods (as shown below) that insurers can employ in providing indemnity. The option as to which method is to be employed is normally given to the insurers by the wording of the policy. Insurers are not, however, intransigent, and often comply with insureds' requests for indemnity to be provided by a specific means. However, they would not look favourably on a method which increased their costs.

Figure 6.2: How indemnity may be provided

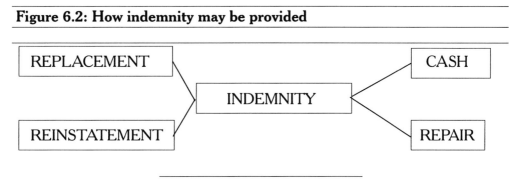

The standard fire policy highlights three methods of providing indemnity where, in its operative clause, it states:

the company will pay to the insured the value of the property at the time of the happening of its destruction or the amount of such damage or at its option reinstate or replace such property or any part thereof.

Other, non-fire, property policies often contain a wording along the lines of 'the company may at its option indemnify the insured by payment of the amount of the loss or damage or by repair, reinstatement or replacement'.

Cash payments

An insurance contract is a contract to pay money and, in the vast majority of cases, the claim is settled by giving the insured a cheque for the amount payable under the policy. In liability insurance, cash (or rather, cheque) payments are always made although, in the majority of cases, the money is paid to the third party direct. This saves the trouble of the insurance company paying the insured and the insured having to pay that amount to the third party.

Repair

Insurers make extensive use of repair as a method of providing indemnity in motor insurance, where garages are authorized to carry out repair work on damaged vehicles.

Evidence of insurers' interest in motor repairs is the Motor Repair Research Establishment at Thatcham, where a great deal of work is done on new and improved methods of repairing damaged vehicles.

A substantial step on from repair work being carried out by authorized garages is for insurance companies themselves to own garages. In certain European countries this practice has grown and insureds can drive or have vehicles towed into the insurer's garage, complete a claim form, have the vehicle examined and have the work carried out all under the one roof.

Replacement

The most common example of replacement is found in glass insurance, where windows and other items are replaced on behalf of insurers by glazing firms. Insurers normally enjoy a discount in view of the vast amount of work paid for by them. Replacement can also be used in special cases where it seems the most acceptable method to both parties.

An example may be where a diamond is lost from a ring containing two stones. The best method of settlement may be for the insurers to direct the insured to a jeweller in order that an attempt may be made to match the existing diamond in replacing the lost one. An increasing use of replacement is being made by some motor insurers where a nearly-new car is destroyed and replaced by a similar model. The insured obtains a new car and the insurers enjoy the benefit of any discount.

Reinstatement

This is a much overused word in insurance. It is used here as a means by which indemnity can be provided, and later under the heading of 'Extensions in the operation of indemnity', on page 164.

As a method of providing indemnity, it refers to property insurance and the case where an insurer undertakes to restore or rebuild a building damaged by fire. Fire policies give the insurer the option of substituting the contract to pay money with one to provide a building. However, such a decision is fraught with difficulties. The insurers must restore the property substantially to the same condition as before the loss. If the property falls short of the original in any material way, the insurer will be liable in damages for breach of the building contract.

Unless the policy provides otherwise, the insurers cannot limit their expenditure to the sum insured, because they are bound by their decision to reinstate substantially irrespective of cost. After they elect to reinstate, insurers have to be their own insurers while work is in hand and they are liable to the insured for bad workmanship. In one particular case they were held to be liable in damages where building regulations would permit only a smaller building to be built.

For these reasons, it is almost certain that an insurer would now never contemplate an election to reinstate a building.

Measurement of Indemnity

A claim under a policy of indemnity has been said to be a claim for unliquidated damages. This means that the exact amount of the compensation is not known before the loss occurs. This is clear in the case of damage to property, liability insurances and other non-life policies, but in the case of life assurance and personal accident policies the amount of money to be paid in the event of a claim is, generally, a liquidated amount: it is known before the claim takes place.

The method by which indemnity is to be measured depends on the nature of the insurance involved. The main forms are considered below.

Property insurance

The general rule is that the measure of indemnity in respect of the loss of any property is determined not by its cost but by its value at the date of the loss, and at the place of the loss. If the value has increased during the currency of the policy, the assured is therefore entitled to an indemnity on the basis of the increased value, subject of course to policy limits such as sum insured or average being applied. In assessing the amount of this value no allowance is to be made for loss of prospective profits or other consequential loss, or for mere sentimental value.

These are very general guidelines and examples of their application in specific cases follow.

Buildings

In practical terms, the indemnity sum for loss or damage to buildings has been calculated as the cost of repair or reconstruction at the time of loss less an allowance for **betterment**. Betterment can take two forms. Firstly, when property is repaired or replaced, certain aspects may be in a better condition than immediately before the loss: for example new plumbing, electrical wiring, decoration. If a deduction was not made for the amount of wear and tear or obsolescence of the previous plumbing, wiring or decoration, the insured would be better off after the loss than before it in the value of his asset. The other way in which betterment can arise is where the repaired or replaced article is better than the original one was when it was new, as when an extra storey is added to a building or sprinklers are installed during the reconstruction when the building was previously unsprinklered. This latter type of betterment is never the concern of the insurer in an indemnity only policy; the extra cost has to be borne entirely by the insured.

At one time, the market value of a building was frequently higher than its replacement cost and buildings were usually replaced in their old form. Nowadays, this is often no longer the case. The industrial base of the UK is changing and it would be uneconomic to replace some buildings in the same materials or in the same design or size. Market value is frequently lower than the cost of replacement or even the cost of repair.

The current position with regard to building losses may be summarized as follows:

● if the insured intends to repair or reinstate the property in its previous form, then indemnity is the cost of that work less an allowance for depreciation as appropriate;

● if the insurer contends that the insured does not intend to reinstate, the onus is on the insurer to prove it. In the absence of such proof, indemnity will be the reinstatement costs less depreciation;

● if the insurer contends that market value is the measure of indemnity, the onus is to prove (i) that there is a market for such a building, and (ii) the level of value in that market;

● where there is evidence that the insured is a willing seller of the property at the time of loss, the market value less site value will be the measure of indemnity.

Household goods

There are particular problems encountered here.

However, sentiment is **subjective value**, not capable of any objective measurement, and if you are to be placed in the same **financial** position after a loss then such a settlement must exclude any thoughts of sentiment. As indemnity is based on the cost of replacing at the time of loss, subject to wear and tear deductions, it is essential to review sums insured annually to keep abreast of price increases, for these increases certainly exceed depreciation, especially in the case of durables such as kitchen equipment, and furniture.

Pecuniary insurances

In **guarantee policies** the measure of indemnity is comparatively easy to ascertain: it is the actual financial loss suffered by the insured as a result, say, of the dishonesty of a cashier. In **consequential loss** insurance it is a little more difficult to establish indemnity, but this is one of the very few policies where the steps to be taken in the event of a claim are detailed. With the help of the insured's accountants it is necessary to try to establish what profit the firm would have made if the fire or other insured peril had not occurred. This is compared with the profit actually made, the difference providing the basis of indemnity.

Liability insurance

Indemnity is most easily established in liability insurance. It is the amount of any court award or negotiated out-of-court settlement, plus costs and expenses arising in connection with the claim.

Salvage

Where property is destroyed to the extent that it has ceased to exist then the problem of salvage obviously does not arise. Where property is not damaged to this extent but remains in a deteriorated or damaged condition the question of salvage does arise. For example, take a shoe shop where stock has been damaged extensively by fire. The shoes are not destroyed but are damaged by smoke; they are in other words in a deteriorated condition. The insured can claim only the value of the loss to him, which would probably amount to having the shoes cleaned, unless he agrees to hand over the shoes that are left to the insurers.

If the insured does not agree to treat the property as wholly destroyed, he cannot insist on having it wholly made good to him. This was established as long ago as 1873 in the case of *Rankin v. Potter*; on the basis of that decision, property insurers are entitled to any materials left following damage where they have agreed to pay a loss in full. In the shoe shop example the insurers would take over the salvaged shoes, or more likely a loss adjuster would do so on their behalf, and sell them to reduce their overall outlay.

If property is not wholly destroyed, the choice of whether it is treated as a total loss or not rests with the insurers. The insured cannot 'abandon' the salvage to the insurers without their consent except in marine insurance. This is the common law position, but sometimes insurers insert a clause in their contracts to emphasize the point.

Abandonment

This applies only in marine insurance. In the event of a **constructive total loss**, the assured is entitled to abandon all rights in the subject matter to the assurer and claim for a total loss. According to the Marine Insurance Act 1906, S60, there is a constructive total loss where:

> the assured is deprived of the possession of his ship or goods by a peril insured against, and (a) it is unlikely that he can recover the ship or goods, as the case may be, or (b)

the cost of recovering the ship or goods, as the case may be, would exceed their value when recovered.

The definition imagines a situation where the property is not destroyed completely, as in the case of a total loss, but is as good as lost as far as the insured is concerned; for example in the case of a ship which runs aground on a sandbank and cannot be refloated. The insured abandons her to underwriters and the claim is dealt with as if it were a loss, with the vessel becoming the property of the insurers. Abandonment is not permitted in fire or non-fire damage under property policies.

Indemnity and Insurer's Liability

In settling losses, the amount of the insured's loss should first be assessed and then the policy terms looked at to ascertain if the insurer is liable for the amount of that loss. In many cases, by choice of the insured or by poor insurance arrangements, the insurer will not be liable to pay a full indemnity. In other cases, the insurer's liability will be more than indemnity because of extensions to a basic indemnity contract.

Factors Limiting the Payment of Indemnity

There are several factors that can have an impact on the payment of indemnity. These are now considered.

The sum insured

The maximum amount recoverable under any policy is limited by either the sum insured or the limit of indemnity. In policies with a sum insured, the insured cannot recover more than that sum even where indemnity is a higher figure. Indemnity very often exceeds the sum insured, especially where policies have not been updated for a number of years.

In policies having a limit of indemnity, or limit of liability, that limit is the maximum amount payable. An exception to this general rule is where costs and expenses in connection with liability claims are paid over and above the limit of liability.

Occasionally, there is no limit except to indemnify the insured. An example of this is in employers' liability insurance where, although the Employers' Liability (Compulsory Insurance) Act 1969 requires a minimum limit of £2 million, many insurers do not have an upper limit.

The use of the phrase 'maximum amount recoverable' does not imply that this is the amount payable to the insured. The actual amount payable is governed by a number of considerations. All that is implied here is that the sum insured or limit of liability is the maximum recoverable.

Average

Where there is underinsurance, the insurers are receiving only a premium for a proportion of the entire value at risk and any settlement will take this into account using the formula:

$$\frac{\text{Sum insured x loss}}{\text{full value}}$$

Example

An insured suffers a fire loss of £40,000, due to an insured peril. His property is insured for £100,000. The insurers find that the actual value of the property is now £160,000. Average will be applied, using the formula above.

$$\frac{100,000 \times 40,000}{160,000} \quad = \; 25,000$$

The insurers pay £25,000 towards the loss.

When average operates to reduce the amount payable the insured really receives less than indemnity but, theoretically, he is being considered his own insurer for a portion of the risk and in a sense should 'indemnify himself' for the balance not received from the insurers.

Note: One interesting development in recent times has been the move towards applying some form of average on household insurance policies, a class of business traditionally free of average. Household insurers have been experiencing large losses, partly due to underinsurance, and the application of average is considered by some to be an answer to this.

Excess

An excess is an amount of each and every claim which is not covered by the policy. Excesses are quite common on private car policies where, for accidental damage to the car itself, the insured might agree to pay the first £25, £50 or some other amount of the cost of repairs. Theoretically, the insured is really his own insurer for the value of the excess. However, when the excess applies the insured does receive less than the indemnity from his insurer.

Franchise

As with an excess, a franchise is a fixed amount which is to be paid by the insured in the event of a claim. However, once the amount of the franchise is exceeded the insurers pay the whole of the loss, including the value of the franchise.

The franchise is not in common use but is sometimes found in marine insurance, and a time franchise (seven days) is sometimes found in personal accident and illness insurance.

Let us contrast the operation of an excess with that of a franchise by using the following example:

> Frank has insured an article for £10,000. This is its true value. The article suffers £5,000 of damage. Who will pay how much if Frank has (i) an excess of £3,000; and (ii) a franchise of £3,000?
>
> (i)   Frank will pay £3,000, and the insurer will pay £2,000: the amount of the loss, minus Frank's excess.

(ii)   The insurer will pay the whole £5,000, as the franchise figure has been exceeded.

In both cases, if the loss had been less than £3,000 Frank would have had to pay all of it.

Limits

Many policies limit the amount to be paid for certain events by the wording of the contract itself. A household contents policy normally has a wording that says:

> no one curio, picture, work of art ... is deemed to be of greater value than 5% of the sum insured on contents.

In the event of a work of art valued at more than £300 being destroyed in a household fire, where the contents sum insured was £6,000, if the insured had not intimated to the insurers that he wished the item covered, he would receive less than indemnity.

A different wording to the one used above is:

> in the event of a loss not more than £100 will be paid in respect of any one item.

In this case the insurers acknowledge that items in excess of £100 may exist, but any claim payment will be limited to that figure.

In either case it is for the insured, and his advisers, to ensure that he is adequately protected.

Deductibles

One aspect of commercial insurance that has increased over recent years, and shows signs of increasing further, is the use of deductibles. A deductible is the name given to a very large excess. An industrial insured may consider that it has the resources to meet fire claims up to £50,000 in any one period of insurance and is confident in its own ability to prevent fires. It may approach an insurer and receive a discount from the premium. In the event of a claim it will not receive indemnity because it has decided that it will settle for less than indemnity in order to obtain the savings in premium.

Extensions in the Operation of Indemnity

In some circumstances an insured may receive more than indemnity. We shall now look at the situations in which this might occur.

Reinstatement

The insured can request that his policy be subject to the **reinstatement memorandum**, and as a result the method of settlement will provide the insured with an amount that has been calculated without deduction of wear, tear and depreciation. The insurers agree to pay the full cost of the reinstatement, at the time of reinstatement. This would mean that the settlement includes indemnity, plus wear, tear and depreciation, plus the effects of inflation between date of loss and eventual date of reinstatement. This is a very valuable cover, and in the case of the example on page 156 would have given the insured the full £30,000 subject to any other limitations not applying. The problems posed by betterment still exist, and insurers protect themselves by saying that they will pay for reinstatement to the position when new but that the property must not end up in a better or more extensive condition than when new.

Reinstatement cover is not paid for by an increase in the rate per cent, but by the fact that the sum insured has to represent not less than the cost of reinstatement at the time of reinstatement. Sums insured are therefore substantially higher on reinstatement policies than on indemnity contracts, and consequently the premium paid is also greater.

Household contents insurance 'new for old'

This is similar to the reinstatement covers described above, and is found in different forms on different policies. At its basic level the insurer agrees to pay for reinstatement of contents if they are destroyed within a certain number of years of their purchase, without deduction of wear and tear. In a fuller form, 'new for old' cover is offered without time limit for all contents with the exception of items such as clothing and linen.

Agreed additional costs

In property insurance the insured often incurs additional costs as a result of a fire or other damage. He may have to remove debris from the site, comply with public authority requirements when rebuilding, and incur architects' and surveyors' fees. These costs can be included within the insured's cover, and any payments relating to them will amount to more than strict indemnity.

Valued policies

Where there is an article of particular value, for example a piece of jewellery or work of art, the insured could obtain the advice of an expert on value and arrange a policy where the amount to be paid in the event of a total loss is determined at inception. It can be argued that valued policies do not modify indemnity, because in the case of partial losses indemnity still operates and in the event of a total loss all that has been done is to agree the measure of indemnity before the loss.

Student Activity 2

Before reading the next section of the text, answer the following questions and then check your answers against the pages indicated.

1. How does indemnity link with insurable interest? *(page 157)*

2. Are life and personal accident policies contracts of indemnity?

   (page 157)

If your answers are basically correct, then proceed to the next section. If significant parts of your answers are wrong, then study the whole of the relevant sections again in detail. Note your areas of weakness, and be prepared for further questions on these areas in the self-assessment section at the end of this unit.

6.3   Subrogation

Subrogation is a very important concept in the study of insurance. We shall look at its various aspects below.

Subrogation Defined

Subrogation is the right of one person, having indemnified another under a legal obligation to do so, to stand in the place of that other and avail himself of all the rights and remedies of that other, whether already enforced or not. As far back as 1882, in the case of *Burnand v. Rodocanachi*, the principle was put forward that an insurer, having indemnified a person, was entitled to receive back from the insured anything he may receive from any other source.

The fundamental point is that the insured is entitled to indemnity but no more than that. Subrogation allows the insurers to recoup any profit the insured might make from an insured event. It also allows them to pursue, always in the name of the insured, any rights or remedies that the insured may possess which may reduce the loss.

It is important to note here that the insured is not prevented from recovering from a source in addition to his own insurers; what is being said is that should he succeed in so doing the money he acquires is not his but is held in trust for his insurers who have already provided an indemnity.

Corollary of Indemnity

Subrogation applies where the contract is one of indemnity. The authority for saying this is found in the case of *Castellain v. Preston* (1883):

> *that doctrine (subrogation) does not arise upon any terms of the contract of insurance: it is only another proposition which has been adopted for the purpose of carrying out the fundamental rule i.e. indemnity which I (the judge) have mentioned, and it is a doctrine in favour of the underwriters or insurers in order to prevent the assured from recovering more than a full indemnity; it has been adopted solely for that reason.*

Preston was in the course of selling his house to Rayner when it was damaged by fire. He recovered from his insurers, Liverpool London and Globe, and when the conveyance of the property was completed, which was prior to repairs being carried out, also received the full purchase price from Rayner. The insurers sued in the name of their chairman, Castellain, and were successful in recovering their outlay.

The contract of sale placed an obligation on Rayner to pay the full contracted price of £3,100 even though the building had been damaged and not repaired. In accepting that figure, Preston had enforced his rights against Rayner. The recovery from Preston of £330, being the estimated cost of repair, is an example of an insurer availing himself of rights which had already been enforced.

Normally, if the insured has been indemnified by the insurer, any recovery will come from the third party, because the insured will not have exercised his rights until asked to do so by the insurer.

It follows therefore that life contracts, for example, are not subject to the doctrine of subrogation because they are not contracts of indemnity. If death was caused, say, by the negligence of another person then the deceased's representatives may be able to recover from that source in addition to the policy moneys.

Extent of Subrogation Rights

Because of the link between subrogation and indemnity, an insurer is not entitled to recover more than he has paid out. In other words the insurers must not make any profit by exercising their subrogation rights. An insured may receive a full indemnity but may later succeed in recovering more than the claim payment from the third party. Insurers can subrogate only to the extent that they have provided indemnity.

Where the insured has been considered his own insurer for part of the risk, as in the case of an excess or the application of average, he is entitled to retain an amount equal to that share of the risk out of any money recovered. Where the insurer makes an *ex gratia* payment to an insured then the insurer will not be entitled to subrogation rights should that insured also recover from another source.

This follows from the fact that an *ex gratia* payment is not indemnity, and subrogation rights arise only out of the need to support the concept of indemnity.

How Subrogation May Arise

Subrogation rights arise in four ways. The rationale behind subrogation is the support of indemnity, in order that a person should not recover from another source in the event of his having been already indemnified by an insurer. What will be considered here are the ways in which insurers may find that they have the right to recover their outlays from some party other than the insured.

Rights arising out of tort

The briefest definition of a tort is that it is a non-contractual civil wrong. Tort forms part of the common law of England and incorporates negligence, nuisance, trespass, defamation and other legal wrongs.

Where the insured has sustained some damage, lost rights or incurred a liability due to the tortious actions of some other person then his insurer, having indemnified him for his loss, is entitled to take action to recover the outlay from the wrongdoer (known as the tortfeasor) involved.

This arises in very many ways. A motorist driving negligently may strike and damage buildings; tradesmen may negligently leave factory doors open and thieves may steal some stock; a painter may drop ladders onto a machine so that it is damaged and production lost. In each of these cases the person suffering the loss could have had a policy to indemnify him; a household buildings policy, a theft policy and an engineering extraneous damage policy. In addition to the indemnity from his insurers the insured would have a right, in tort, against the motorist, tradesman and painter. The insurers assume these rights and attempt to recover their outlays from the appropriate party. Any action the insurers take is in the name of the insured, and his permission will be sought if legal action is found to be necessary.

Another practical reason for seeking the insured's permission to take legal action is that he may well have an uninsured claim he wants to include. The law does not allow a plaintiff to sue a person more than once arising out of the same event.

Rights arising out of contract

Another part of the common law is contract. Subrogation is concerned with those cases (a) where a person has a contractual right to compensation regardless of fault, and (b) where the custom of the trade to which the contract applies dictates that certain bailees are responsible, for example a hotel proprietor or common carrier. The insurers then assume the benefits of these rights.

Common examples of rights arising out of contract are found in many tenancy agreements where tenants agree to make good any damage to the property they occupy. Prudent property owners would also maintain a policy of insurance, and in the event of damage to the property may find it easier to recover under that in the first instance. Where they do recover they are not also entitled to the compensation from the tenant, and the insurers assume the rights to any money from that quarter.

Rights arising out of statute

Under the Public Order Act 1986, where a person sustains damage mentioned in the act and is indemnified, his insurers have a right in their own name to recover their outlays from the police authority.

Since the insurers have only 14 days after a riot in which to make their claim against the police authority, policies that cover riot usually give the insured only seven days in which to finalize his claim against the insurer.

The Railway Fires Act (1905) Amendment Act 1923 removed a defence normally enjoyed by the railways for damage by sparks and cinders, but only in respect of agricultural land or uncut crops to a value of £200; later this figure was voluntarily increased by British Rail to £400.

Rights arising out of the subject matter of insurance

Where an insured has been indemnified in the case of a total loss he cannot also claim the salvage, because this would give him more than indemnity. It can be argued therefore that when insurers sell salvage, as in the case of disposing of damaged cars, stock or machinery, they are really exercising their subrogation rights in support of the principle of indemnity.

When the Right of Subrogation Arises

The **common law** right of subrogation does not arise until the insurers have admitted the insured's claim and paid it. This could, however, give rise to some problems, because the insurers would not have complete control from the date of the loss, and their eventual position could be prejudiced by delay or other action on the insured's part.

To ensure that their position is not prejudiced, insurers place a **condition in the policy** giving themselves subrogation rights **before** the claim is paid. The insurer cannot, of course, recover from the third party before he has actually settled with his own insured, but the express condition allows the insurers to hold the third party liable pending indemnity being granted to the insured.

The subrogation condition on the standard fire policy confirms this:

> *Any claimant under this policy shall at the request and at the expense of the insurers do and concur in doing and permit to be done all such acts and things as maybe necessary or reasonably required by the insurers for the purposes of enforcing any rights and remedies or of obtaining relief or indemnity from other parties to which the insurers shall be or would become entitled or subrogated upon their paying for or making good any destruction or damage under this policy, whether such acts and things shall be or become necessary or required before or after their indemnification by the insurers.*

Irrespective of whether an express subrogation condition appears on a policy or not, any action must be taken in the insured's name. The only exception to this rule is the case of the Public Order Act, when the insurers can proceed in their own name.

The rights which pass to the insurers by virtue of subrogation are the rights which the insured has. Because the insurers could not maintain an action against the third party in their own right, certain obligations are placed upon the insured – namely to assist the insurers in enforcing claims and to do nothing that might prejudice the insurers' chances of recovery.

It is worthwhile also to note that although subrogation is intended as a back-up to the principle of indemnity it has one other useful side-effect, in that in many cases if a person receives indemnity from his insurers he may decide not to proceed against some other person who may be liable, say in negligence, to him. Subrogation has the effect then of ensuring that these negligent persons are not 'let off the hook' simply because the insured was prudent enough to arrange insurance.

Modifications to the Operation of Subrogation

In very many cases, the exercising of subrogation rights by one insurer involves him in claiming money back from another insurer. In the case of a motorist hitting property, the property insurer would be exercising subrogation rights against the driver, who in turn would pass the claim on to his own motor insurers. As one can imagine, insurers would find themselves involved in correspondence for each such event and in view of the volume of business would probably also find that they were exercising subrogation rights against a company one day and paying out to that same company the next, when roles were reversed.

This situation is very noticeable in motor insurance and in consequence subrogation rights are waived by certain insurers, who have become parties to the 'knock for knock' agreement dealt with later in the course.

Other agreements exist, for example one between motor insurers and property insurers who cover impact damage by motor vehicles, whereby the companies agree to contribute towards losses by a predetermined proportion.

In employers' liability, subrogation is waived where one employee causes the injury of another. In the absence of this rule there would be the unacceptable situation where insurers would be taking action against one employee on behalf of the insured, his employer. This rule is itself waived where there is some knowledge that the employees concerned are acting together to obtain some financial benefit from their employers.

This agreement among insurers was reached following the case of *Lister v. Romford Ice and Cold Storage Ltd* (1957). In this case an insurance company indemnified its insured, an employer, in respect of damages to an employee who had been injured by the negligence of a fellow employee. The insurer was then successful in suing the negligent employee in the name of the insured.

6.4   Contribution

At the beginning of this unit it was suggested that several policies might cover a particular loss.

In each of these examples, several insurers will receive a premium in respect of an interest or piece of property which is common to another insurer, and it is equitable that they should share any loss of the common part.

In addition, and as a corollary of indemnity, it is important that the insured does not receive more than an indemnity through having several policies covering the same incident.

Contribution Defined

Contribution is the right of an insurer to call upon others similarly, but not necessarily equally, liable to the same insured to share the cost of an indemnity payment. The fundamental point is that if an insurer has paid a full indemnity, he can recoup an equitable proportion from the other insurers of the risk. If a full indemnity has not been paid, then the insured will wish to claim from the other(s) also to receive an indemnity and the principle of contribution enables the total claim to be shared in a fair manner.

How Contribution May Arise

At **common law**, contribution will apply only where the following conditions are met:

- two or more policies of indemnity exist;
- the policies cover a common interest;
- the policies cover a common peril which gave rise to the loss;
- the policies cover a common subject matter;
- each policy must be liable for the loss.

Policies do not have to cover identical interests, or perils or subject matter of insurance, provided there is an overlap between one policy and another.

A policy insuring A's interest would contribute in respect of that interest with one insuring A's and B's interests in the same property.

A policy covering fire only would contribute with one covering fire, explosion, and aircraft in respect of fire loss to the property insured.

A policy covering the insured's stock in his Glasgow premises would contribute with one covering his stock in all his premises.

A common interest

The leading case in contribution is *North British & Mercantile v. Liverpool & London & Globe* (1877), also known as the '*King and Queen Granaries*' case. Merchants Rodocanachi had deposited grain at the granary owned by Barnett. The latter had a strict liability for the grain by the custom of his trade in London, and had insured it. The owner had insured it to cover his interest as owner. When the grain was damaged by fire, the bailee's insurers paid and sought to recover from the owner's insurers. Because the interests were different, one as bailee and one as owner, the court held that contribution should not apply.

A common peril

The perils insured by each policy do not have to be identical under each contract, so long as it is the common peril that causes the loss. In *American Surety Co. of New York v. Wrightson* (1910), an insurance covering dishonesty of employees was held to be in contribution with one covering dishonesty of employees and fire and burglary. The dishonesty was the common peril.

A common subject matter

This is frequently some form of property, but not necessarily so, as seen in the *American*

Surety case just mentioned. Similarly it could relate to a legal liability.

When Contribution Operates

At **common law**, when an insured has more than one insurer, he can confine his claim to one of them if he so wishes. That insurer must meet the loss to the limit of his liability and, at common law, can call for contribution from the other(s) only after he has paid. This is still the position in marine policies, and it means that the unfortunate insurer has to lay out all of the money until such time as he makes a recovery. He also has the trouble of negotiating the method of sharing the loss.

To overcome this difficulty, most non-marine policies contain a **contribution condition**.

The condition in most policies states that the insurer is liable only for his **rateable proportion** of the loss. The insurer is liable for his share only, and the insured is left to make a claim against the other insurer(s) if he wishes to be indemnified. You should note that **the condition does not require the insured to claim** from the other policies, although in practice he will elect to do so.

The Basis of Contribution

Whether insurers are in contribution by common law or by a contractual condition, the end effect is that the loss will be shared by the insurers in their 'rateable proportions'. The purpose of the condition is really to prevent the insured claiming from one insurer only, with that insurer laying out the total loss value until such time as the contribution recoveries are made.

Other property policies

In the case of policies that are subject to average, or where an individual loss limit applies within a sum insured even when such policies are non-average, the independent liability method must be used to calculate the proportions. The 'independent liability' is the amount an insurer would have to pay if he were the only insurer covering the loss.

As more and more policies become subject to average, and as limits become more common, this method will become almost universal in use.

Non-contribution Clauses

Sometimes the equitable right to contribution is removed by a clause in one or both of the policies, such as:

> *This policy shall not apply in respect of any claim where the insured is entitled to indemnity under any other insurance.*

This means that the policy would not contribute if there was another insurance in force.

Alternatively, the following words may be added to the clause given above:

except in respect of any excess beyond the amount which would have been payable under such other insurance had this insurance not been effected.

Under this full clause the insured may have a claim under the policy containing it, but only if the other policy does not pay indemnity, and then only for the balance of loss. There is not 'rateable' sharing.

However, the courts do not favour such clauses and if both policies contained such a clause, both insurers would contribute rateably.

More Specific Insurance Clauses

Where a policy is issued covering a wide range of property, a clause similar to that quoted above is sometimes inserted to prevent contribution between the wide-range policy and any that might be more specific in their cover.

An example is fire insurance of mercantile stocks in the UK, which would insure the balance of loss only after the liability of more specific policies had been exhausted. Similarly, a fire policy on stock would not contribute with a marine cargo policy in a dockside warehouse except for any excess of value not covered by the marine policy.

Market agreement

Many insurers are party to an agreement in relation to injuries suffered by employees being carried in the employer's vehicle in the course of their employment. In these circumstances there could be a claim in law under the motor policy and the employer's liability policy. The market agreement states that such claims will be dealt with as employer's liability claims and that there will be no contribution with the motor insurers.

Conclusion

The exercising of an insurer's subrogation or contribution rights must not interfere with or delay the insured's right to be indemnified within the terms of the policy. For example, if an insured has given his name to an insurer for an action against a third party, the insurer is not entitled to withhold settlement of the claim whether a recovery from the third party has been made or not.

In the event of insurance being inadequate to provide full indemnity, the insured is entitled to retain from any third party recovery an amount which together with the insurance claim payment will give him a full indemnity. The balance of the subrogation recovery is then distributed among the contributing insurers in proportion to their claim payments.

Self-assessment Questions

Short answer questions

1. List the perils relevant to an insurance claim.

2. Give an example of a condition precedent to recovery.

3. Define indemnity.

4. List the four ways in which indemnity may be provided.

5. Explain why subrogation and contribution are corollaries of indemnity.

6. How may subrogation rights arise out of the Public Order Act 1986?

7. List the five conditions necessary for contribution to arise.

(Answers given in Appendix 1)

Specimen Examination Questions

1. A theft policy excluded losses due to war. During an enemy air raid one night, all street lights were extinguished so as not to illuminate targets for the enemy aircraft. Under cover of this blackout, a thief broke into a warehouse and stole some the insured property. Explain, with reasons, whether or not the loss was covered by the insurance policy.

2. A property is insured against fire for £12,000 subject to average but its value at time of loss is £16,000. Calculate the insurers' liability where the insured suffers a fire loss of £9,000 ? Give reasons for your answer.

(Answers given in Appendix 1)

7

INSURANCE DOCUMENTATION

Objectives

After studying this unit, you should be able to:

- identify the basic issues surrounding the transaction of insurance;

- describe the changes in the promotion of insurance in recent years;

- explain the basic structure of proposal forms, for various classes of insurance;

- outline the basic structure of policies, for various classes of insurance, including cover notes, certificates and renewals.

7.1   Introduction

Having looked at the marketplace in which insurance is transacted, we can now turn to the transaction of insurance itself. The specific detail as to how the different classes of insurance are transacted will be dealt with in the various technical subjects that follow later in the syllabus. In the meantime we shall look at the basic issues surrounding the transaction of insurance, in a general sense.

Insurance is a contract. One party contracts with another to perform a particular service. The contractual basis of insurance is so important that an entire subject is devoted to it and forms one of the three core subjects which every student must study. We shall not dwell on these contractual issues in this unit, but concentrate on the more practical aspects of how insurance is transacted.

In Figure 7.1 we have illustrated the triangular nature of the insurance transaction.

Figure 7.1: The Insurance Transaction

THE RISK

THE INSURED   THE INSURER

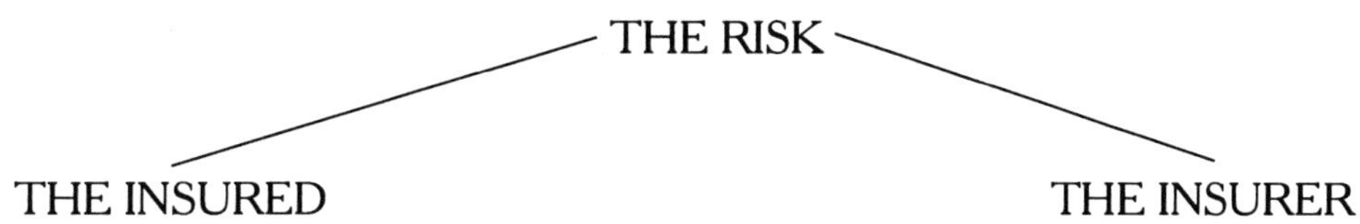

At the apex of this triangle there is the risk. This could be the risk of fire, theft, motor accident, liability, death, and so on. The insured is the person or company having the insurance in force and the insurer is the insurance company that has contracted with the insured to provide cover of one form or another.

Looking at this triangle from the insured's side we could say that:

- The insured knows the nature of the risk from his side (or its side in the case of a company or organization arranging insurance).

- The insured has to describe the risk to the insurer. At this stage the insured could more properly be termed the proposer, because he is at the point of describing the risk to the insurer in order to obtain insurance.

- The proposer will look for acceptable protection. He may have a particular form of insurance cover in mind, or want a special clause included or even excluded. The proposer knows, or should know, what he wants and will go into the marketplace in an effort to satisfy his needs.

- The proposer's main determinant in selecting an insurer will be price. He will also be concerned with service and security, but price will be extremely important.

From the point of view of the insurers:

- They will be told about the risk by the proposer.

- In many cases the insurers will not rely on this source of information alone, but will make their own enquiries. This may involve using skilled risk surveyors to look at proposals and make physical inspections.

- The insurers will decide on the level of cover they are prepared to offer to the proposer.

- Finally, the insurers will have to determine the price they are to charge for the cover they are willing to offer. This price will have to reflect a number of factors, as we shall see.

Clearly, this triangle is not the whole story. At the insured end of the triangle we also have intermediaries (often insurance brokers) who assist insureds or proposers at various stages in the transaction of insurance. For many large industrial insureds, the use of a broker is almost essential and the role they perform is of crucial importance.

At the insurer end of the triangle we have reinsurers operating, and we shall look at the role they perform later. Essentially the reinsurer is offering the same kind of protection to the insurer as the insurer offered to the insured.

We shall try to work our way through the process of transacting insurance in some kind of logical manner, taking each stage in the process in turn. We will start with publicity and work our way through proposal forms, underwriting, policies, claims and reinsurance.

7.2   Publicity

This does seem a logical place to start. Insurers have a service to sell and this must be marketed in such a way as to attract consumers or potential consumers. Over the last couple of decades there has been a substantial increase in the level of publicity undertaken by insurers and brokers. Insurers, in particular, have embraced modern concepts in marketing and some of their advertisements are regarded as 'classics' in their own right. Readers will be familiar with many television advertisements that appear regularly, promoting the products available from insurance companies:

Advertising and the marketing of products is not limited to television. Insurers make substantial use of a whole range of techniques and students can select an option in marketing at a later stage in their insurance studies. The inclusion of a marketing option within the syllabus does itself underline the importance placed on the topic.

At some point the potential consumer has to be provided with an idea of the product being offered. The television advertisements, billboards, sports sponsorship, and so on may all generate interest, but at some stage the proposer will want something to read which he can understand and which will indicate what the insurer can offer by way of protection.

This has always represented something of a problem for insurers. They are in the business of providing a service and cannot offer the proposer the opportunity to see or touch the product. There is no possibility of testing the product and in many cases the proposer hopes that he will never have to use the service of the insurer. This places the insurer in a rather unique position, quite unlike the seller of a physical product such as a car or an item of clothing.

In the past many insurers presented a rather austere image to potential consumers. There was a certain mystery about the product and the marketing message was not always clear. Often the only printed publicity material available came in the shape of the proposal form. However, this is a generalization and there have always been insurers who have been excellent in their marketing.

When we look at the printed material now available, we see quite a change in the practice of insurers. You should try to obtain as much as possible for comparison purposes. In the best examples, the essential aspects of the cover are detailed. For a motor prospectus this will include things such as total loss of the car, authorizing repairs and using the car abroad. The leaflet will be easy to read and free from jargon which may be off-putting to a potential insured.

A typical leaflet for businesses will provide information on a range of covers for small businesses. There will be little said about the actual covers since these can be complex and may detract from the value of the leaflet in the first place. The emphasis will be very much on the help which the insurer can offer to the proposer. Those who want further information can complete the form and obtain more specific details.

The same style of leaflets is also used for life assurance products. The emphasis will be on general features such as the strength and security of the insurer, the level of service and brief details of the product range.

There is therefore a general move away from trying to describe, in detail, the cover which is afforded by different policies and a move towards emphasizing the merits of the insurer linked with the more general benefits of insuring.

7.3 Proposal Forms

The proposal form is the most common mechanism by which the insurer receives information about risks to be insured. In most classes of insurance a proposal form is completed by the proposer and submitted to the insurer. These forms may be requested from an insurer direct or could have been provided by a broker.

In the past, the proposal form also acted as a form of advertising and there is still an element of this today. However, advertising (as we have seen) is much more sophisticated now and the proposal form is less likely to be the only, or even main, form of advertising.

There are certain classes of insurance for which proposal forms are not normally required. The main examples of this are fire and marine insurance. In the case of fire insurance the actual details of the risk could be so complex that it would be impossible to confine them to a proposal form. It would be very difficult to describe a large manufacturing plant on a proposal form, or to list hundreds (possibly thousands) of premises which a company may own or occupy. For these and other reasons, the insurers often use their own risk surveyors to visit premises or to discuss risks with proposers. Brokers play an important part in this process, often preparing full details of a risk for an insurer. This saves both the insurer and the proposer a great deal of time and allows the risk to be presented in a form that can be readily understood by the insurer.

In marine insurance, other than the insurance for certain smaller craft, it is not common for a proposal form to be used. A broker, acting for a proposer, would normally describe the risk and take the 'slip' containing the details of the risk to an underwriter at Lloyd's.

Rather than look at proposal forms for every single form of insurance that is offered, we shall look at some examples and attempt to draw some general conclusions. We shall do this under the two headings of personal and business insurances.

Personal Insurances

When we look at various proposal forms we can see at least three features:

- The forms are of variable length, dependent on the nature of the risk and the information an insurer will need to be able to underwrite the risk. There are very few questions on a travel proposal form, more on a household form and more again on a private car proposal.

- There will be questions that are not necessarily specific to the actual class of insurance. Certain questions are common across a range of personal matters. They may not appear on every single proposal, but they are not exactly specific to the risk itself. These include:

- the name and address of the proposer, occupation and age;

- details of past claims and in some cases past or present insurances of a similar nature;

- the period of time over which the insurance is required;

- the basis upon which the premium will be calculated. In the case of household cover this would be the sum insured for contents or buildings. In life assurance it would be the age of the proposer plus the sum assured.

● There are questions that we could call risk specific, in the sense that they relate to the form of risk for which cover is being sought. These are the questions that will assist the underwriter in determining whether or not he will accept the risk and on what terms and price.

These may include the following:

● On a motor proposal details of drivers are required. Clearly the underwriter will want to know who will be driving the car as this is a fact which could certainly influence the price of the insurance, if it is in fact accepted.

● On a household proposal there are some questions concerning the level of physical protection at the house. One question may ask about any intruder alarms which may be used and a further question may ask about neighbourhood watch schemes in which the proposer may be involved. These questions will provide the insurer with relevant information on at least one aspect of the many risks covered by the household policy.

● On a life proposal there are a number of questions concerning the health of the proposer and these questions are obviously of crucial importance to the life underwriter.

The pattern that emerges is one of a form that carries both general and specific questions, all of which are of value to the insurer. The forms should be simple to understand and easy to complete. In many cases the details from the form will be transferred to a computer file and this is reflected in many of the styles of question and response required, specifically the confining of answers to boxes.

Business Insurances

Much of what we have said for personal insurances applies also to business insurances. The level of information required is greater and in many cases will be supplemented by additional information provided by the proposer or broker. The proposal may be the first stage in assessing the risk and the insurer may well use a surveyor or other assessor to gauge the level of the risk.

If you look at a range of commercial proposal forms you will see that a similar pattern emerges to that of personal insurances:

- The forms are of different lengths. A liability form, for example, is comparatively brief when put beside a retailer's form. This is understandable and simply reflects the scope of the cover and the range of information that the underwriter requires for each.

- There will be fairly general questions which may appear in one form or another on many business proposal forms. They would include:

    - the name of the proposer. This would be the corporate, or business name;

    - the business address along with the addresses of the various locations from which the company operates and for which it may require cover;

    - the exact description of the trade, business or profession carried on by the proposer;

    - the basis upon which the premium is to be calculated. In the liability form this would be the wage roll and/or turnover. In the retailer's form there are a number of different types of cover and each one may be priced differently. The basis upon which the premium is calculated could be the sum insured for damage to contents, the sales figure for the business interruption or the value of frozen food in a cabinet, where cover for damage to that stock is required;

    - the period of cover required;

- A number of risk specific questions would also be included. For example:

    - on a liability form it would be important to know the level of the potential noise risk. Noise-induced deafness in industry is a growing problem and the underwriter would want to be in a position to assess the extent of the risk;

    - on the retailer's form there would be a large number of risk-specific questions, such as the construction of the property, the nature of the stock and the use of the premises.

You should endeavour to obtain a range of proposal forms and study them carefully, in order to build up a solid picture of what is normally included. What we have described here is only a very small sample.

Before we leave the proposal form, there is one important point that should be raised. It relates to two features that appear on each of the forms. Each proposal form will include a declaration and a warning or important note.

The **declaration** appears near to the end of the form. It says that the proposer confirms that the information supplied is true to the best of the proposer's knowledge and belief.

The second feature on every form is a related point. Each of the forms contains a warning or statement about what facts should be disclosed and the dangers if all material facts are not disclosed.

These codes form part of the protection offered to insurers and are in line with a great deal of consumer legislation which has been passed over the last decade. Before the codes, many proposal forms asked proposers to warrant the truth of statements made. This had the effect of allowing insurers to avoid liability under the policy if a fact emerged that had not been declared. This would have been quite reasonable, provided that the fact had been known to the proposer and could have been declared. The problem arose where the fact was completely beyond the knowledge or belief of the proposer at the time the form was completed. The declaration wording which we have seen takes care of this point by including the phrase '... to the best of my knowledge and belief ....'. In addition, the warnings or important notes urge the proposer to reveal facts even where they are in doubt as to whether or not they should be revealed.

7.4   Policies

The proposer or potential insured has now made a proposal to an insurer. When the insurer accepts this proposal, terms have been agreed and the premium has been paid (or there is an agreement to pay the premium), then there is a contract.

Every insurer has its own form of policy for the various classes of business that it offers. They vary considerably in style and length. Style is normally determined by company or corporate approaches to documentation. Some companies produce policies in A4 format, others have them bound in plastic folders, while others have smaller booklet type documents. The length of the document is determined more by the actual class of business rather than any corporate attitude. A simple personal accident policy may be very brief, but a retailer's policy, or even the normal household policy, could be reasonably lengthy.

When looking at different policies you will notice differences in style. The retailer's policy tends to be very lengthy. The household policy is equally lengthy and an interesting feature is the index which many insurers now use. One or two of the policies also include helpful hints in the event of a claim. This does seem to make sense because, after all, the potential of a claim is the reason the policy was effected in the first place.

We shall not concentrate on the actual cover provided by these policies at this stage. What we will do now is to look at the components of these policies and see if there are any common features we can draw from them.

Components of the Policy

In the early days of insurance, each individual policy would be prepared by hand and issued to the insured. As time passed, this became less and less practical and standard policy documents were pre-printed. These documents would have blank spaces where the individual details of an insured would be inserted. This narrative form of policy eventually gave way to what we have today, which is a scheduled policy. Looking at these policies, a number of component parts emerge.

The heading

Each of the policies has a heading which includes the name of the insurer, and in some cases the address and company logo. The fact that there is a heading goes without saying and hardly needs to be mentioned.

Preamble

At the very beginning of each of the policies there is a wording which is referred to as the preamble. The actual wording varies a little from policy to policy, but in essence there are three points which are covered by all the preambles we have illustrated:

- The proposal form is stated as being the basis of the contract and incorporated in it. This has the effect of making the proposal a part of the contract even though it is not actually reproduced and printed with the policy document. This means that the insured has to be particularly careful when completing the proposal form, because it will become part of the contract. This fact is part of the reasoning behind the earlier point we made in relation to the ABI Statement of Practice and the disclosure of material facts. You will recall that the proposer signed a declaration at the end of the form. This declaration says that the proposer confirms that the information which has been supplied is true to the best of the proposer's knowledge and belief and it now becomes a part of the contract. If the wording had been to the effect that the information was true, with no qualification, then this would also have been part of the contract but much harsher and not in keeping with the Statement of Practice.

- The preamble also makes mention of the premium. It normally states that the premium has been paid or that there is an agreement that the insured will pay. Clearly, there can be a valid contract only when the insured has paid the premium or, if the policy is prepared ahead of the premium having been paid, has agreed to pay it.

- The preamble also states that the insurer will provide the cover detailed in the policy, subject to its terms and conditions.

Read through each of the preambles and you will find that these three points are common. There are other matters raised in certain of the preambles, but the three points we have listed are the essentials. In the two life policies the preamble is included in the introduction section of the rules page of the document.

Signature

Under the preamble, or close to it, will be the signature of an official from the company.

Operative clause

The most important section of the policy is the part where the actual cover provided is outlined. What cover is to be operative is detailed quite fully in each of the policies we have illustrated. Each operative section of a policy normally begins with the phrase 'The company will ...' and then goes on to say exactly what the company is promising to do. This is the cover under the policy.

Again, you should collect together a number of different policies. As you read the operative clauses you will find that they all perform the same function, although they may look quite different. The insurer is stating quite clearly what it is agreeing to do. In the case of the two life policies the style is slightly different.

Exceptions

One of the occasions on which insurance often gets a bad press is when exceptions are applied to a policy and, as a result, a claim is not met. Exceptions are the inevitable consequence of having a scheduled style of policy. The alternative would be to have an operative section which was large enough to embrace all the various exceptions within the details of the cover which the company agrees to give. This would be no better than having a list of exceptions and there is really little alternative to detailing what is not covered, as well as what is.

We could probably say that disputes over claims are an almost inevitable consequence of transacting insurance. There will always be insureds who feel that, as they have paid a premium, they are entitled to have any claim met. All that insurers can hope to do is to make clear that there are exceptions and word them in simple terms.

When exceptions do appear they can be particular, in the sense that they apply to a part of the cover provided by the policy, or general, as they apply to the whole contract. A retailer's policy is a good illustration of this. The basic cover deals with loss or damage to the trade contents. In the main this would be stock, furniture and fittings in the shop premises. A number of particular exceptions will apply to this section. One, for example, will exclude loss or damage to movable property in the open caused by wind, rain, hail, sleet, snow, flood or dust. The exception is quite clear and the insured, if he has read it, should understand what is not covered. Later in the policy document there will be a number of general exceptions which apply to all sections of the policy. For example, there will be one exception dealing with war risks and nuclear contamination. You will recall that these are regarded as fundamental risks and as such are not traditionally insurable.

Conditions

Each of the policies also contains a list of conditions. They appear at different parts of the policy but cover very similar points. Common conditions include:

● A condition stating that the insured will comply with all the terms of the policy.

- The requirement that the insured notify the insurer of any changes in the risk.

- What procedure is to be followed in the event of a claim. This will vary from cover to cover, but will include reference to the time within which a claim is to be notified.

- The effect of fraud.

- Reference to the fact that the insured is to take all reasonable care to minimize the risk of loss or damage or of incurring liability. In other words the existence of a policy of insurance is not to be regarded as a mandate for carelessness.

- A condition about arbitration which relates to the amount to be paid under a claim and not liability for the claim itself. In other words, if the insurer agrees that there is a valid claim under the policy but cannot agree the actual amount which is to be paid.

- A condition which outlines what is to happen if there are other policies in force covering the same loss. This concerns one of the basic doctrines of insurance, contribution: a great deal will be said about that in another subject.

- There may also be a condition allowing the insurer to cancel the policy and saying how this is to be done.

- Many premiums are based on an estimated figure and adjusted once the actual figure is known. For example, an employers' liability policy premium will be based on the payroll of the insured. The insured provides an estimate of the payroll, on which the premium is calculated and charged when the policy is effected. At the end of the insurance year the actual payroll figure is declared and any adjustment made in the premium. A condition will lay down the time within which the insured is to provide the actual figure and also what is to happen if he fails to do so.

These conditions all appear on the printed policy and as such are regarded as **express conditions**. The reason for having this distinction is that there are also **implied conditions**, which do not appear on the policy but are nevertheless important conditions. These implied conditions include the fact that the subject matter of the insurance actually exists and can be identified, that the insured has insurable interest and that there has been utmost good faith in the negotiations leading up to the formation of the contract. The terms insurable interest and utmost good faith are also basic doctrines of insurance and are dealt with in some detail in another subject. In brief, the former is concerned with the fact that the insured has a financial relationship with the subject matter of the insurance, whereby he stands to benefit if it is not lost or damaged and will suffer in the event of any loss or liability. The latter is a doctrine dealing with the duty of disclosure of all facts which may be material in the forming of the insurance contract.

There is one further classification that it is worth mentioning at this stage. So far we have said that conditions can be expressed in the policy or implied. These conditions are obviously important otherwise they would not be there, and a breach of the conditions will be serious. The effect of a breach, however, will vary and this leads us into the further classification. All conditions fall into one of three classifications:

Conditions precedent to the contract

These are conditions that must be fulfilled prior to the formation of the contract itself. The implied conditions fall into this category. If they are not complied with then there is doubt as to the validity of the entire contract.

Conditions subsequent to the contract

These are conditions that have to be complied with once the contract is in force. For example, any condition relating to the adjustment of premiums, or notification of alterations to the risk.

Conditions precedent to liability

These conditions relate to claims and must be complied with if there is to be a valid claim. For example, this would include the prompt notification of claims in the proper manner.

Before leaving these conditions you should look at the ABI Statements of Practice in the appendices at the end of this book. Under the heading of 'Claims' there are certain restrictions laid down on the application of conditions. For example, the general insurance statement says that the insurer should not repudiate (refuse to pay a claim) on the grounds of a breach of a condition, where the condition was not connected with the circumstances of the loss.

The policy schedule

The final component of the policy we shall look at is the policy schedule. The parts of the policy we have looked at so far are pre-printed and apply to all insureds; there was nothing which related it to the individual insured. The schedule is the place where the policy is made personal to the insured.

Typically, the schedule will include information on:

- the insured;
- the address of the insured;
- the nature of the business;
- the period of insurance;
- premiums;
- the sums insured or limits of liability;
- the policy number;
- reference to any special exclusions, conditions or aspects of cover.

Cover Notes and Certificates

The policy is evidence of the contract and contains all the details of cover, exceptions, conditions, period of cover, premiums and other relevant information. In certain cases, it is also necessary to issue further documents in connection with the cover afforded by the policy.

Cover notes

It is not always possible to issue an actual policy document as soon as the terms of the contract have been agreed. The sheer practicalities of preparing the appropriate schedule and issuing the document all take time. In the meantime, there may be the need to prove that cover is in force. This is particularly true in the case of motor insurance where, as we will see later, there is the legal requirement to have insurance. In this case a **cover note** is prepared by the insurer and issued to the insured.

It simply states that insurance is in force and gives brief details of the cover. These cover notes are temporary and are superseded once the policy and permanent certificate of insurance are issued. Confirmation that cover is in force for other classes of business need not always be in the form of a pre-printed cover note. It could take the form of a letter from the insurer to the insured. This may be useful where the insured has need to prove to some other party that insurance has been effected.

A rather different situation exists in life assurance. Once the proposer has sent his completed proposal form to the insurer he will receive a letter of acceptance. This **letter of acceptance** is really an offer to the proposer, which is accepted once the premium has been paid. The difference between this and the cover note (for example in motor insurance) is that the life assurance policy will come into effect only once the premium has been paid. The motor cover is in force once the cover note is issued although the premium may still have to be paid.

Certificates

Where insurance is compulsory in law, the law also requires that certificates are issued that prove that a policy is in force.

What is to be shown on a certificate is dealt with in a later unit.

It is also compulsory for those who employ people to have an employers' liability policy. This provides protection to them in the event that they are legally liable to pay damages to an injured employee. Once again, it is necessary to prove that there is a policy in force and the law requires that insurers issue a certificate and send this to the insured.

It is very similar in content to the motor certificate. The law states that the certificate must be displayed at all places of business. Some of these may be outdoor sites and so a suitable covering will be provided by the insurer.

Renewals

The vast majority of policies are for periods of 12 months. Insurers are obviously anxious to have the person insure for a further year, in other words to renew the contract. There is no obligation on either side to renew, but in most cases the insurer will take steps to secure the business for another year. In periods of soft market conditions, when there is stiff competition for business brought about by overcapacity, this can be difficult.

In the normal course of events, the insurer will issue renewal papers to the insured. These renewal papers take the form of a **renewal notice**. This notice brings to the attention of the insured that the period of insurance is nearly at an end and that the premium to renew the policy is as shown. There is no obligation on the insurer to issue this notice, but it is clearly in their interest to do so in order to secure renewal of the policy.

The insured then sends his premium to the insurer and receives a **confirmation of renewal** together with any certificate that may be appropriate to the form of insurance.

There are one or two points that should be noted in connection with the renewal of business.

Non-payment of premiums

Non-payment of a premium implies that the contract is not to be renewed and it will therefore lapse on the renewal date. However, there may be cases where the premium has not been paid by the renewal date even though there was still an intention to renew. This could happen, for example, where the renewal papers have been lost or the insured has innocently overlooked the renewal. To cope with cases like this, insurers offer **days of grace**.

These days of grace extend to 15 or 30 days after the renewal date, during which time the insured can pay the premium. However, it is necessary to say that days of grace are not an extension of cover. They are 15 or 30 days into the next period of insurance. Once the premium is paid the cover applies from the renewal date, not the day on which the premium was paid. This is understandable, because otherwise the insured would use the days of grace as at extension of cover and end up with 12 months plus the days of grace.

Motor insurance is different in that the premium must be paid by the renewal date and days of grace do not apply. If the premium is not paid then the policy ceases. We shall look at this aspect in more detail later.

Long-term agreements

We have already mentioned the strong competition that can exist for business, particularly good business. This competition is at its keenest whenever there is renewal of a policy: insurers and brokers are trying to secure the best deal for their insureds.

One way in which insurers try to retain business is by offering insureds a discount from the premium, provided that they agree to offer the business for renewal over a period of years. This normally means a 5% discount if the insured undertakes to offer the business to the insurer each renewal date for three years. Both parties to the contract benefit, the insured enjoys the reduction in premium and the insurer has the knowledge that business will be renewed.

Declarations

When we looked at policy conditions we mentioned the adjustment of premiums. This arises when a premium is based on an estimated level of cover and then adjusted once the actual amount is known.

This is often the case with an employers' liability policy. The premium is calculated by applying a rate to the wages paid by the insured. These wages may be split into different categories on the declaration, because different types of employees attract different rates, dependent on the level of risk to which they are exposed. At the start of the insurance year the premium is based on the rates applied to estimated wages. At the end of the year the actual wages are declared and any adjustment carried out. Notice that the declaration states it must be returned whether the policy is renewed or not. This is because the declaration applies to the past year of insurance, not the future year.

Student Activity

Before reading the next section of the text, answer the following questions and then check your answers against the pages indicated.

1.   Give two examples when certificates of insurance will be required.

(page 186)

2.   Give an example of a type of insurance where cover notes are commonly in use.
(page 186)

3.   Why do insurers give days of grace?   *(page 187)*

If your answers are basically correct, then proceed to the Summary. If significant parts of your answers are wrong, then study the whole of the relevant sections again in detail. Note your areas of weakness, and be prepared for further questions on these areas in the self-assessment section at the end of this unit.

Summary

In the course of this unit, we have followed the transaction of insurance from the original publicity material, through the proposal form to the policy document (including cover notes, certificates and renewals). In the next unit we shall consider underwriting, reinsurance and claims.

Self-assessment Questions

Short Answer Questions

1. What is the purpose of a proposal form?

2. Which part of the policy defines the actual cover provided?

3. What information would usually be included in the policy schedule?

4. What are the two most common types of compulsory insurance?

(Answers given in Appendix 1)

Specimen Examination Question

Compare and contrast the proposal forms that are needed for different types of insurances.

(Answer given in Appendix 1)

8

UNDERWRITING AND CLAIMS

Objectives

After studying this unit, you should be able to:

- define the need for, and the basic principles of, underwriting;

- explain the basis for premium calculations, particularly which factors need to be considered;

- outline the claims procedure, from notification by the insured to handling by the insurer and final settlement.

8.1   Introduction

In the previous unit we looked at proposal forms, the nature of insurance policy documents and the renewal of policies. What we did not look at was the important link in the chain between the proposal and the policy. Clearly, not every proposal is accepted by the insurer and not all proposals that are accepted are taken on exactly the same terms or premiums. The proposal form plays an important role in providing information to the insurer and, based on this information, decisions can be made by the insurer.

If it were a straightforward matter of accepting all risks there would hardly be any need for the completion of proposal forms. There is obviously a link between the proposal and the policy, which we could refer to as underwriting. In this unit we shall look at the nature and process of underwriting and this will lead on to an examination of reinsurance. We shall conclude the unit with a look at premiums and, lastly, claims.

8.2   Underwriting

In the early days of marine insurance, the details of a ship or cargo to be insured were described on a slip. This slip was taken to Lloyd's and the person who was to carry the risk read the details, then signed the slip under the details of the risk. In this way, the person carrying the risk became known as the underwriter. The underwriting process is far more complicated nowadays but the term still applies.

When we looked at the nature of insurance in Unit 2, we talked about it as a common pool. The contributions of many people were made to the pool and the losses of the few were met from it. In essence, the task of the underwriter is to manage this pool as effectively and profitably as he can. Thinking of the role of the underwriter in this way, we could say that he has to:

● assess the risk which people bring to the pool;

● decide whether or not to accept the risk, or how much to accept;

● determine the terms, conditions and scope of cover to be offered;

● calculate a suitable premium.

In the various technical subjects that follow later in the syllabus the actual practice of underwriting is examined in some detail, as it relates to different classes of insurance. In this unit we shall concentrate on the principles of underwriting in a general sense, rather than the application to particular types of insurance.

Hazard

The first task of the underwriter is to assess the risk which each person brings to the common pool. You will recall that in Unit 1 we looked at various definitions of risk and a number of different associated terms. One of the terms we examined was 'hazard'. We differentiated hazard from peril by saying that peril was the event giving rise to the loss itself, such as collision, fire or theft. Hazard was the factor that might alter the frequency or severity of the peril.

In the light of this, we could say that the underwriter has the task of assessing the hazard which is associated with the various perils brought to the common pool. There are two aspects of hazard, physical and moral, with which the underwriter is concerned.

Physical hazard

Physical hazard is the hazard attaching to the physical characteristics of the subject matter of insurance. For example:

Property loss or damage

The construction of a building would be an aspect of physical hazard, as would the provision of fire-fighting apparatus. Buildings of wooden construction would represent a much higher level of physical hazard than ones built of brick. In the same way, the provision of automatic fire sprinklers would represent a very good physical feature.

Liability

The presence of dangerous chemicals in the workplace would be a high physical hazard, as would the absence of suitable guards on machinery, or excessive noise or dust.

Motor

People who aggregate a very high mileage, such as salesmen, represent a higher physical hazard than someone who does a very low mileage. The place where the car is garaged or normally used also has some impact on the physical hazard.

Life assurance

People with certain, potentially dangerous occupations may present a high physical hazard, as would a person who has a recurring illness.

All of these examples attach to the physical nature of the subject matter of insurance. Even in those examples that mentioned people, the emphasis was on the hazard attaching to the subject matter of insurance. We were not commenting on the personal attitude of the insured. This is where moral hazard comes in.

Moral hazard

This is the hazard that attaches to the attitude of the insured or proposer, rather than what is being insured. In insurance underwriting the prime source of moral hazard is the insured and the underwriter must attempt to identify this aspect of hazard when risks are being assessed.

Examples of moral hazard as experienced in insurance include the following:

● One of the most common examples of moral hazard is lack of care on the part of the insured. There are people who believe that because the risk is insured, they can forget any form of vigilance concerning the particular perils insured. We saw in the previous unit that there is normally a condition on policies stating that the insured must continue to exercise reasonable care to prevent loss or minimize its impact. Despite this we still have ample evidence of cars being driven in a dangerous manner, workplaces that are not kept tidy and free from the risk of fire, machine guards not being provided, and so on.

● Moral hazard can also be seen in the regular claimants, the people who look upon insurance as a kind of investment. They think they have a right to receive back in claims each year at least what they have contributed. What these people forget is that they have also had the security of knowing that they were protected all year, regardless of whether a claim arose or not. Often these people are also particularly difficult to deal with when there is a claim.

● A final example is the case of the dishonest insured. This could manifest itself at the time of claim or at the time of proposing for insurance. If not dishonest, it could be exaggerated claims which many people regard as quite acceptable.

As we saw in Unit 1, many textbooks (particularly American texts) divide moral hazard into morale and moral hazard. The first two examples we provided would be morale hazards and the last one moral hazard. The need for such a distinction is probably more academic than real and in underwriting it is more important to identify the general moral hazard, rather than to be able to categorize it.

It is worth noting that moral and physical hazard are not necessarily mutually exclusive. Poor management in a factory could be regarded as a moral hazard. However, this may manifest itself in an untidy or dangerous workplace, which is a physical hazard. What is important to the underwriter is that the hazard which the insured brings to the pool is properly assessed and taken into account in any decision about accepting the risk and in calculating the premium which is to be charged.

The Underwriting Process

The actual process by which risks are underwritten vary from one class of business to another and depend also on an insurer's general approach. What we can do is to look at underwriting in a general sense in relation to personal insurances, life assurance and commercial insurances.

Personal insurances

The underwriting of personal insurances is relatively straightforward. The main source of information about a risk will be the proposal form, and if there is anything further that the underwriter wants to know he will write to the proposer. A large volume of proposal forms for various classes of personal insurance will be dealt with by branch offices of insurers. Much of the work will be mechanical in nature and the vast bulk will be processed with little difficulty.

In many cases the underwriting is delegated to some other person, quite outside the insurance company. This is the case in travel insurance where the policy is sold by a travel agent or airline. A proposal form is completed by the proposer and the policy issued almost immediately from a pad of policies. Much the same has emerged for many household insurances. The broker has authority to issue policies, possibly with an upper monetary limit on the sum insured. Underwriting in these cases is almost a matter of making sure that a completely undesirable proposer is not allowed cover. There will be little discrimination among those cases which are accepted and the broker, or other agent, will have little or no flexibility in pricing.

Life assurance

The underwriting of life assurance is in quite a different category from other forms of personal insurances. This is because the underwriter assesses the risk at inception only. The company is then guaranteeing cover for sometimes up to 30 years, or even throughout life. Life assurance underwriting involves looking at medical, occupational and avocation factors as well as the individual's lifestyle. In particular, the extra risk posed by AIDS has led to an increased number of questions on proposal forms, or on a separate questionnaire, about lifestyle, which are designed to identify if the proposer is likely to be in a high risk group for AIDS or HIV.

Additional information is often required by the underwriter in order to reach a decision.

This can be in the form of detailed questionnaires, a report from the proposer's own doctor (Medical Attendant's Report), an examination by an independent doctor (Medical Examiner's Report) and/or specific tests. The cost of this additional information is borne by the insurer.

Commercial insurances

The underwriting of commercial, business insurances is a much more complicated and involved task. Commercial insurances range from small shops and factories to large multinational corporations, with operations in many countries throughout the world. The degree of complexity of the underwriting required will obviously vary with the sheer size of the risk, but certain basic principles are still recognizable.

The essence of the task is that the underwriter has to evaluate the hazard associated with the risk which is being proposed. In small cases he may be able to do this from reading a proposal form and corresponding with the proposer. It may be that a local inspector is asked to call and see the shop or factory for himself. In large cases this is simply impossible. Details of the risk could not be confined to a proposal form since there is just too much information to condense, no matter how large the form may be.

This is where the broker may help. As we mentioned earlier, the broker in these large cases will be in a position to prepare the case for the underwriter. This may mean site inspections by the broker and the preparation of plans and reports on the relevant aspects of the risk. This documentation, which may be extremely extensive, is then passed to the underwriter and negotiation can commence on the terms, conditions, cover and price.

Risk surveys

Even where a broker is involved, and certainly when there is no broker, the underwriter will involve a surveyor. This risk surveyor is the person who acts as the 'eyes and ears' of the underwriter. Many companies employ specialist surveyors in the different areas of risk such as fire, security, liability, business interruption and so on.

For a business risk the surveyor is interested in occupation, construction, services, fire protection, security, management, special perils, all risks, adequacy of sum insured, previous losses, estimated maximum loss, risk improvements and future developments. He will also give his opinion of the risk and recommend when it should be surveyed again. The special forms developed by different insurers will provide a framework. There may be *aide-mémoires* for employers' liability, public liability and products liability, and the form will indicate the nature of the enquiries that the surveyor should be carrying out. The risk is of course different from that of fire but the principle is the same: the surveyor is attempting to assess the risk on behalf of the underwriter.

The surveyor will eventually prepare a report for the underwriter, and in the case of many property risks will also draw a plan. The report will cover a number of features, including:

● A full description of the risk. This may include a plan of the premises in the case of a property risk, the process being carried on at the premises, details of the insured, and so on.

- An assessment of the level of risk. This will take into account all the relevant hazard factors, both moral and physical, and provide the underwriter with some idea of the degree of risk which he is being asked to accept. The surveyor will also be able to comment on surrounding property, which in the case of fire insurance, for example, may have an impact on the level of risk.

- A measure of the maximum possible loss (MPL), or estimated maximum loss (EML) as it is known by some. This is the maximum that the surveyor believes will be the subject of a loss.

This is simple to illustrate in the case of fire insurance. Say there is a building which has a value of £300,000. It is one building with no divisions and if a fire starts in one area it is likely to spread throughout the entire property. The MPL in such a case would be £300,000; in other words, in the worst situation the whole building could be destroyed. Now imagine that the building has been divided into three equal size sections.

The wall that creates the section at the left of the building is a fire wall. This wall means that it is most unlikely that a fire would spread through either way. The other dividing wall has a door in it and the likelihood is that any fire would spread between these two sections. Each section has the same value, let us say, and the conclusion would be that the MPL is £200,000. In the worst case, the fire would start in one of the sections at the right of the building and then spread through the dividing wall to the other. The section separated by the fire wall would be saved.

This MPL calculation takes no account of any good features which may be present. The underwriter must then consider the impact of good features and may reduce the MPL. In a fire risk the underwriter may take account of fire fighting apparatus of various kinds, such as automatic sprinklers.

One point the surveyor would have to remember is that the MPL he has just calculated is only for fire damage. The building could, for example, be in the flight path for a major airport and run the risk of being destroyed by aircraft. Dividing walls would be little protection against such a risk. The reason for calculating MPLs is to give the underwriter an idea of the maximum that is likely to be lost.

The surveyor will also make known to the insured what steps should be taken to protect against the risk. In a few cases these recommendations will be in the form of requirements, which the insured must implement if cover is to be granted.

The surveyor will assess the adequacy of the insurance being requested. The responsibility for ensuring that the cover is adequate rests with the insured. He may seek advice from a broker or other expert, but at the end of the day he will have to satisfy himself that the insurances are adequate.

For many classes of insurance, adequacy will mean the level of sum insured. This will be true for many classes of property insurance. In the case of liability insurance there is no sum insured, but a limit of indemnity. Adequacy in these cases will mean a limit of indemnity large enough to cater for the expected claims. The adequacy of cover is an extremely important issue and the underwriter will want to ensure, as far as is possible, that the insured is not underinsuring the risk.

At the end of the process the underwriter is left to decide whether to accept the risk and, if he does, on what terms.

Assuming that a risk is acceptable in all matters relating to the level of hazard, the decision as to how much of this risk can be accepted is, in part, dependent on the financial capacity of the insurer. The insurer may have some limit on how much of a particular type of risk it wants to accept in any year. Questions relating to the financial capacity of the insurer lead us into the area of reinsurance.

Student Activity 1

Before reading the next section of the text, answer the following questions and then check your answers against the page indicated.

1. Give an example of moral hazard for motor insurance. *(page 192)*

If your answer is basically correct, then proceed to the next section. If significant parts of your answers are wrong, then study the whole of the relevant sections again in detail. Note your areas of weakness, and be prepared for further questions on these areas in the self-assessment section at the end of this unit.

8.3   Premium Calculation

Earlier in this unit we listed the tasks of the underwriter as:

- assessing the risk that people bring to the pool;

- deciding whether or not to accept the risk, or how much to accept;

- determining the terms, conditions and scope of cover to be offered;

- calculating a suitable premium.

So far we have looked at the role of the underwriter, the underwriting process itself and examined the way in which risks are accepted by insurers. We have two final aspects of the insurance transaction to examine. The first, which we deal with in this section, is the whole business of pricing and paying for the insurance service, and the second is the setting of claims.

The last task of the underwriter, as we listed them, was to calculate a suitable premium. The premium an insured pays represents that insured's contribution to the common pool. This contribution must be fair and must reflect the degree of hazard which that insured brings to the pool.

In general, the premium must be sufficient to:

Cover expected claims

The insurer is in a position to estimate the level of claims which it expects. We touched on this when we looked at the measurement of risk in earlier units. It is not possible to say exactly how much is to be paid out in claims, but the law of large numbers does allow the insurer to make a reasonably accurate assessment of the likely loss costs. At the very minimum, the premium must be sufficient to meet these expected claims. This could mean that a number of insureds must pay premiums which in total will cover claims, or it could mean, in the case of very large insureds, that the one insured must contribute a premium which it is estimated will meet expected claims costs.

Create an estimate for outstanding claims

Not all claims will be settled during the year for which the premium has been paid and hence the premium must take into account those claims still to be settled at the end of the year. This is particularly true in the case of claims involving personal injury. They can take several years to settle and the insurer must bear them in mind when calculating the premium.

Provide a reserve

The insurers must also take into account the fact that there can be contingencies, beyond their control, which may involve a liability to meet claims at some time in the future. Insurers do this by making reserves. For example, most insurers will make provision for an IBNR reserve, for claims which are incurred but not reported. A claim may have been incurred for which an insurer could be liable, but it has not yet been reported to the insurer.

Take the case of an industrial disease. An employee may have contracted some disease which will eventually form the basis of a claim against his employer. The employee does not know that he has the disease, but when it manifests itself he will seek damages from his employer. The employer will then make a claim under his employers' liability policy, for indemnity in respect of the legal liability to pay these damages. The notification of the claim to the insurer could be several years after the injury was caused. The claim had in fact been incurred but the insurer did not know about it, which is why a reserve has to be made.

Meet all expenses

The insurer has a number of operational expenses to meet in the running of the business which include:

● salaries to staff;

● office costs of all forms;

- advertising;

- commission.

These operating costs must be covered from the aggregate premiums, collected from the insureds.

Provide for profit

Lastly, the insurer must ensure that there is provision for a reasonable profit. The majority of insurers are answerable to shareholders and must provide a reasonable return on the investment which these shareholders have made in the company. In the case of mutual companies, the members will still be aiming for a reasonable surplus, in order to meet the objectives of the mutual.

However, arriving at the premium is not simply a matter of calculating the correct figure using a mathematical formula. A number of important commercial considerations must be borne in mind. These will include:

Inflation

The insurer must be aware of the changing value of money. Claims will be met in the future, out of premiums received today. This means that the cost of settling a claim may rise, not due to any increase in the magnitude of the claim itself, but simply due to the fall in the value of money. This is something which insurers cannot ignore in their premium calculations.

Interest rates

We have already seen that insurers are major investors of funds. These funds generate substantial investment income upon which insurers depend. Variability in interest rates also has to be taken into account in premium calculation.

Exchange rates

We have seen that a substantial volume of premium income is derived from outside of the United Kingdom. Whenever there is movement of money across national borders, there is the added problem of exchange rate risk. The insurer has to take account of this risk and the cost of managing it has to be recovered through the premium which insureds pay.

Competition

The final commercial factor is that of competition. The insurer is not alone in the market-place and increasingly there is strong competition. Charging too high a premium may result in the loss of business, but charging too little could mean running at a loss. This is a difficult tightrope along which insurers must walk.

Premium Calculation

Premiums are normally arrived at by applying a premium rate to a premium base. The rate could be a rate per cent or per mille, applied to a figure which is the premium base. The rate is intended to reflect the hazard associated with the particular insured and the premium base is the measure of the exposure.

Fire insurance is a good illustration of this. A rate per cent is normally applied to the sum insured. The rate for an explosives factory will obviously be higher than that for one involved in something much less hazardous, such as metal working. In this way, the rate reflects the hazard which the insured brings to the pool. However, not every insured will be identical in size. The exposure can vary considerably from the large manufacturing plant to very small factory units. The premium base is intended to take account of this. The sum insured reflects the differing exposures and, when the rate is applied to the sum insured, it is hoped that a realistic premium results.

While the sum insured is a suitable premium base for many property insurances, it would not be appropriate for liability insurance. In the case of employers' liability, the wage roll of the insured is used. Different rates, based on the hazard associated with different occupations, are applied to the total wages paid by the insured for each of these occupations. Public liability is often rated on turnover and professional indemnity on fees earned.

Other forms of insurance will have different premium bases, but the concept is the same: the premium base will reflect the exposure rather than the hazard.

Adjustable premiums

We mentioned the need for adjustable premiums when we were examining policy conditions in Unit 7. In certain cases, the premium base will not be known at the start of the insurance year. All that will be possible is to give an estimate of what the figure might be. This would be the case in employers' liability insurance. The insured will be able to estimate what the total wage bill for the coming year will be. The rate will be applied to this estimated figure and at the end of the year he will submit a declaration, showing the actual wages paid. At this point the premium will be adjusted up or down, depending on the wages figure.

Another form of adjustable premium often applies in the case of insurance for the loss of, or damage to, stock. The actual values of stock will vary a great deal throughout the year and it would be very difficult to decide what the sum insured should be, for the purposes of arriving at the premium. Rather than take some kind of average figure for the year, the insured can pay an estimated premium and declare the value of stock each month. At the end of the year, it is then possible to calculate exactly how much premium is required for the risk which the insurer has run.

Flat premiums

In a few cases it is the practice of the insurers to charge a flat premium, rather than apply a rate to a premium base. This is the case in motor insurance. The insured pays a flat premium in the vast majority of cases, unless the car has a particularly high value when some adjustment to the premium would be required. This flat premium is arrived at by consulting rating tables, which take into account the hazard associated with the individual insured and car. In this way, young drivers pay more than older drivers and high performance cars attract higher premiums than family saloons.

The various factors that will influence the premium are revealed on the proposal form. These factors are often held in a computer program and it is possible to derive the premium by feeding in the appropriate information. Many brokers operate a computerized motor quotation system which provides motor premiums according to rating factors it asks for.

Life Assurance Premiums

Life assurance premiums are made up of four components:

- mortality;

- expenses;

- investment;

- contingencies.

Mortality is concerned with the risk of death. Actuaries have compiled comprehensive mortality tables for different groups of people. These tables tell us the number of people in a group who will survive for given numbers of years. These tables are based on very large numbers and are accurate when dealing with large numbers of people. Using them the life underwriter is able to determine the risk of having to make a claim payment, either once a person dies, or under an endowment policy because the life assured has survived to the end of a certain number of years.

It should be noted that the premium which is charged will, most likely, be a level premium. In other words, the life assured will be told what premium he or she has to pay each year or each month and that premium will not increase. The reason for making this point is that the level of the risk increases each year as the person gets older, but this is taken into account at the outset and a flat premium is charged.

In addition to covering the mortality risk, which is similar to the expected level of claims in general insurances, the life assurance company must also cover all its expenses. It has the same expenses as we listed for a general insurer and these must all be recovered in the premium. One factor which is slightly different is that the life assurer normally pays a much higher commission in the first year than at renewal. This **indemnity** cover cannot all be recovered in the first premium and it is, in fact, spread over a number of years.

We saw in Unit 2 that the life assurance industry is a major investor. The premiums which individual people pay are combined and invested by life assurers in considerable amounts. These investments earn substantial income for the life assurers and this source of income must be taken into account when arriving at the premium. The life assurer calculates the value of these future investment earnings and they are reflected in the premiums.

The final component of the premium is a form of reserve, for unexpected events. The life assurer always has to have in mind the possibility that a quite unexpected level of loss may arise. The contingency factor provides this safety margin.

8.4 The Impact of Legislation and Competition on Pricing

Non-life Insurance

The non-life insurance market is cyclical over time. This is known as the **underwriting cycle** and varies according to the type of business. It means that during a time when more claims are being made, underwriting profit will disappear and premiums are pushed upwards. Once the market becomes profitable again, new companies enter the market and existing companies try to gain a larger slice of market share to gain more profits. This then causes a downward pressure on premium rates. Eventually rates become too low and losses are experienced.

Explanations for the underwriting cycle include the following:

●   the effects of regulation on premium rating;

●   market interest rate movements;

●   the impact of large claims;

●   the need to increase reserves;

●   incorrect expectations of losses assumed in premium calculations;

●   competition.

In recent years, deregulation and an increase of competition have had a significant impact on the non-life market. In particular, the emergence of direct insurers, who compete on costs and favour the better risks, has pushed down premium rates and cut profit margins.

Long-term Business

Profits arise in life business in any of the following three ways:

●   Actual mortality is less than expected mortality (as assumed in premium rates).

●   Actual expenses are less than expected expenses.

●   Actual interest rates are higher than interest assumptions made.

Every life office is required by the DTI to undertake an annual valuation. This means valuing assets against expected liabilities. The excess is known as a 'surplus' from which reserves can be taken to increase the life office's contingency fund. The amount left is the 'divisible surplus'. A mutual company will distribute 100% of this divisible surplus to policyholders in the form of bonuses. A proprietary company is required to distribute a minimum of 90% of the divisible surplus to policyholders, with a maximum of 10% being distributed to shareholders in the form of dividends.

The long-term market has undergone a number of important changes in the last decade, including:

- The Financial Services Act, involving increased costs of compliance and training, leading to higher expenses.

- Emergence of the bancassurers as direct competition to the traditional life offices.

- More recently, new disclosure rules introduced in 1995 which make charges and life office costs transparent to policyholders.

- Direct writing, with Direct Line, for example, extending into the long-term market, and Virgin Direct offering simple, low-charge products over the telephone.

8.5   Claims

In a real sense, the claim is the tangible result of insuring. We have talked quite a lot about peace of mind and security, but at the end of the day most people will judge the value of the cover by the way in which a claim is handled. The actual procedure for handling claims varies according to the type of cover, the amount of the claim and whether it is a personal or commercial claim insured.

In this section we shall concentrate on the notification, handling and settlement of claims. The main concern of this section is the general procedures for claims notification, handling and settlement rather than the more detailed issues which may be specific to different types of cover. These details of actual claims handling will be dealt with in the technical insurance subjects, which follow later in the syllabus.

Claims Notification

The first and most important point to make is that the notification of a claim is the responsibility of the insured. We shall see later that the insured also has certain other duties, but at the outset he has the onus of intimating the claim. We saw in Unit 7 that one of the conditions on policies relates to the notification of claims. The insurer will want speedy notification of the claim and will often lay down time limits within which a claim should be intimated.

The reason for wanting claims notified quickly is easily illustrated. Take the case of a liability claim, where an employee has been injured in an accident at work. The insurer will want to be able to take statements from witnesses as soon after the accident as possible. This will also be the case in motor accident claims and in any other incidents where statements from witnesses are important. It is not only the taking of statements that is important. In the case of thefts the insurers will want to make sure that the claim has been intimated to the police, to allow the maximum opportunity to recover stolen property. Even in the case of damage to property the insurer requires speedy notification, so that remedial or loss reduction action can be recommended as soon as possible.

The means by which the claim is intimated is normally a claim form.

Questions on the claim form fall into two broad categories.

First there are the questions that deal with general matters, such as the name of the insured, the policy number, the contact point, the date and place of the incident. These questions are important from an administrative point of view and are crucial in checking that the policy was in force when the event took place.

The second group of questions are more specific in nature and deal with the details of the claim itself. A household claim form asks a range of questions about the nature of the loss or damage and provides ample space for the insured to list all the items lost or damaged. A motor claim form asks for full details of the accident, the drivers, the damage and other parties involved. These specific questions are dependent upon the type of cover, whereas the general questions could appear on many different forms.

We would see this same pattern if we were to look at a few forms relating to claims under commercial policies. There are the same general questions, with the possible addition of the description of the business. Specific questions are very detailed and in some cases the questions are extensive, reflecting the scope of cover under the policy.

Although the claim form is the main means by which insurers receive notification of claims, it is not always used. In many cases, including large losses or losses involving a great deal of detail, the insurers would appoint a loss adjuster and we shall look at the role of the adjuster later.

Life assurance claims

It is important to point out that what we have said so far relates to general insurances. The procedure for notification and handling of claims under life assurance policies is quite different. One simple reason why this should be so is the fact that, in many cases, the life assured may be dead and this is the reason for the claim.

It is important to have mechanisms in force to ensure that the insurer receives proper proof of death and that the proper, legal recipients of any proceeds from a claim are identified taking into account any wills or assignments of the proceeds which may have been made. These procedures often involve the use of the courts.

Claims Handling

Small, personal claims are often dealt with by someone other than the insurance company. We have seen that brokers and others can have delegated authority to issue simple personal policies. In certain cases, these brokers may also have authority to handle claims. There may be a limit on the value of claims that can be dealt with in this way, but the process is speedy and the claimant deals with the person or organization issuing the cover in the first place.

However, the majority of claims will be dealt with by the claims department of the insurer. The onus is on the insured to prove that he has suffered a loss, by a peril which is insured by the policy, and in the majority of cases this will have been done by the completion of a claim form. The insured also has the onus to prove the amount of the loss in all cases other than those involving life assurance, personal accident or liability. He cannot simply make a claim for a lost or damaged item without proving the value of the item. This proof could take the form of a purchase receipt, a repair account or valuation. The point is that it is not for the insurer to prove the value of the loss. Agreeing the value of a loss can be difficult as we shall see later.

The insurer has to ensure that:

- The cover was in force at the time of the loss.

- The insured is the correct insured.

- The peril is covered by the policy.

- The insured has taken reasonable steps to minimize the loss.

- Conditions have all been complied with.

- No exceptions are appropriate.

- The value of the loss is reasonable.

These steps can involve a great deal of work and the claims departments of insurance companies are often among the busiest. However, there is a limit to the number of staff which even the largest companies could afford to have in-house to deal with claims. Not only would the cost be huge, but the level of expertise required would be costly in terms of recruitment and training. The alternative is to retain experts. Such experts are chartered loss adjusters. Not only are they used for large or detailed claims, but many insurance companies also retain the services of a loss adjuster to deal with the majority of their property losses.

Loss adjusters are experts in processing claims from start to finish. They are normally involved at the very early stages of a claim and see it through to the conclusion. This will involve ensuring that all the interests of the insurer are preserved, in checking that the cover was in force and was adequate at the time of the loss. The adjuster will also act to minimize the extent of the loss and is in a position to use his considerable experience to bring about a swift settlement of the claim.

In this latter respect, the adjuster can be of considerable help to the insured. Take the case of a fire at a factory. The insured will have suffered a traumatic experience and will need guidance on the immediate steps that should be taken following the fire. The insured is unlikely to have any experience or knowledge of loss minimization, or even of how to begin the task of rebuilding or repair. The loss adjuster can be of considerable value in all these problems.

The loss adjuster's report covers basic facts about the insured and the loss. This is very similar to the answers that might be expected for the general questions on a claim form. In addition, the preliminary report suggests the amount the insurer should reserve as the possible settlement figure, comments on the adequacy of the cover, gives a full description of the premises and tells the insurer what steps are now being taken in the handling of the claim. Under the heading of 'Initial Measures' the adjuster will identify detailed work which is carried out by him for the benefit of both the insured and the insurer.

The final report gives full details of what has taken place and gives the final adjustment of the loss. There will be reference to the application of average in the report if appropriate. These reports would be checked by claims officials in the insurer's claims department and then settlement would be arranged.

Claims Settlement

The final stage in the claims procedure is the actual monetary settlement. The claim has been notified, all parties have carried out their respective duties and all that remains is for the claim to be settled. The actual settlement, or the amount payable, depends upon a number of factors including the nature of the cover, the adequacy of the cover and the application of any conditions that limit the amount payable.

It is possibly easier to decide on the amount payable under a life assurance policy, rather than other forms of policy. The life assurance policy normally has a fixed sum assured so that both the assured and the assurer understand exactly what is to be paid and under what circumstances it will be paid. There may be complications in specific circumstances, but normally the amount payable in the event of a claim is stated on the policy and is not the subject of discussion or negotiation at the time of the claim.

Contrast this with the case of a fire claim at a factory. The policy of insurance did have a sum insured, but this is only the limit of the liability of the insurer and is not the amount which they have agreed to pay in the event of a claim. The eventual cost of the claim will depend on the extent of loss or damage and on the nature of the cover afforded by the policy. In most property policies there are two kinds of cover, indemnity or reinstatement. These terms will become very familiar to those of you who go on to study general insurances.

We have already seen that indemnity is one of the basic doctrines of insurance which says that an insured is to be placed in the same financial position after a loss as he enjoyed before the loss. As a value cannot be placed on a person's life or limbs, we can say that life assurance and personal accident policies are not contracts of indemnity; however, property and liability policies are. Take the case of a fire at a factory, this presents obvious problems in ascertaining the value of the loss. A machine bought five years ago for £50,000, which has been used for all of those five years, is clearly not worth £50,000 today and this would not be the value of the loss. Trying to place the insured in the same financial position after the machine has been damaged as he enjoyed before any damage will be difficult. Where the machine is completely destroyed, the measure of indemnity would be the replacement cost less an amount for wear and tear. In the case of partial damage, indemnity would be the repair cost less wear and tear.

Let us assume that the machine has a life expectancy of ten years. It has been in use for half its life and this is a measure of the wear and tear. The cost of replacing the machine today is

£90,000. Indemnity would then be half of the cost of replacement, that is £45,000, and this would have to be the sum insured. Notice that this figure depends on the level of wear and tear and the replacement cost. As replacement costs will rise each year it is likely that the final sum insured will have to rise.

Clearly this can cause a great deal of work and, potentially, a few problems for both the insured and the insurer.

Reinstatement, on the other hand, provides the insured with the cost of reinstatement. This is a form of 'new for old' and many household insurers use that phrase in their marketing. Offering reinstatement avoids much of the difficulty in ascertaining the value of a loss under an indemnity contract. In the case of the machine we used in the earlier example, the insured would have to fix the sum insured at the cost of reinstatement. We know this to be £90,000, but the loss may not happen until the last day of the insurance year. What the insured needs to calculate is the cost of reinstatement at the time of reinstatement, and this may be higher than the cost of replacing the machine today. It may even be that there is a time delay in ordering new machines of this type and all of these factors have to be taken into account.

With liability claims it is a little easier to decide on indemnity. A liability policy provides indemnity to the insured in respect of his legal liability to pay damages. The policy does not define the amount, this is left in many cases to the court, but it does lay down how indemnity is to be calculated.

Adequacy of cover

Earlier we said that the amount payable under a claim depended upon a number of factors, including the nature of the cover, the adequacy of the cover and the application of any conditions that limit the amount payable. We have looked briefly at the nature of the cover, so now turn to the adequacy of the cover and limits on the amount payable.

The amount an insurer pays will be limited by the sum insured, in the case of property policies, or the limit of indemnity, in liability policies. Consider property claims, for example. A machine may be insured, under a contract of indemnity, for £75,000, and after a total loss it is estimated that the cost of replacement less wear and tear is £100,000. Clearly there is underinsurance and the insured cannot expect to receive £100,000 in settlement of the claim. The value of the machine was £100,000, but it was insured for only £75,000 or 75% of the actual value. The maximum the insured could hope to receive would be 75% of the value of any loss, which in this case is the sum insured. In the event of partial damage, say to the extent of £20,000, the same principle would apply and the loss would be reduced by the proportion which the sum insured bore to the actual value at risk. In our example, this proportion is 75% and so the insured would receive £15,000. You will recall that this is termed the application of average.

Under a liability policy, the adequacy of cover refers to the limit of indemnity. Average is not applied and the insured will suffer only if the award of damages exceeds the limit. Certain policies have an aggregate limit, in the sense that there is an upper limit on the total amount of indemnity provided in any one year. In such a case, an insured could find himself with inadequate cover if there were a number of claims which in aggregate exceeded the limit.

The amount payable may be further limited by the application of an excess or deductible. Excesses are very common, for example, in private car insurance. An insured may agree to pay the first £100 of accidental damage to the car and a discount from the total premium is given. Should there be accidental damage, the insured must then pay the first £100.

In commercial insurances, excesses are often very large and the term deductible is often preferred. A public liability policy may have a £25,000 deductible, meaning that the first £25,000 of any claim will be met by the insured. This means that the premium will be much lower than it would have been, had the risk been insured from the first pound upwards. What the insured has really done is to limit the cover to very large claims and has agreed to be his own insurer for claims at the lower end.

Disputes

The vast majority of claims are settled speedily and to the satisfaction of both the insured and the insurer. Unfortunately, a few claims are the source of dispute and these can cause a measure of poor publicity for the industry as a whole, regardless of the merits of any one case.

When a dispute does arise it can revolve around a number of factors. In the main, disputes tend to be about either the liability of an insurer to pay a claim, the amount which should be paid or the speed with which claims are handled.

Where the insured is in dispute with an insurer about whether or not a claim is covered by a policy, or the liability of the insurer to pay a claim, the insured has the right to take his case to a lawyer and seek a resolution of the dispute in that way. Ultimately, there is nothing to stop the insured taking the insurer to court.

Disputes concerning the amount to be paid, liability under the policy having been admitted, are usually the subject of policy conditions. Policies normally carry an arbitration condition, which states that the insured must refer any such disputes to arbitration. This involves appointing an independent arbitrator who will look at the merits of the case and make a judgment. His decision is binding on both parties, otherwise there would be little value in having arbitration.

However, very few insureds ever took cases to arbitration. This may have been because they did not trust the process, or simply did not know that such a route was open to them.

In 1981, a group of insurers set up an entirely independent mechanism for dealing with disputes when they established the Insurance Ombudsman Bureau. The Ombudsman is concerned only with personal insurances and hence excludes all business insurances, which remain subject to the rules we have mentioned above concerning arbitration.

The most recent annual report of the Ombudsman reveals that some 360 insurers are now members of the scheme, including the Corporation of Lloyd's. It is estimated that this membership accounts for over 90% of all personal insurance business.

During 1994, over 8,500 cases were referred to the Ombudsman covering disputes on policy terms, amounts payable, delays in settlement and other areas. The Ombudsman first insists that the matter has been referred to the senior management of the insurer concerned and then, if this does not give satisfaction, that it is passed to him within six months of the insured having received a reply from senior management. This ensures that all possible steps have been taken to resolve the dispute before he is called in.

The insured can either accept or reject the Ombudsman's decision. Accepting it results in the insurer being required to pay any award, up to a monetary limit. An insured can use the scheme only if the insurer is a member.

In 1994, a separate Personal Investment Authority (PIA) Ombudsman scheme was created. In most cases, the PIA Ombudsman will now deal with disputes concerning life assurance business, whether the dispute is in respect of advice, mis-selling or administration.

Disputes over pension schemes are also dealt with differently. The Occupational Pensions Advisory Service has a network of 250 advisers, contactable through the Citizen's Advice Bureau, for help and advice on all types of pension scheme. Policyholders can also refer the complaint to a separate Pensions Ombudsman if not satisfied with the outcome.

Certain companies who did not become members of the Insurance Ombudsman Bureau launched another organization, the Personal Insurance Arbitration Service. Its primary role and function is to provide a less formal method of resolving disputes between insurers and their insured.

Claims Reserving

Insurance companies have substantial funds at their disposal, broadly categorized into:

- **Technical Reserves** which are necessary to cover the outstanding liabilities to policyholders.

- **Free Reserves** which are the remaining funds, not tied to any specific liabilities.

Technical reserves: Non-life business

Technical reserves held to meet liabilities under non-life business can be divided into six headings:

- **Unearned Premium Reserves**
  The part of this year's premium income which relates to that part of the policy year falling in the next accounting period.

- **Unexpired Risk Reserves**
  Where the unearned premium reserve is insufficient to meet liabilities left over from the previous year, this is used to increase that reserve to the required level. This may be a result of unexpectedly high claims, for example.

- **Outstanding Claims Reserves**
  Claims that have been reported but not settled in the particular accounting year must have a reserve created out of that year's premium income.

- **IBNR Reserves**
  'Incurred but not reported' reserves are in respect of losses that have occurred before the end of the year but which have not been reported.

- **Catastrophe Reserves**
  Created to allow for exceptionally adverse claims experience.

- **Claims Equalization Reserves**
  Created in a 'good year' to allow for a 'bad year' which may follow.

Technical reserves: Life business

Level premiums are paid by the policyholder each year but, in the early years, the actual risk is less than the premium paid. The excess is therefore invested and built up in order to cover claims in future years. The ability to invest these reserves allows the life office to earn interest and make capital gains which make a vital contribution to the office's profits.

Free reserves: Non-life business

Known as 'shareholders funds', these are not tied to any specific liabilities and can be used as the insurance company wishes. Part of these will be retained to comply with the solvency rules. The rest will provide dividends to shareholders and a contingency fund for unexpectedly high levels of claims.

Free reserves: Life business

This is the 'surplus' explained earlier, from which reserves for unexpected claims may be taken. The divisible surplus is then distributed between policyholders and shareholders, or policyholders only in the case of mutual companies.

Student Activity 2

Before reading the next section of the text, answer the following questions and then check your answers against the pages indicated.

1. What are adjustable premiums? *(page 199)*

2. When would a loss adjuster be appointed? *(page 203)*

If your answers are basically correct, then proceed to the Summary. If significant parts of your answers are wrong, then study the whole of the relevant sections again in detail. Note your areas of weakness, and be prepared for further questions on these areas in the self-assessment section at the end of this unit.

Summary

In this unit, we have followed the process of transacting insurance from the proposal form, through to the settlement of claims. We have considered the need for underwriting and how this is carried out. The basics of reinsurance have been introduced, as have the main considerations for premium calculations. Lastly, the main stages in the claims process have been outlined. We now go on to consider life assurance and other forms of personal insurance.

Self-assessment Questions

Short Answer Questions

1. Define moral hazard.

2. What are the four elements that make up a life assurance premium?

3. What is required for proof of death for life assurance?

4. Give the full name of OPAS.

5. Define the type of dispute dealt with by the PIA Ombudsman.

6. What is the Personal Insurance Arbitration Service?

7. Is the Insurance Ombudsman's decision legally binding

    a) on the insured?

    b) on the insurance company?

8. In what year was the Insurance Ombudsman set up?

(Answers given in Appendix 1)

Specimen Examination Questions

1. Outline the role of the loss adjuster and describe the information he or she will provide to the insurance company.

2. A policyholder is unhappy with the administration of his pension scheme and wishes to complain about the service received and a possible loss of return due to a delay in investing a large contribution. What course of action should he take?

(Answers given in Appendix 1)

9

LIFE ASSURANCE AND PERSONAL INSURANCE

Objectives

After studying this unit, you should be able to:

- state the main elements of the basic products available in the marketplace, including: whole-life, endowment, term assurance, annuities, index-linked contracts, unit-linked contracts, unit trusts, investment trusts, personal equity plans, Tessas;

- explain the particular features of products, including: bonuses, surrender values, paid-up policies, bid and offer prices;

- identify the major taxes which impact upon life products;

- say to what extent tax relief is available for life products.

9.1   Types of Life Assurance Policy

Introduction

The array of life assurance policies is extensive and very varied.

It is the general rule that a life assurance policy is effected on a single life, but sometimes more than one life is directly insured under one policy. For example, a policy can be effected on two lives such as husband and wife jointly. Under joint life first death policies the sum assured is payable at the time of the first death. Under joint life last survivor policies the sum assured is payable when the last survivor dies. There are very few policies issued which insure more than two lives.

Occasionally the payment of the sum assured under a policy depends not only on the death of the life assured but also on some other contingency, for example the prior death of some other specific person. When the payment of a sum assured is dependent upon an additional factor of this sort the policies are called contingent assurances.

Broadly speaking, conventional life assurance products take one of three forms:

- term assurance (sometimes known as temporary assurance);

- whole-life assurance;

- endowment assurance.

Term Assurance

The payment of the sum assured is dependent on the life assured dying within a stated period of time (the term of the policy).

If at the end of the term of the policy the life assured is still alive, the contract ceases and no payment is made. In its most straightforward form the sum assured does not vary during the term of the policy. This is known as level term assurance, but sophistications can be introduced.

For example, the sum assured under a term assurance can be of a **decreasing** nature. This means that the sum assured is reduced each year (or sometimes more frequently) by a stated amount, perhaps reducing to nil by the end of the policy term. On the other hand the sum assured might be of an **increasing** nature, being enhanced each year by a fixed annual rate of, say, 10%.

Decreasing term assurance might well be used in connection with a mortgage where the annual repayments are reducing the capital amount of the loan outstanding.

Increasing term assurance might be utilized when it is considered essential to keep the sum assured in line with 'real money' values.

A **renewable term assurance** gives the option at the end of the term to effect a further term assurance to be offered at normal premium rates with no evidence of health requirements. Normally such an option would stipulate the same sum assured for the further term, and it may restrict the length of the further term to a maximum age of 55 or 60.

A further type of option sometimes available in connection with a term assurance is that of allowing, at any time during its currency, to connect to a whole-life assurance or endowment assurance for the same sum assured to be effected at normal rates of premium, again without medical evidence of health requirements. This is known as a **convertible term assurance** and may be initiated by a person wishing to effect a long-term savings type of policy but whose present financial commitments preclude this.

Some companies are now marketing a unit-linked term assurance contract. The premium paid is invested in units in the fund chosen, while each month units are cancelled to pay for life cover and charges. The remainder is invested. Should investments perform well, there is the possibility of a small surrender or maturity value; if they perform badly, the premium may have to be increased to maintain the same level of cover.

A variation of the term assurance contract is the **family income benefit policy**, which is really a form of decreasing term. On death, the sum assured is paid as an income rather than a lump sum, and these annual (or monthly) amounts are paid from the date of death until the expiry date. Policies can be effected on single or joint life benefits, and index-linked benefits are also available.

Whole-life Assurance

This provides cover throughout the life of the life assured.

The sum assured is payable whenever death occurs. Unlike a term assurance, a whole-life policy is permanent assurance. Because the life assured is certain to die at some time or another, the only area of doubt is the question of when this will happen. The sum assured is certain to become payable.

Endowment Assurance

These are fixed-term contracts; in this respect they resemble term assurances. However, as well as providing for the sum assured to be payable should death occur during the policy term, an endowment assurance provides for the sum assured to be payable should the life assured survive to the end of the policy term. This is known as the maturity date.

There are many combinations and varieties of the three basic forms of cover.

The Pure Endowment

This type of contract should be distinguished from an endowment assurance. A pure endowment policy is effected for a stipulated term of years, but under such a contract no sum assured is payable should the life assured die during the term. It is payable only at the end of the term (the maturity date) if the life assured survives. It is possible therefore to view an endowment assurance as having two component parts: a term assurance for the term of the policy plus a pure endowment for the same term.

Non-profit and With-profits Contracts

These different bases on which life assurance policies are written reflect the uncertainties involved in setting premiums.

The premium for any life assurance contract will include three basic aspects. The first is mortality - what is the scientific likelihood of survival of the life assured to a particular age? Secondly, interest - what interest is likely to be earned on the money that has been invested from inception until maturity or a death claim? Thirdly, what are the expenses in terms of initial and maintenance costs of the particular contract?

Non-profit contracts

A non-profit life assurance is basically a life assurance on guaranteed terms. It follows that if the mortality, interest and expense factors reflect the best estimates, it is reasonable to add directly to the premiums a marginal loading for possible adverse fluctuations in each of the categories. In practice, this is exactly what does happen.

With-profits contracts

There are difficulties inherent in predicting mortality, interest and expense elements so that they accurately reflect what is going to happen in the future. Because of this, most life offices prefer transacting conventional main class ordinary life assurance contracts on a with-profits basis. The unguaranteed bonus element will follow the fortunes of the performance of the life office funds. Unless there is a major catastrophe, with-profits policies are almost certain to contribute to the surplus of the life office.

On balance, with-profits contracts tend to give policyholders better value for money than non-profit contracts, at the expense of some loss in guarantees.

Whole-life and endowment assurances are usually offered on either a with-profits or a non-profit basis. However, there are some minor classes such as term assurance where non-profit type policies only are issued.

Distribution of Surpluses

The life office is bound to carry out a valuation by an actuary, under the terms of the Insurance Companies Act 1982. Assets must be valued at market price, where this can be determined, and there is a format of accounts which needs to be completed for the Department of Trade and Industry (DTI).

Once the office has carried out its valuation and arrived at the amount of the surplus, it then seeks to distribute that surplus fairly.

Bonuses

The most common way is by declaring the policyholders' bonus in reversionary form. 'Reversionary' simply means 'payable at a future date'; that is, when the policy matures or death intervenes. These bonuses are generally declared at the end of each year, as a percentage addition to the sum assured. If they are applied to the basic sum assured they are known as simple reversionary bonuses. If added to the sum assured plus bonuses already allotted they are known as compound reversionary bonuses. This allocation of surplus to the policyholders forms the bulk of the surplus declared. A small part will go to the special reserves of the life office, and in the case of a proprietary office to the shareholders' account as well. If the company proposes to reduce the proportion of the actuarial surplus which it makes available to with-profits policyholders by more than half a percentage point on the previous year, then it must give written notice to the DTI and advertise the fact in the London and Edinburgh *Gazettes* (and in any other way that the DTI may direct). So, if the policyholders are entitled after a valuation to share 91% of the divisible surplus, but after the next valuation the company intends to reduce it to 90%, then these requirements operate.

Since 1971 certain years have produced increases in interest earnings (and at times earnings from capital appreciation) which are exceptionally high, making it possible for offices to develop very high rates of bonus. Because of this, many offices have declared special bonuses or terminal bonuses as well as the more traditional bonuses.

Special bonuses

These have varied in form from insurer to insurer but they invariably favour the longer-term policies. The bonuses may take the form of an extra percentage for each year in force, a percentage of the bonuses accrued to date, or an amount that will raise all past bonuses to the current level.

Terminal bonuses

These apply to claims whether by death or maturity, within a short period (not exceeding a year) following the declaration. After expiry of this period they may be held, increased or decreased, usually according to the state of the equity market at the time. The rates of terminal bonus may also vary according to class of policy, year of entry, and so on. These bonuses are temporary and are intended to ensure that claims values reflect the current level of the value of the investment.

It is important to note that ordinary reversionary bonuses and special bonuses once they have been declared increase the benefits under the policy permanently. Terminal bonuses apply only if a claim occurs within a certain limited period.

Special With-profits Products

The with-profits system has been adapted to develop certain other types of contract. A number of these are featured below.

Low-cost whole-life assurances

These are basically whole life policies operating normally on the reversionary bonus with-profits system. They have the added feature of a guaranteed death benefit which is greater than the basic sum assured. When a death claim arises, the guaranteed death benefit is payable unless and until the basic sum assured plus bonuses exceeds this sum.

Low-cost endowment assurances

These operate in a similar way to low-cost whole-life assurances. The amount payable should a death occur is either the basic sum assured plus bonuses or the guaranteed death benefit, whichever is the greater. The basic sum assured is usually fixed at an amount anticipated to exceed the guaranteed death benefit once bonuses are added. Although a guarantee attaches to the death benefit, no corresponding guarantee attaches to the maturity amount. The amount payable at the maturity of the policy is the basic sum assured plus bonuses in exactly the same way as a straightforward with-profits endowment assurance.

Flexi-endowment assurances

These policies tend to provide a very favourable guaranteed surrender value should the policy be surrendered during the first ten years of its term. They are usually written on a with-profits basis but with a policy term much longer than ten years. However, what they provide on encashment after ten years is more in the nature of a maturity value than a surrender value. These policies are usually issued on the basis of a stipulated premium rather than a stated sum assured. Sometimes they are issued in small bundles of policies rather than as a single document, to facilitate the surrender of one or two units from time to time if required. This avoids the necessity of surrendering the whole policy.

Index-linked Policies

The lack of guarantee attached to with-profits policies is a fundamental feature of the with-profits system. There are other types of policy which provide guaranteed bonuses or other guaranteed additions to the sum assured each year. Such guaranteed bonuses are not paid out of the declared surplus of the life office; they are provided on a non-profit principle. The policies are therefore essentially non-profit contracts. All index-linked contracts fall into this category.

The principle of index-linking is a straightforward one. Because policies effected for a fixed sum assured provide lower cover in real terms as time passes, index-linking provides a means of keeping up with inflation. The usual index used is the retail prices index. This is used for both premium and sum assured. Index-linked term assurances are relatively common.

Unit-linked Policies

There is a disadvantage, from the investor's point of view, associated with traditional contracts issued by life offices. It arises from the fact that the information regarding mortality rates, interest and expenses is effectively hidden from the policyholder. With-profits policyholders have reversionary bonuses added to their sums assured as a result of a calculation determined by an actuary. It follows that the individual investor may be unsure of the basis upon which this has been calculated.

What has now proved extremely popular has been the introduction of unit-linked policies.

Except for the crash of 1987, ordinary shares have tended to show good increases in capital values. The distribution of capital surplus has been largely achieved with traditional contracts through the with-profits system by enhancing reversionary bonuses and introducing terminal bonuses.

The unit-linked contracts are more explicit than conventional contracts. Fundamentally, a unit-linked contract provides for benefits to be payable which are formally linked to the value of units in a specified fund.

The fund may be an authorized unit trust, but more often it is a special unitized segregated internal fund managed by the issuing company. If it is a single premium contract, the number of units purchased at the outset is known. Because of reinvestment and distributions of investment income, that number may subsequently be increased. For those contracts with regular annual (or more frequent) premium payments the policy document indicates the percentage of each such premium which is to be utilized for the purchase of units. Management charges, which form part of the balance, usually allow for future increase if necessary. There are two prices that apply to the units. The offer price is the price at which units are obtained by the policyholder by payment of premium and the bid price is the price of units when cashed. At any point in time the bid price is lower than the current offer price. A bid/offer spread is often of the order of 5%.

Authorized unit trusts have various specialized characteristics in their investment make-up. There may be separate funds where investments are confined solely to ordinary shares, fixed-interest stocks or property. Facilities often exist to enable a policyholder to switch from one fund to which his contract is linked to another of his choice subject to a relatively small charge. To this extent the policyholder has a certain freedom of investment choice and bears certain of his own investment risks.

Single premium bonds

These bonds are written as whole-life contracts and the policyholder can continue the policy indefinitely. Occasionally, partial surrender is permitted so that effectively an income may be maintained. The death benefit under these contracts is normally at least the value of the units, although it can be substantially more.

The contracts may be either single life, joint life or last survivor contracts.

Annual premium unit-linked whole-life policies

These **Universal** or **Flexible** whole-life policies are often marketed as 'plans for life'. They are whole-life policies funded by regular premiums, but the sum assured can be varied between minimum and maximum levels to suit different lifestages. For example, a young married man with a family may require the maximum level of life cover while his family is fully dependent, but this may not be needed once the children leave home. The varying levels of life assurance cover allow a corresponding increase or decrease in the remainder of the premium for investment. Hence, a contract with a low level of life cover acquires a higher cash value in a shorter time period, compared with a contract for a similar premium and life assured with a high level of life cover. In addition to the flexibility allowed in changing the sum assured, these policies also offer various 'bolt-on' options such as waiver of premium, critical illness, permanent health insurance and accidental death benefit.

Unit-linked endowment assurances

A specified percentage of the premium for these contracts is used to purchase units in a fund of the policyholder's choice. When a death claim arises, either a guaranteed death benefit or the bid value of the units allocated to the policy (whichever is the higher) becomes payable. On the maturity of the policy the amount then payable is the bid value of the units. There may be a penalty charge if surrendered in the early years.

Unitized With-profits

In recent years, a new type of policy has been developed with the aim of combining the security of traditional with-profits with the flexibility of unit-linked.

Premiums are used to buy units, but there is usually a guarantee that unit prices will only increase, reflecting the addition of bonuses each year.

Some insurers have now stopped offering traditional with-profits business altogether.

Surrender Values

There are certain policies that acquire no surrender values at all. These include term assurances, which are designed to provide cover against death during a specified period.

The expenses in connection with the issue of conventional ordinary life assurance policies are heavy in the first year, and indeed to some extent in the second year, although the office annual premium is calculated on the assumption that these expenses will be recouped over the years that the policy remains in force. The level premium system has been adopted in order to achieve this end. The net effect is not to allow a surrender value even under policies such as whole-life or endowment assurances during the first two years of their existence. Even after this period it is unusual for a life office actually to guarantee a scale of surrender values. The exception is unit-linked contracts, when the bid price determines the surrender value.

The general principle applied by life offices is that the surrender value for any policy should be less than the nominal amount of cash it has in hand in respect of the policy. This is because expenses have been incurred which have been 'spread' assuming that the policy will run its full term and, of course, the life cover has been provided. This last point is often overlooked by those wishing to surrender their policies.

There is clearly a point at which the policy, even though it has not run its full term, has acquired a value which is in excess of the premiums paid.

Paid-up Policies

Surrendering the policy is not the only option a policyholder may have if he or she wishes to discontinue payment of premiums. It may be possible, in the case of endowment and whole-life policies particularly, to have the policy converted into a paid-up policy. When this happens, no further premiums are payable and the policy remains in force with a reduced sum assured. The normal basis used by life offices is to reduce the sum assured on some proportional basis relating the premiums paid to the term of the policy. For with-profits policies the reversionary bonuses already allotted to the policy remain, but the policy may not necessarily share in any further surplus distributions.

Student Activity 1

Before reading the next section of the text, answer the following questions and then check your answers against the pages indicated.

1.   Explain the options provided under a renewable term assurance.

(page 213)

2.   Distinguish between reversionary and terminal bonuses.   *(page 215)*

3.   A low-cost endowment is taken out in conjunction with an endowment mortgage. What guarantees are provided:
    i)   on death within the term?

    ii)   on maturing of the policy?   *(page 216)*

4.   Outline why the surrender value under an endowment or whole policy will be less than the premiums paid if the policy is cancelled in its early years.

(page 219)

If your answers are basically correct, then proceed to the next section. If significant parts of your answers are wrong, then study the whole of the relevant sections again in detail. Note your areas of weakness, and be prepared for further questions on these areas in the self-assessment section at the end of this unit.

9.2   Annuities

In addition to transacting life business, life assurance offices also transact annuity business. The two are closely related. Life annuities are annual payments (although in practice they may be paid more frequently) made throughout the life of the annuitant.

They may be paid in advance, say on attainment of age 70. In this case the first payment is made on the 70th birthday. This is called an annuity due. If it is paid monthly in arrears it is called an immediate life annuity (although this term may seem somewhat misleading).

An annuity may be apportionable (sometimes termed a 'with proportion' annuity). In this case a proportionate payment is made to account for the period of survival since the last payment date up to the date of death.

Usually the consideration payable for a life annuity is a lump sum known as the 'purchase price'. Sometimes, however, when the annuity is deferred, an annual (or more frequent) payment may be made. Whether the amount is paid as a lump sum or by annual amount, it has to be paid before the annuity is due to commence.

Underwriting Considerations

While the adoption of strict underwriting standards is required for life assurance (to avoid selection against the insurer), the opposite is true for annuity business. This still poses a problem for the underwriter because it is inevitable that those who believe they will not survive very long will equally not be prepared to fund an annuity, and so the office suffers from being able to sell policies only to those who are likely to benefit greatly from them.

Payment of Annuities

An immediate annuity provides a series of payments throughout the life of the annuitant in return for a lump sum. A deferred annuity provides for an annuity to become payable as from some future date known as the vesting date. It is payable thereafter throughout the annuitant's life. Sometimes the contract provides for an option exercisable at the vesting date to take a cash lump sum instead of the annuity payments.

There may be a **guaranteed period** of payment. In normal circumstances payment would stop upon the death of the annuitant. Clearly the amount of the annuity is reduced if there is a guarantee period. This provision does, however, have a 'value for money' appeal because the death of the annuitant shortly after the vesting date would mean that very little had been paid out by the life office.

Temporary annuities are available which continue to pay the annuitant, subject to survival, for a limited period of years (perhaps ten) or until the annuitant attains a specific age such as 60.

A **joint life annuity** may be effected and in this case the annuity payments continue until the first of the two dies. If it is a joint life last survivor annuity, the annuity payments continue until the last survivor of the two dies.

There are also **contingent reversionary annuities**. Under these the annuity payments are made to a specified person commencing on the death of another specified person, subject of course to the former still being alive. This may typically be used for a husband and wife, with the annuity payments being to the wife and commencing on the husband's death. If the wife predeceases her husband no annuity payments are made.

Increasing Annuities

Increasing life annuities seek to provide some measure of protection against inflation. They may be increased by a fixed percentage, say 5% each year, or by a percentage equalling the increase in the retail prices index, or some other reasonable basis. The life office in issuing such contracts tends to match its own liabilities by index-linked government stocks so that both are linked to changes in the RPI.

9.3 Health and Disability Insurances

Permanent health insurance (PHI)

This policy covers inability to work due to sickness or accident and provides a regular income to replace that which the insured is no longer able to earn for himself. The benefit becomes payable only once the insured has been disabled for a specified period, the deferred period, which may be 4, 13, 26 or 52 weeks. Policies can be effected on a level or increasing sum insured basis. Benefits are payable until retirement age, return to work or death, whichever is sooner.

Waiver of premium

This is an optional extra to most PHI, pension and unit-linked policies which provides for the payment of premiums on a policy should the life assured be unable to follow his own occupation due to illness or accident. A deferred period applies and the benefit is paid until retirement age or return to work, whichever is sooner.

Critical illness

Originally known as 'dread disease' cover, this was first launched in the UK in 1986 and currently over 70 offices sell this type of policy.

The sum assured is payable on diagnosis of a number of disorders as specified in the policy. These usually include coronary artery disease, heart attack, stroke, cancer, kidney failure, major organ transplant and paralysis. Competition among offices has led to an increase in the number of disorders covered by the policy. It can be sold as a stand-alone policy, or be attached to a life policy to provide accelerated payment of the benefit.

Long-term care

This is a new product in the UK market but has been widely sold in the USA. By paying regular amounts or a lump sum into the plan, the aim is to provide funds to meet the cost of care in later life, either in a private nursing home or at home. Disability is normally established by reference to a number of 'activities of daily living' such as eating, washing and dressing.

9.4 Taxation

The following section outlines the different types of taxes as they relate to life assurance, annuities and permanent health insurance.

Tax Relief on Life Assurance Premiums

Following the Finance Act 1984, income tax relief is no longer allowable in respect of premiums paid for life assurance policies taken out after 13 March 1984. This applies even to policies effected before that date if they are altered by an increase in benefits or a change in term.

Those policies taken out on or before 13 March 1984 which remain unaltered and which meet certain qualifying conditions still gain some income tax relief on the premium paid. This is known as LAPR: Life Assurance Premium Relief. The rate for relief for 1995/96 and 1996/97 was 12.5% and is given by the policyholder deducting the relief from the premium and the life office claiming it back from the Inland Revenue by block monthly claims.

Taxation of Life Assurance Policy Proceeds

There are three main facets to the taxation of life assurance policy proceeds and these are considered below.

Income tax

The general rule is that no income tax is paid on the proceeds or benefits arising under a policy that ranks as a qualifying policy under the terms of the Income and Corporation Tax Act 1970. However, income tax may become payable if the qualifying policy is surrendered or made paid-up within ten years (or within three-quarters of the maturity term if that is shorter). For non-qualifying policies, on death, maturity or surrender, income tax may be payable.

In either case, tax is payable on the 'chargeable gain', but only if the policyholder is in, or close enough to, the higher rate tax bracket. Even then, the 'chargeable gain' on the policy is taxed only at the difference between the basic and the higher tax rate.

Wherever a chargeable event occurs, the life office will issue a certificate to the Inland Revenue. The policyholder's Inspector of Taxes will be responsible for calculating any tax due on any gain.

Capital gains tax

No capital gains tax is normally paid on the proceeds of a life assurance policy. Tax is chargeable only under policies that have been sold to a third party, and then only on subsequent disposal, maturity or death. The gain is calculated by deducting the total acquisition costs, indexed to take account of inflation, from the policy proceeds.

Taxation of Annuities

The premium paid for an individual life annuity relates to a contract that does not have a capital sum element on death. In view of this there is no relief from income tax. Certain limited relief may be available in respect of premiums payable under a deferred annuity which is taken out in connection with a pension scheme.

Benefits from individually purchased life annuities are subject to preferential taxation treatment. The income is treated as having two components. The first is the capital content of the annuity payment and is treated as a return of the capital paid for the annuity; it is therefore not subject to tax. The other component is treated as an interest element and is therefore subject to income tax. The capital element is calculated by reference to the annuitant's life expectancy, calculated from mortality tables prescribed by the Inland Revenue.

The actual payment of an annuity is made net of income tax at the basic rate on the interest element only. Should an annuitant be subject to a higher rate of income tax then this is a matter to be dealt with directly between the annuitant and the Inspector of Taxes. The reverse is also true where an annuitant may be subject to less income tax than has been deducted by the life office. In this case a refund is due, again dealt with on a direct basis. Annuitants can elect to have annuity payments made gross by completing an R89 form.

Annuities for beneficiaries under trusts or wills are taxed in full as investment income.

Taxation of Permanent Health Insurance

There is no tax relief available on the premiums for permanent health insurance.

From 6 April 1996, benefits paid under a PHI policy were made tax-free.

Student Activity 2

Before reading the next section of the text, answer the following questions and then check your answers against the pages indicated.

1. Distinguish between a temporary annuity and a guaranteed annuity.

    (page 221)

2. How much can be withdrawn from a Tessa without affecting the tax exempt status?

    (page 225)

3. List the types of investment that were allowable in a general Pep.   *(page 226)*

4. Explain how benefits payable under a PHI policy are treated for income tax purposes.   *(page 224)*

If your answers are basically correct, then proceed to the next section. If significant parts of your answers are wrong, then study the whole of the relevant sections again in detail. Note your areas of weakness, and be prepared for further questions on these areas in the self-assessment section at the end of this unit.

9.5 'Non-life' Investments

The following section outlines some of the investments available.

National Savings

National Savings products are offered by the government through the Post Office network and, more recently, information has been made available through off-the-page advertisements in the press and direct by telephone. These products should be completely secure because they are guaranteed by the government.

Products include the tax-free National Savings Certificates and Children's Bonus Bonds, plus a range of other products which are taxable, such as pensioners guaranteed income bonds ('granny bonds'), income and capital bonds, and bank accounts.

You should obtain the latest leaflets from National Savings to assess the range of products available and compare the rates of return offered from each.

Tessas

Tax Exempt Special Savings Accounts (Tessas) were introduced in the 1990 Budget to encourage saving and were offered by all the major banks and building societies in the UK. The first Tessa became available on 1 January 1991.

The interest paid on this account is free from income tax as long as the capital remains invested for the full five-year term. However, there are maximum investment limits :

- Overall maximum investment is £9,000.
- First year maximum £3,000.
- For the four subsequent years, maximum is £1,800.

A special rule applies for maturing Tessas, whereby the total capital of £9,000 (but not the accrued interest) can be rolled over into a new Tessa immediately as long as this is transferred within six months of maturity.

There are no minimum requirements imposed by the Inland Revenue, but banks and building societies impose their own minimum investment, ranging from £1 to £100. Tessas are available to any individual over the age of 18. No joint accounts are allowed.

The capital must remain invested for the full-five year term to obtain the tax exempt status. However, an amount equivalent to interest net of basic rate tax can be withdrawn each year. Withdrawing any capital from the Tessa means that all tax exemptions are lost - but this simply puts the investor back in the same tax position he would have been in with an ordinary savings account. Tessas can be transferred from one provider to another, but a charge may be applied, or the end-of-term 'loyalty bonus' lost.

In 1997 the government announced that Tessas would lose their tax-free status in 1999, when the new Individual Savings Accounts (ISAs) were introduced.

Unit Trusts

Most unit trusts are authorized by the Department of Trade and Industry. The trust manager is then permitted to invest only in specified securities. Many different types of unit trust exist. Their aims are often very different. Some aim specifically at capital growth and others at high income. There are virtually all shades in between. Some are of a specialist character: North American equities are a good example. There are even recovery trusts that invest in low-priced shares thought to have some recovery potential.

The income from unit trusts is taxable. Income is received net and basic rate taxpayers have no further liability. Higher rate taxpayers need to account for the difference between standard rate (which is deducted at source) and such higher rate. Non-taxpayers need to claim back the tax that has been automatically paid. Capital gains tax is payable on profits made from sales.

As with unit-linked contracts the selling price of units back to the trust is a number of percentage points below the buying price: the bid/offer spread which is usually 5% or 6%. This allows for charges and management fees. Any income distributed to unit holders is also normally subject to a small annual charge.

An important feature of unit trusts is that they are 'open-ended'; as many units can be issued as demand requires.

Investment Trusts

An investment trust is a limited liability company whose purpose is to invest shareholders' money in other stocks and shares. The name is a misnomer because it is not a trust.

Each investor is a part-owner of the investment trust company and receives dividends as well as potential capital growth through the value of shares increasing over time. An investment trust is 'close ended' because, unlike unit trusts, there is a finite number of shares available to buy and sell.

Investment trusts are an example of a pooled investment, but may be riskier than unit trusts because they often take the lead in launching new companies and providing development finance for other companies. In addition, they can take advantage of gearing, which means raising money by borrowing; this is beneficial if the investments produce more than is required to repay the loan.

The income received and capital gains made by an individual from holdings in an investment trust are taxed in a similar way to ordinary shares.

Personal Equity Plans

Personal equity plans, or Peps, were introduced by the government in 1987 to encourage wider share ownership by individuals. Peps were investment plans managed by investment managers but owned by an individual and represented a tax-efficient way of investing in shares, unit trusts and investment trusts. Planholders had to be resident in the UK and aged 18 or over.

The maximum investment in a general Pep in any tax year was £6,000 and investments were restricted to UK or EC ordinary shares and unit trusts or investment trusts with at least 50% invested in UK or EC shares. In 1995, the investment restrictions were extended to include certain UK corporate bonds, convertibles and preference shares in UK or EC companies.

In addition to a general Pep, single company Peps were available with investment in some of the major UK blue chip companies. The maximum investment was £3,000 per tax year.

Peps were free of both Income Tax and Capital Gains Tax, making them a particularly suitable investment for higher rate taxpayers.

In 1997 the government announced that Peps would lose their tax-free status in 1999, when the new Individual Savings Accounts (ISAs) were introduced. Peps are no longer available.

Self-assessment Questions

Short Answer Questions

1. Consider the types of contract that have been covered in the chapter so far.

   Recommend the most suitable contract in each of the following circumstances.

   a) A young married man is seeking the cheapest form of protection for his wife and two children in the event of his death.

   b) A client requires cheap protection in the event of death, but has limited funds available. He would like the flexibility to change the policy to a long-term contract in the future.

   c) A client wishes to save £50 per month in a contract with some life assurance cover. He would like some control over his investment and is prepared to take some risk.

   d) A retired couple are currently receiving a good pension from the husband's company scheme, but his wife is not provided for. They wish to invest a lump sum to provide an income should he predecease her.

2. Construct a table showing the differences between unit trusts and investment trusts.

3. a) Explain why it is so important for a self-employed person to consider Permanent Health Insurance cover.

   b) Consider the likely level for such a client of:

   i) cover;

   ii) deferred period; and

   iii) term necessary.

   (Answers given in Appendix 1)

Multiple-choice Questions

1 Which of the following disorders would NOT be covered under a Critical Illness policy?

   a) kidney failure;

   b) coronary artery disease;

   c) multiple sclerosis;

   d) AIDS.

2   Which of the following statements are true. Payments under an annuity contract

a)   cannot be paid gross;

b)   can be paid gross by completing an R85 form;

c)   can be paid gross by completing an R89 form;

d)   are always paid gross.

(Answers given in Appendix 1)

Specimen Examination Questions

1.   Explain how life assurance contracts can be used for family protection.

What are the advantages of placing such life policies under trust?

2.   A client wishes to invest £200 per month and requires some guidance on the most suitable type of investment for him. Compare the relative advantages and disadvantages of a regular premium, unit-linked endowment savings plan and a regular unit trust savings plan.

What further information would be required before making a final recommendation?

3.   What is the difference between simple reversionary and compound reversionary bonuses?

(Answers given in Appendix 1)

10

PENSIONS

Objectives

After studying this unit, you should be able to:

- describe the operation of pension schemes including the state pension scheme;

- outline the reasons for and restrictions relating to additional voluntary contributions (AVCs);

- identify the scope of personal pension plans;

- suggest applications of Executive Pension Plans.

10.1   Introduction

The whole area of pensions has to be viewed against the background of what is already provided by the state and the restrictions, and in some cases incentives, that apply to particular methods of pension provision.

10.2   Provision by the State

The State pension consists of two components:

- Basic State Pension.

- The State Earnings Related Pension Scheme (Serps).

Basic State Pension

Most individuals are entitled to a basic state pension, but the amount is dependent on the number of years' National Insurance Contributions (NICs).

An individual who has paid NICs for at least 90% of his working life is entitled to a single person's basic pension of £59.15 per week for 1996/97. This is available at State Pension Age, which has now been equalized at 65 for both men and women. For women born before 6 April 1950 the State Pension Age is 60.

Married women who have had significant breaks in their working lives may not be entitled to a full basic state pension in their own right. If this is the case, they may have to rely on their husbands' NIC record, and then when the husbands reach State Pension Age, they are entitled to a married couple's pension. This is £94.45 per week for 1996/97.

State Earnings-Related Pension Scheme (Serps)

Serps was introduced in 1978 to replace the State Graduated Pension Scheme. It was set up by the Social Security Act 1975 and is available only for employed people.

In addition to the basic pension, Serps was available at a rate of 1.25% of middle band earnings for each year of contribution. For people with more than 20 years of contributions, the formula was applied to the average of the person's best 20 years' middle band earnings. All middle band earnings are revalued to State Pension Age in line with National Average Earnings.

Social Security Act 1986

The prompting for this act was the government's concern that the long-term cost of Serps could not be sustained and that consequently some alternative arrangements had to be made. The complete removal of Serps was not generally supported. The government's stated aim was that each individual should save for his or her own additional pension by means of contributions paid by the employer and employee to occupational and private pension schemes. The modifications made to Serps are as follows:

For those retiring or widowed after 5 April 2000:

- earnings-related pension will be calculated on lifetime average earnings rather than the best 20 years' earnings;

- the benefits will be based on 20% of earnings between lower and upper earnings levels rather than the previous 25% level;

- the widow's pension will be 50% of the member's entitlement and there will be a widower's benefit on a corresponding basis.

From 6 April 1988, compulsory membership of an occupational pension scheme was, in general, abolished.

10.3   Personal Pensions

Personal pension plans offer a further alternative means of both investment and protection. The growth of the market for personal pension plans has been assisted by government policy which has encouraged people to leave the State Earnings-Related Pension Scheme (Serps) and provided the ability for employees to opt out of an occupational scheme to make their own arrangements for retirement.

The following benefits can be provided by a personal pension plan:

- a pension for life;

- a tax-free cash lump sum at retirement;

- a lump sum on death;

- a widow's or widower's pension;

- waiver of premium.

Term assurance benefits may be written in conjunction with a personal pension plan. This policy can be written up to age 75 and can be effected under trust. A spouse's or dependant's pension cover can also be provided whereby the pension commences on the death of the life assured and continues until the death of the pensioner.

The maximum premium payable for death-in-service benefits is 5% of net relevant earnings. An added attraction is that tax relief is available on premiums paid, subject to statutory limits; this is in contrast to ordinary term assurances.

Personal pension plans are used to provide for retirement. Benefits may be taken at any age between 50 and 75 unless the policyholder is in an occupation where an earlier retirement age has been agreed by the Inland Revenue, and part of the benefit may be taken as tax-free cash. There are maximum contribution levels for personal pension plans; these are based on the age of the life assured.

Contributions into personal pensions are restricted by reference to net relevant earnings. The maximum contributions are as follows:

Age on 6 April	% of net relevant earnings
35 or under	17.5
36 - 45	20.0
46 - 50	25.0
51 - 55	30.0
56 - 60	35.0
61 and over	40.0

The maximum contributions are further restricted by reference to a maximum earnings figure. This was introduced in 1989 when the maximum figure was set at £60,000. The figure increases in line with the Retail Prices Index each year, although for tax year 1993/94 it was frozen at the 1992/93 level of £75,000. The earnings cap increased to £82,200 for 1996/97.

Where the maximum possible contributions have not been used in a tax year, there are rules which allow for them to be carried forward in later years. For this to happen the full entitlement for the current year must have been used; the policyholder is then allowed to go back and use this earlier figure for up to six years.

At the chosen retirement age the policyholder is permitted to utilize an open market option. This option permits him to require the office to transfer the value of the benefits to another office from which he will take an annuity contract. Thus, the policyholder is able to seek the most competitive annuity rate at the time of retirement rather than the rates of the office with which he took the personal pension plan. Income arising under the annuity is taxed as earned income and it may be advantageous to boost income by taking the cash sum and purchasing an immediate annuity where only the interest content is liable to tax. A maximum of 25% of the fund excluding any protected rights may be taken as tax-free cash. The annuity may be payable during the lifetime of the annuitant or may continue for the lifetime of the widow or widower at a reduced level thereafter. Some annuities are written to increase in payment, for example, at a fixed rate.

Since 1 April 1995, personal pension planholders are able to defer the purchase of an annuity at retirement date, irrespective of whether or not they take the tax-free cash at retirement date. The reason for this is to avoid planholders having to buy annuities when interest rates are low. The planholder is allowed to draw a reasonable income from the pension plan fund until such time as annuity purchase is made. Annuity purchase cannot be deferred beyond the planholder's 75th birthday. Planholders who do this have to balance the opportunity for a larger annuity in the future against the risk of the future falls in interest rates and the danger of depleting their fund before annuity purchase is made. Any income withdrawal amounts have to be reviewed by the provider every three years to see that the pension fund is not too rapidly depleted.

Personal pension plans may be non-profit, with-profit or unit-linked. It is also possible to incorporate waiver of premium benefits into the plan - this enables premiums to be maintained when the life assured is disabled and may otherwise be required to cease contributions as a result of having no relevant earnings.

A further option is to include a permanent disability benefit. This provides that, where the life assured becomes permanently disabled, the policy will boost the level of pension to that which would have been payable had the life assured not been disabled and the policy continued until the anticipated retirement age.

Pension Mortgages

Pension mortgages are now more and more popular, especially since LAPR was abolished in 1984. At first retirement annuity contracts were used and now personal pensions can be used in the same way. They work in a similar way to an endowment mortgage in that the borrower's payments to the lender consist only of interest. Instead of taking out an endowment policy, however, the borrower effects a personal pension plan. The contract is so arranged that the estimated tax-free cash sum on retirement will be equal to the amount of the loan, using conservative assumptions as to bonuses (for with-profit policies) or unit growth rates (for unit-linked policies). There is a statutory prohibition on assignment of the pension so it cannot be mortgaged to the lender in the same way as an endowment. Instead, most lenders require the borrower to sign an undertaking to use the cash sum to repay the loan, although this has no effect on the life office which must pay the sum to the policyholder if so requested. The policyholder also naturally receives a pension for life in addition. The lender normally requires the borrower to arrange life cover for the duration and amount of the loan.

The advantages of pension mortgages are as follows:

- Full income tax relief is allowed on the premium, thus the net cost can be as low as 60% for a 40% taxpayer. This includes the life cover where this is written as part of the pension plan and compares very favourably with ordinary endowments, where tax relief is no longer available.

- The pension premiums go into a fund which pays no income tax or capital gains tax, whereas the office's life fund where endowment premiums are invested pays both these taxes. Potential benefits thus build up faster.

- The cash sum on retirement is tax-free (although this is equally true of the endowment sum assured) and there is a pension in addition.

The major drawback is that part of the retirement benefits are utilized to repay the mortgage, thus reducing the amount available to the life assured after retirement.

10.4 Occupational Pension Schemes

For an employee whose employer has a pension scheme this is often the best way of planning for retirement. If an employee does not like the scheme, however, he does not have to join it and can elect to arrange his own personal pension. The employer does not have to contribute to the personal pension plan if he does not want to.

One of the main benefits of an occupational scheme is that the employer pays some, or all, of the cost. The pension that can be provided by an approved scheme is limited by Inland Revenue rules. If an employee cannot get the maximum pension under the scheme he can pay extra amounts himself to increase the pension to the statutory maximum. These payments are known as additional voluntary contributions (AVCs) and are limited to 15% of pensionable remuneration minus any compulsory contributions to the scheme. There are two types of AVC. The first is effectively a bolt-on extra to the employer's scheme and the second is a free-standing AVC (FSAVC) which is under the employee's own control. New AVCs cannot now provide a lump sum on retirement.

As with personal pensions it is usually beneficial to take the maximum lump sum from the occupational scheme at retirement. This is tax-free and can be used to buy a purchased life annuity if desired, where part of the annuity will be tax-free. The maximum figure is based on years of service and is set at 3/80ths of final remuneration for each year of service up to a maximum of 40 years.

The maximum salary mentioned under personal pensions earlier also applies to new occupational schemes with effect from 14 March 1989, and to new entrants to existing schemes from 1 June 1989.

For anyone who is a member of a pension scheme, the possibility of arranging family protection cover within the scheme should not be ignored. Many schemes provide a death-in-service benefit. This can be arranged on a discretionary trust basis so that it will be free of Inheritance Tax on the member's death. The normal procedure is for the member to complete an 'expression of wish' form telling the trustees whom he would like them to pay. The trustees would normally comply with his wishes but because of their discretion do not legally have to do so. The maximum benefit that can be paid on death is four times remuneration plus a pension to a widow or dependant. The maximum pension that can be paid is two-thirds of the maximum pension that could have been approved if the member had retired through incapacity.

Many schemes provide for a spouse's pension if death occurs before retirement. This is payable for the spouse's life and is taxed as earned income. Protection after retirement can be obtained by arranging for the member's pension to be on a joint life last survivor basis with the member's spouse. Thus, if the member dies first the pension continues throughout the life of the survivor. Again the pension is taxed as earned income. This is consistent with the bases for personal pension plans mentioned earlier.

Any amount paid by the member into an approved pension scheme qualifies for full tax relief. Any contributions by the employer also gain full tax relief as a business expense.

Types of Occupational Scheme

Money purchase

This is a defined contribution scheme where the employer decides on the level of contributions both he and the employees make. This is usually a percentage of salary. The contributions are invested, and the fund at retirement is used to purchase an annuity. There is no guarantee as to the benefit levels in retirement, but there is the advantage of known cost to the employer.

This scheme can be used to contract out of Serps. The employer pays the contracted-out rebate, currently 4.8% of middle band earnings, into the scheme, in addition to any other regular contributions. The benefits from the rebate contributions are known as protected rights, to which special rules apply.

Final salary

The employer provides a pension scheme which guarantees the employee a fraction of final pensionable salary per year of service. For example, if a 1/60 scheme is offered, and an employee has 40 years' service, he is guaranteed an annual pension of 40/60 times his final pensionable salary in retirement.

Although this scheme is of great benefit to the employee, who is guaranteed a certain level of pension in retirement, the employer must contribute sufficient to the fund to ensure that the guarantee is maintained. The employer, therefore, has no real control over cost.

A final salary scheme can be used to contract out of Serps. In this case both employer and employee pay lower NICs, and the scheme promises to provide a Guaranteed Minimum Pension (GMP), that is a pension which is at least equivalent to Serps.

Executive pensions

These are usually money purchase occupational schemes for directors or key employees. They are individual arrangements governed by occupational scheme rules and are usually non-contributory. The Inland Revenue has recently introduced strict limits on the funding of such schemes.

SSAS

Small self-administered schemes (SSAS) are occupational schemes with fewer than 12 members with special advantages for small companies. They allow the company to set up the scheme but to use the scheme's assets to provide loans to the company or to purchase property. Strict rules apply to 'self-investment' and a Pensioner Trustee must be appointed to ensure the scheme is run within Inland Revenue rules.

Student Activity

Before reading the next section of the text, answer the following questions and then check your answers against the pages indicated.

1.   What is the difference between AVCs and FSAVCs?   *(page 234)*

2.   Explain how a personal pension can be used to fund a mortgage.   *(page 233)*

If your answers are basically correct, then proceed to the next section. If significant parts of your answers are wrong, then study the whole of the relevant sections again in detail. Note your areas of weakness, and be prepared for further questions on these areas in the self-assessment section at the end of this unit.

10.5   Approval and Taxation

Pension schemes are submitted to the Pension Schemes Office (PSO) of the Inland Revenue for exempt approval to obtain the relevant tax concessions summarized below:

- Tax relief at the highest rate paid on members contributions.

- Fund growth is free of both Income Tax and Capital Gains Tax.

- Tax-free cash sums are available on retirement (subject to limits).

- Benefits on death are free of Inheritance Tax.

- Any employer contributions are allowable as a business expense for Corporation Tax purposes and are not treated as a benefit in kind for Income Tax purposes.

Self-assessment Questions

Short Answer Questions

1. What are the two component parts of the State pension?

2. What type of approval gives pension schemes the full tax concessions available?

3. Who is responsible for approval of pension schemes?

4. A self-employed person is aged 60 at the beginning of the tax year. How much can he contribute to a personal pension plan?

5. What is an appropriate personal pension plan?

6 . What is the limit on the tax-free cash lump sum that can be taken from a personal pension plan?

7. What is meant by a defined benefit scheme?

8. Why is the death benefit under an occupational scheme free of inheritance tax?

(Answers given in Appendix 1)

Specimen Examination Question

A member of an occupational scheme wishes to increase his pension benefits because he joined the scheme at age 40 and is concerned that the state will not provide for him when he retires. He would like your advice on the various options available to him to increase his pension benefits. Outline the options open to him, indicating the advantages and disadvantages of each.

(Answer given in Appendix 1)

11

HOUSEHOLD AND OTHER
PERSONAL INSURANCES

Objectives

After studying this unit, you should be able to:

- identify the main underwriting and claims considerations for these various covers;
- state the cover available under each type of policy.

11.1   Introduction

Household insurance falls into two main categories, although there are many extensions of cover available. The major categories are household buildings and household contents. Household cover is not compulsory by law in the way that motor insurance is. However, as we shall see later, it is often necessary to insure at least the fabric of the building if a mortgage has been taken out by the individual. The mortgagee (the person lending money on the security of the house) will want to protect his interest and will therefore insist upon an approved insurance policy. Insurers provide buildings and contents cover under a variety of different brand names.

Before looking at the specific range of cover available for buildings and contents it is worth establishing what the terms **buildings, fixtures and fittings**, and **contents** actually mean. Precise definitions are difficult but the following guidelines are helpful in determining which is which. The term **buildings** relates to permanent fitted items as well as the fabric of the building itself. It would include permanent kitchen or bedroom fitments. It would also include electrical fittings and double glazing. Items that are removable (even if sold with the property) are considered to be **contents**. Items such as fitted carpets would come into this category.

11.2   Buildings Cover

The main concern when buildings cover was first contemplated was the risk of damage by fire. Indeed this is still the major catastrophe of concern to most people. There are many other contingencies now covered by household buildings policies. There is no such thing, however, as a standard form of cover – numerous variations exist between the different products offered by different insurance companies. There are some common areas and we have drawn these together to identify the cover provided by most household buildings policies:

- Fire (or smoke damage).

- Lightning, explosion and earthquake.

- Riot and civil commotion (including strikes and political disturbances).

- Damage by malicious persons (normally termed malicious damage).

- Theft or attempted theft.

- Storm, tempest and flood. Not every insurer continues to use the term 'tempest'. There is an exclusion of damage caused by frost, subsidence or landslip as well as an exclusion relating to the destruction of or damage to gates, hedges and fences. There is also an excess.

- Falling trees or parts of trees (subject to an excess).

- Impact by vehicles, animals or aircraft.

- Subsidence and/or heave of the site or landslip excluding:

  - the bedding down of new structures,

  - coastal erosion,

  - damage to or resulting from the movement of solid floor slabs unless foundations beneath the external walls of the building are damaged at the same time,

  - damage to swimming pools, patios, terraces, footpaths, drives, gates, fences, hedges or garden walls unless the building is damaged at the same time,

  - the use of defective materials or arising from faulty workmanship in the course of constructing the foundations,

  - there is an excess applicable to this section normally amounting to £500.

- Escape of oil or water from fixed domestic installations. There is an excess applicable to this cover.

- Accidental damage to water, oil, gas, sewage and drain pipes, underground telephone, television and electricity cables serving the building.

- Accidental damage to fixed glass in walls, doors and roofs and double glazing units. Also included is damage to fixed wash basins, lavatory pans and cisterns, baths, splash backs, shower trays and screens, bidets and other sanitary fittings.

- Rent and alternative accommodation – the cover here is in respect of ground rent for a maximum period of two years and loss of rent for any part of the premises, not occupied by the insured, which has become uninhabitable as a result of an insured peril. The insurer's maximum liability is limited to 10% of the sum insured.

- Reasonable legal fees and architects' and surveyors' fees (not exceeding those authorized by their professional bodies) necessarily incurred in the reinstatement of the buildings following loss or damage are included. This cover does not include any cost involved in preparing the insured's claim. The cost of demolition or shoring up the property and removing debris is also included.

- Automatic reinstatement of the sum insured following a loss is a standard feature. Most indemnity insurance contracts require an additional premium for this. This is not so for a household buildings policy.

Liability (As Owner)

Household buildings policies include a section that is designed to protect the owner of the property against all sums **which he shall become legally liable to pay** in respect of:

- accidental bodily injury to or disease contracted by any person other than a member of the insured's family permanently residing with him;

- accidental loss of or accidental damage to property not belonging to nor in the custody or control of the insured or any member of the insured's family permanently residing with him.

The bodily injury or property damage must happen within the British Isles or elsewhere while the insured or any person in the employment of the insured is on a temporary visit.

It is not the intention of this cover to provide indemnity in respect of injury to members of the insured's family. It is however intended to cater both for the domestic employees which the insured may have as well as members of the public.

The maximum amount payable in respect of any number of claims arising out of one cause will:

- be without limit in the case of accidental bodily injury to or disease contracted by any person in the employment of the insured;

- otherwise not exceed (say) £1m.

Insurers will also pay costs and expenses incurred with their written consent and solicitors' fees if it is necessary for the insured to be represented at any Coroners' Inquest, Fatal Enquiry, or Court of Summary Jurisdiction. The latter cover applies in respect of any event which **may be** the subject of indemnity under this particular section.

The intention of the wording is to protect the insured in respect of claims made against him or his family in his private capacity.

Defective Premises Act 1972

Certain liabilities exist for premises previously owned if they prove to be defective after having been sold to a third party. As the insured may, therefore, have a liability by virtue of this act in respect of premises previously owned, the policy provides an indemnity for up to seven years.

Contracting Purchaser

The policy covers the purchaser who completes the purchase of the building once he has signed the contract. It is a contingency cover and does not apply if he has insured it himself.

Extensions of Cover

There are a number of additional covers available. Many of these have been introduced in an effort to gain a marketing edge on competitors. Those that follow are now fairly commonplace in the market:

- **Accidental damage cover.** This would extend to include events such as putting one's foot through the ceiling when climbing around in the loft.

- **Family legal protection.** This provides payments for solicitors' fees in the event of the insured pursuing or defending a claim.

- **Free help line facility.** A contact telephone number is provided which is manned to ensure that legal advice is available in relation to domestic matters.

- **Emergency services facility.** Some insurers have arranged for an approved tradesman to assist in an emergency situation such as a burst pipe. Because of the amount of work 'guaranteed' by the insurer, the tradesmen respond very quickly.

It is possible that some of these extra covers are available at an additional charge. Others may be included by some insurers as standard cover.

Underwriting Factors

The main considerations for a underwriter when considering a proposal for household buildings insurance are as follows:

- **The construction of the building.** Is it of standard construction (built of bricks or concrete and roofed with slates or tiles)? As we have said before, insurers set their premiums to reflect average risks and any deviation from the 'norm' would need to be adjusted for in setting the rate. Therefore if the property is, for example, a stone-built cottage with a thatched roof it would need to be rated differently from normal risks. A timber-built property would also require different rating.

- **Previous claims.** The previous claims history is always important in any class of insurance. The particular focus so far as householder's cover is concerned is a history of frequent losses, whether significant in amount or not. The type of cover requested will affect the insurer's judgment. If there are a number of situations that could reasonably be regarded as carelessness on the part of the insured and the wider form of accidental damage cover is required this will have an impact on the insurer's view as to whether he should accept the risk or not.

- **Convictions.** Offences would be viewed in relation to the cover which is being provided. Any convictions relating to arson or fraud would be viewed very seriously by the insurer.

- **Sum insured.** The premium for the risk traditionally is dependent upon the amount of insurance sought although, as we shall see shortly, other methods are now being employed by some insurers.

Calculating the sum insured has its problems. The best guide is probably the Royal Institute of Chartered Surveyors which publishes the cost of re-building a house for various geographical areas of the United Kingdom on the basis of a cost per square foot. This is designed to reflect the current building prices. Insurers make use of the guide, as do surveyors employed by building societies and other lenders.

The sum insured has to take into account the following:

- demolition of the building;
- site clearance and removal of debris;
- architects' fees for re-building;
- digging up of foundations and laying of new ones.

The number of bedrooms and square footage of the property are criteria used now by some insurers to calculate the premium. Those who do this tend to issue policies which do not show a sum insured selected by the insured. This does not mean that there is no limit to what will be paid in the event of a claim but it will avoid the necessity for precision in fixing sums insured. There is usually an overall limit which is high enough to deal with the vast majority of householders' properties offering the particular size of living accommodation.

Index-linking

Building insurers have adopted index-linking in an effort to ensure that sums insured keep pace with building costs. The premiums also increase at the same rate. Index-linking means an adjustment that takes into account an index figure appropriate to the item in question. All indices start from a particular date at a reference point of 100. The index then moves up or down by a number of points each month according to the latest statistical information. An appropriate percentage increase (or decrease) is then found which corresponds to the index movement over the past 12 months.

Proposal Forms

The proposal form is designed to be as 'user friendly' as possible. The number of questions has been reduced to a minimum consistent with asking enough to ensure that all predictable material facts have been addressed. Typical questions are:

- name, address of proposer and property to be insured;

- construction of walls, outbuildings and roofs;

- previous claims;

- previous convictions;

- ownership;

- sum insured;

- number of bedrooms;

- type of house – semi-detached, detached, etc.;

- type of cover.

Claims

We shall now consider the procedure relating to claims that occur. The claims conditions of the policy require the insured to notify the insurers immediately and send a completed claim form as soon as possible after any event giving rise to the claim. The claim form itself asks certain questions similar to those on the proposal form. These are cross-checked by the claims official to ensure that there is consistency.

The insurers require to know how the claim arose and the full circumstances surrounding it. An estimate of the cost of repairs/re-building should be sent as soon as possible. Depending upon the cost, the insurers either deal with the loss in their own claims department or alternatively appoint a loss adjuster to deal with the claim on their behalf. The loss adjuster negotiates and makes recommendations as to settlement to the insurer. The loss adjuster, although remunerated by the insurer, is governed by a code of conduct requiring him to be impartial and he therefore seeks to settle the claim fairly from both parties' viewpoint. Before committing themselves to paying a claim insurers will wish to be satisfied that the event giving rise to the claim is actually covered under the policy and that the notification procedure has been adhered to. They will also check on the practical aspect of whether the last premium has been paid.

A further important consideration is the actual value of the property itself. We have already talked about the need to ensure that each risk must pay its fair contribution to the insurance pool. It would therefore be unfair for the majority of policyholders to declare the full value of their property and for others to be able to declare a lower sum than the full value. It is true that in circumstances where there is a total loss by, say, fire the insured would lose out by insuring for a lesser sum than the full re-building cost. However, the vast majority of claims are for partial losses and insurers have had to decide how to deal with this situation when it arises. It is unusual for very small amounts of under-valuing to be taken into account in a claims settlement. On the other hand, where there is clearly a sizeable understatement of the actual rebuilding cost an insurer may settle a claim on a proportionate basis.

In some commercial property insurances this basis is formalized as what is known as the **pro**

rata average condition. This states that if the sum insured at the time of the loss is less than the re-building cost then the insured should be considered his own insurer for the difference and bear a rateable share accordingly. It is unusual to find this kind of clause in a household buildings or contents policy although this does not imply that insurers are happy with underinsurance.

It is important to bear in mind that the insured, in making the declaration regarding the sum insured, has confirmed that the sum stated represents the full re-building cost of the property (or replacement cost of the contents).

In circumstances such as these it is likely that a compromise will be struck which will effectively scale down the payment of the claim according to the proportion that the sum insured bears to the total re-building costs.

Example

Let us assume that a house has a re-building value of £100,000 and it is insured for only £50,000. This means that the insured is paying premiums based on a total value of £50,000 when he should be paying premiums on the basis of £100,000 sum insured.

There is fire damage to the house which is covered by the policy and the cost of the damage is £5,000. A loss adjuster calls on the householder to discuss the claim and recognizes that the value of the house is clearly understated. The loss adjuster notifies the insurers, and rather than repudiate the claim they operate the principle of average;

$$\text{the claim settlement would be} \qquad \text{value of loss} \qquad \times \qquad \frac{\text{sum insured}}{\text{value of property}}$$

In this example the claim will be settled at

$$£5,000 \qquad \times \qquad \frac{£50,000}{£100,000} \qquad = \qquad £2,500$$

You may feel that this is unfair treatment of the policyholder. However, first the insurance is not a 'first loss' type of policy. The insured has not entered into a contract where he buys a certain amount of cover. He has entered into a contract where he has affirmed the adequacy of the sum insured and has agreed that this shall form the basis of the policy between the insurer and himself. His premium has been geared to an overall re-building figure set at what he has declared to be the re-building cost. This has resulted in an inadequate (and unfair) contribution to the pool or fund.

11.3   Household Contents Cover

The objective of this form of insurance is to provide cover for personal possessions. It is primarily designed to cover items in the home. There are certain extensions of cover as we shall see later which do give a measure of protection outside the home. Virtually everyone has possessions that could be insured. Unfortunately a very high proportion do not arrange any insurance cover. You will remember the earlier illustration of the man whose house was devastated by fire.

Rather like buildings insurance, the cover originally offered for those wishing to insure their household contents was very basic. Fire and theft cover were offered, but it has developed now into a highly complex range of covers and these vary from insurer to insurer, again under a variety of brand names.

Project

Try to obtain as many sample prospectuses as you can to enable you to make comparisons between the various contracts on offer in the market-place.

There are a number of common areas where cover is provided by the majority of insurers and these are summarized as follows:

- Fire (and smoke damage).
- Explosion, earthquake.
- Water damage - storm, tempest, flood and burst pipes (there is usually no excess for this cover under a contents policy).
- Impact damage, by road vehicles, aircraft or animals.
- Riot and civil commotion.
- Theft (as well as the damage that may be caused in the course of a theft).
- Subsidence, landslip and heave.
- Damage by falling trees.
- Accidental damage to underground pipes that serve the premises.
- Architects' and surveyors' fees.
- Loss of rent in the event of the building becoming uninhabitable up to a maximum of (normally) 10% of the contents sum insured.
- Accidental damage cover to specified items such as televisions and fixed glass and furniture.
- Liability cover in respect of all sums that the insured becomes legally liable to pay in respect of third party personal injury and property damage resulting from his tenancy or occupation of the property.

The perils covered can be extended to include accidental damage cover to all contents in the home and may also include loss or damage outside the home. We shall look at these specific extensions to cover that may be required by particular individuals later in this unit.

All Risks Cover

This is a misleading title because there is no insurance that provides cover against every risk.

There are always exceptions and limitations. Practice varies among insurers as to whether this form of cover is offered. Where it is available there are normally exclusions such as:

- mechanical or electrical breakdown;

- wear, tear and depreciation;

- moth or vermin;

- rot;

- damage by domestic pets;

- processes of repair and renovation.

Basis of Fixing Sums Insured

You will recall the principle of indemnity, which is to put the insured in the same financial position he enjoyed immediately prior to a loss. How does this apply when related to the insurance of household contents? Consider the following situation:

Alan Wells has insured his household contents with the ABC Insurance Company and severe damage has been caused to his dining room table by a localized fire. A candle which was part of a table decoration fell over, set fire to the table cloth and ruined the surface of the table. Which of the following courses of action (assuming that the insurers are satisfied that the loss is covered under the policy) do you think would be appropriate?

(a) the insurer should agree to replace the table at the current cost without any deduction for wear and tear;

(b) the insurer should assess a proper degree of contribution from the insured bearing in mind the age of the piece of furniture (in other words take into account the depreciation aspect).

The fact is that either of these options is possible. It will depend entirely upon the basis of the policy. The insured is asked at the outset to identify the full value of household contents and most insurers will offer either a **new for old** basis or what is known as an **indemnity** basis. It is important to recognize that the 'new for old' option does not disregard the principle of indemnity but is a development of it. It recognizes the fact that, for the vast majority of people, it is not an acceptable solution to purchase a second-hand item in the same condition as the item that is lost or damaged. Nevertheless, it is important that an adequate contribution is made to the insurance pool for the risk which is being presented. For this reason the sum insured must be assessed on exactly the same basis as any potential claims settlement.

'New for Old' Cover

In fixing a sum insured for this form of cover the proposer is required to state the total value of household goods (excluding household linen and clothing) on the basis of the cost to replace each item with a similar new item at current prices. In addition a figure must be provided for household linen and clothing which is based upon an assessment of their value which takes into account wear and tear. The reason for this is that, unlike the three piece suite or the kitchen clock, clothing loses its value very much more rapidly and may even lose its value for reasons totally unconnected with wear and tear - for example fashion.

'Indemnity' Basis

If a proposer opts for this form of cover he will be required to indicate a sum insured that takes account of depreciation of all items according to their age and condition.

Whichever method is chosen, there is still a 'full value' declaration which the insured must sign affirming the total value on whichever basis has been chosen. Naturally, the premium for the 'new for old' cover are more expensive to reflect the greater risk.

Automatic Sum Assured

A method of rating gaining popularity is one whereby the insurers provide cover based upon the number of bedrooms and type of house (detached, terraced, etc.) and the sum insured is automatically fixed at figures designed to cater for 90% to 95% of all potential proposers' requirements. This has obvious attractions from the insurer's viewpoint in that it requires very much less administration than personalized and individual quotations and premium calculations on a policy-by-policy basis.

Underwriting

When considering a risk a number of factors are taken into account. These correspond with the questions asked on the proposal form. Each is important and is likely materially to affect the rate or terms quoted, depending upon the answer given.

The particular aspects that vary from proposal to proposal are as follows:

- value of contents - especially jewellery, furs, works of art and other valuables;

- post code - the reason for this is that the claims experience differs widely according to geographic area and the insurers have a number of different rating areas (perhaps as many as nine) with different premium rates for each;

- the number of bedrooms and type of home are relevant if insurers are using a rating matrix linked to those factors.

Claims

In the same way as an insurer appoints a loss adjuster once claims reach a certain limit under a buildings insurance, the same considerations apply under a contents insurance. It is usually the size of the claim that determines the involvement of the loss adjuster, although precise figures vary from one insurer to another.

There are four basic steps in the procedure:

- A detailed report of the circumstances of the loss is given by the insured. This normally takes the form of a description within the claim form.

- Where loss or destruction of an item is involved, the value has to be supported by proof of purchase incorporating the purchase price, or by some other method (unless a valuation has already been provided for the particular item and the insurers have accepted this).

- Confirmation in the claim form that the loss has been reported to the police with the appropriate details of the police station and the personnel involved (if the item has been completely lost or stolen).

- An allowance is made for wear and tear from the amount of any claim unless the basis of settlement is 'new for old'.

Sometimes settlement of a claim is by replacement of a lost item by a supplier recommended by the insurer.

Example

A gold bracelet worth £750 is lost - the sequence of events in the claims process could be as follows:

- Upon receipt of the appropriate claim form together with the proof of purchase the insurers appoint a loss adjuster.

- Insurers contact the police station shown on the claim form to confirm that the loss has been reported to them.

- The loss adjuster visits the insured to discuss the circumstances of the loss, verify these and check the adequacy of cover.

- The loss adjuster negotiates the settlement with the insured.

- The loss adjuster then makes a recommendation for settlement to the insurers.

- The insurers may well confirm to the insured that the claim will be paid in cash, but may advise the insured to call on a particular jeweller nominated by them with a view to obtaining a replacement bracelet.

Combined Buildings and Contents Policies

Many policies are issued as combined policies, especially through building societies. The advantages are:

- The insured pays only one premium to one insurer.

- In the event of a claim, only one claim form is required even if the claim is for both building and contents items.

● There is no dispute between insurers as to which policy should cater for a particular claim.

In this unit we have dealt with the major aspects of policy cover, underwriting features and claim settlements for household insurance. Although the premiums may be relatively modest, the household contents policy with its extensions is one of the most complex policy documents in the insurance marketplace.

Student Activity 1

Before reading the next section of the text, answer the following questions and then check your answers against the pages indicated.

1. Outline the cover provided under the personal liability section of a buildings policy.

(page 240)

2. What is accidental damage cover?

(page 241)

3. What are the advantages of combined buildings and contents cover?

(page 248)

If your answers are basically correct, then proceed to the next section. If significant parts of your answers are wrong, then study the whole of the relevant sections again in detail. Note your areas of weakness, and be prepared for further questions on these areas in the self-assessment section at the end of this unit.

11.4   Other Personal Insurances

Introduction

There are many other types of insurance for the individual, a number of which are available as optional extensions to a householder's policy. However, they are often also available in their own right as a separate policy and, indeed, if there is some special feature present, or if the risk falls outside clearly defined guidelines, a separate policy would be needed. In all probability very much more detailed underwriting information would be necessary before the risk could be accepted. For example, a boat that exceeds the size requirements for 'small craft' would need to be considered separately; so too would a trailer caravan that is fixed on a permanent site (rather than a touring caravan).

For each of the classes of personal insurance we shall identify the basic policy cover and exclusions, and any special underwriting and claims features.

Personal Possessions

At first sight this may seem like an overlap in cover with the household contents insurance. However, you will recall the limitations under that cover which were essentially that any cover provided (whether specified perils or the wider accidental damage cover) essentially relates to damage in the home. The personal possessions form of cover is designed to cater for situations outside the home.

The insurance itself relates to the property of any member of the insured's household and provides protection for accidental loss of or damage to valuables, clothing and personal effects with a monetary limit for any one item (this could be £500). There is a list of specific exclusions either because separate cover is available for these if required, or because they represent a much higher risk than a standard policy envisages. A typical list of excluded items would be:

- hearing aids, contact lenses;
- china, glass or porcelain articles;
- pedal cycles;
- musical instruments;
- camping equipment;
- sports equipment and any specialized sports clothing.

In addition cover is provided for loss of money used or held solely for private social or domestic purposes. A further list of exclusions exists in relation to this cover to clarify the extent of the cover. Excluded items are:

- securities, certificates and documents;
- any depreciation in the value of money;
- book-keeping errors;
- losses that are not reported to the police as soon as possible .

A further additional cover provided by some insurers is the loss incurred as a result of the fraudulent use of credit cards and charge cards by unauthorized persons. This cover would normally apply only if the loss has been reported to the police and the organization that issued the card, within 24 hours of discovery.

The whole of the cover would apply anywhere in the British Isles and for a limited period (say 60 days) worldwide in any one period of insurance.

Because it is an 'all risks' type of cover there are certain exclusions that apply to this and to the sports equipment and pedal cycle policies which we shall look at next. You should therefore think of these as being general exclusions relating to most 'all risks' covers:

- damage due solely to wear and tear;
- damage caused by any cleaning or repairing process, or any restoration or renovation work;
- damage caused by mechanical or electrical breakdown;

- loss or damage caused by nationalization or confiscation by any authority;
- losses by deception (unless it is entry gained to the home which is by deception).

Sports Equipment

This cover is specifically designed to provide protection for accidental loss of or damage to sports equipment and specialized sports clothing owned by any member of the insured household. There is a sum insured which should be fixed at the total value of such equipment and it is this figure which is used for determining the premium. Cover would normally apply anywhere in the British Isles and for a limited period (say 60 days) worldwide in any one period of insurance. In common with the personal possessions cover, cover for sports equipment has list of exclusions which are designed to clarify the extent of cover or point to some areas where a separate policy would be appropriate. The exclusions are:

- the amount of any excess;
- equipment for certain hazardous pursuits - mountaineering, pot-holing, snow skiing, parachuting, wind-surfing and underwater sports;
- motor vehicles and equipment, trailers, caravans, boats, vessels, aircraft, and their accessories;
- any living creatures;
- clothing that is not specialized sports clothing;
- pedal cycles;
- loss or damage during any organized racing or professional sport;
- loss or damage to rackets, cricket bats or golf clubs while in play;
- lost or damaged golf balls (unless they are in the golf bag at the time of loss or damage);
- camping equipment.

The general exclusions listed for personal possessions apply to this cover.

Pedal Cycles

This is another 'all risks' type of cover designed to provide an indemnity in respect of accidental loss of or damage to pedal cycles owned by any member of the insured's household. In common with the sports equipment there is an extension for a limited period outside the British Isles.

The normal exclusions are:

- the amount of any excess;
- theft of the cycle or parts of the cycle while outside the bounds of the home unless

the cycle is in a locked building or has been immobilized by a security device;

- loss or damage during racing;

- loss or damage to tyres or accessories unless the cycle is lost or damaged at the same time.

You will recognize that some of these exclusions relate to areas of wear and tear, and others are specifically geared to pedal cycles, for example the restricted theft cover.

Summary

The personal possessions, sports equipment and pedal cycle covers are basically appropriate responses to particular needs that individuals have. It is for this reason that they are not generally included as a standard part of a household policy but are available as extensions.

Claims settlements under these types of cover would reflect the options generally available to insurers that they may;

- pay the cost of repairing;

- pay the cost of replacing as new;

- replace as new;

- make a cash payment for any item lost or damaged.

There may well be a proviso relating to clothing and pedal cycles to the effect that where an item is not repaired or replaced a deduction will be made for wear, tear or betterment. The cover would normally otherwise be on a 'new for old' basis.

11.5 Trailer Caravans

The cover provided for trailer caravans is **all risks** and applies anywhere in the United Kingdom plus areas that are accessible by limited sea travel. 'Limited' would normally mean a journey not taking longer than 65 hours under normal conditions. There is also an extension for use in Europe during any one period of insurance. This would be typically up to 60 days.

The definition of the caravan is important. The following is a common definition:

> *Any caravan including its fixtures, fittings, awnings, furniture, furnishings, and utensils owned by any member of the insured's household and described in the schedule.*

There are a number of extras that are standard under some insurers' contracts; they may be optional extras under others. They are :

- Recovery and re-delivery - the reasonable cost of getting the caravan to the nearest competent repairer if it is not roadworthy as the result of an insured event.

- Delivery home.

- Loss of use - which means the reasonable cost of hiring another caravan or alternatively finding other accommodation if the caravan is rendered uninhabitable as a result of loss or damage insured under the policy - there would be a monetary limitation to this extension.

- Salvage charges - designed to provide cover for costs and expenses incurred during any sea transit.

The major exclusions are:

- the amount of any excess (there would normally be at least a modest sized excess as standard);

- use as a permanent dwelling, permanently sited;

- use for business purposes;

- loss or damage caused by domestic pets or vermin, insects, mildew or fungus;

- mechanical or electrical breakdown;

- damage to tyres caused by punctures, cuts or bursts;

- valuables, clothing or personal effects (although these may be insured separately under the appropriate cover);

- money, credit and charge cards;

- pedal cycles, prams and push chairs;

- sports equipment and specialized sports clothing;

- loss or damage to furniture, furnishing or utensils caused by theft or malicious persons when the caravan is left unattended unless to the caravan is fully locked.

Many of the exclusions are there to clarify the cover rather than to make specific restrictions. You will recognize that there are a number of other extensions to the household policy (or separate policies) that are designed to cater for some of the excluded items and we have already considered these.

In addition to the cover for the caravan itself, third party liability cover is included if this arises from the use or ownership of the caravan. A limit of indemnity applies to this section (a fixed sum which could be £250,000 or £1,000,000).

There are certain other exclusions that relate to this cover. The main area is the use of a motor vehicle. This means that legal liability cover arising from towing is not covered under a trailer caravan policy. It is covered under a standard motor policy.

Underwriting and Claims Considerations

You will have noticed from the definition of the trailer caravan that no distinction is made between the caravan itself and its fittings and furniture. This is in sharp contrast to the household buildings and contents policies which make clear distinctions between the two areas. However when we look closely at the way in which caravans are manufactured, it becomes apparent that it would be very difficult to draw that kind of clear distinction. So much of the caravan is fitted furniture and fitted units and, by definition, very little of it is movable. There is therefore a single sum insured and normally a rate of premium which is charged according to the sum insured set for the caravan and contents together.

11.6 Small Boats

There is a definition of what is meant by a 'small boat'. This is normally any boat not exceeding 16 feet in length (or in the case of sailing dingy 16ft 6 inches) and with a design speed of less than 17 knots.

The Basis of Cover

Cover is provided under two main headings - loss and damage (to the boat itself) and third party liabilities.

Loss and Damage

The cover provided is accidental loss of or damage to the boat in the British Isles or its coastal waters. There is normally an extension to cover European coastal waters for up to 60 days in any one period of insurance. Because of the limitations of the size of the boat it may well be transported by a recognized passenger carrying service. In this case, provided the journey does not take longer than 65 hours under normal conditions, the transit risk is included.

There is an extensive list of exclusions for this form of cover. This arises partly because of the special risks attaching to seafaring craft. The main exclusions are:

- the amount of any excess;

- wear and tear (in common with other 'all risks' type covers);

- damage resulting from faulty construction or design;

- mechanical or electrical breakdown;

- unseaworthiness;

- scratching or bruising in transit (this is really something of a maintenance item);

- loss or damage caused by theft of the boat's machinery or equipment unless there is forcible entry to the boat itself or to its store;

- loss or damage caused by theft of an outboard motor unless securely locked to the boat by an anti-theft device or in a locked store;

- loss or damage caused by theft of a trailer unless it is immobilized or kept in a locked store when not in use;

- splitting of sails or protective covers by the wind unless the boat is stranded or in collision with another object or resulting from some other damage to the spars;

- loss or damage while the boat is let out on hire or being used for business purposes;

- loss or damage while towing other craft or being towed except in the case of distress.

There is a further exclusion that normally applies to the vessel while taking part in any race. This cover may be provided at an additional premium.

Although this appears to be a daunting list of exclusions, if you analyse them carefully you will see that a number of these relate to areas that we might regard as being clarification of the cover rather than real restrictions. In other words, it would be unreasonable to expect damage by faulty design to be included. The exclusion makes the position absolutely clear.

It is possible with many insurers to link the sum insured to the retail prices index (consumer durables section). In this case the renewal premium is calculated on the revised sum insured at each subsequent renewal date.

The basis of claims settlement for small boats is the cost of repairing the part that is lost or damaged, or at the insurer's option paying the replacement cost for any item lost or damaged **less a deduction for wear or tear or betterment.**

Third Party Liability

As well as the damage to the craft itself there is a clear need for liability cover in the event that injury or damage is caused by the operation of the craft. The third party liability section covers all sums the insured (or a member of the insured's household - if as an extension of a house contents policy) becomes legally liable to pay in respect of:

- accidental bodily injury, death or disease of any person including passengers;

- accidental loss of or damage to property including piers, docks, wharves and jetties arising out of the ownership or use of the boat.

There are exceptions to this section, some of which follow the exceptions under the 'loss and damage' cover. Additional exclusions that relate specifically to the third party section are:

- accidental bodily injury, death or disease of any person employed by the insured (this is more appropriately dealt with as part of an employer's liability insurance);

- loss of or damage to property owned, occupied or in the custody or control of the insured (this is clearly not a third party liability);

- use or custody of the boat by an operator or an employee of any ship yard, marina, repair yard, slipway, yacht club, sales agency or similar organization (they would normally have their own third party cover);

- transit by road or rail (the 'road' exposure is more properly covered by a motor insurance policy).

There is an overall limit of indemnity which may be set at a fixed sum (some insurers have a standard £1,000,000 limit of indemnity). The limit does not apply to certain additional expenses the insurers will pay. These are the costs of salvaging or attempting to salvage the boat, expenses incurred to reduce or avoid loss or damage to the boat and any other costs, expenses and solicitor's fees paid by the insured provided that the insurers have agreed to this in writing.

Underwriting Considerations

Insurers will apply a scale of rates that broadly reflect the type and value of the boat. This may be on the basis of the length of the vessel, or alternatively by class.

Claims

Claims settlements for the damage section are relatively straightforward to deal with. Essentially, they follow the pattern of other general insurance property claims. However, the settlement of liability claims, particularly if another vessel is involved, may be more complex to deal with because of the nature of maritime law

11.7   Horses and Ponies

The insurance of horses and ponies is a specialist area when it relates to animals used for racing or for working purposes. Insurers are usually prepared to provide cover for horses and ponies used for private hacking, gymkhanas, pony club events and show jumping, either as an extension to a household contents policy or as a separate insurance policy. Cover outside this limited use would normally require specialist consideration. The cover provided is normally under four headings:

- death, unless caused by slaughter (except on humane grounds), destruction in compliance with a statute or other order or death from castration or any other surgical operation except where it has been conducted by a veterinary surgeon to save the animal's life;

- the permanent inability to perform the duties for which it is kept excluding:

    - blemishes which mean that the animal is unsuitable for showing because of its appearance;

- veterinary fees paid for treatment excluding:

    - foaling, or protective inoculations, or fees for castration or other surgical operations unless conducted to save the animal's life;

- loss by theft or straying, excluding:

- theft involving any members of the insured's family or employees.

The death or injury must result from an accident, illness or disease sustained in the British Isles and it must occur during the period of insurance.

There may be an excess applicable to this cover, in which case the insurers will not be liable for that first amount of any loss. The amount payable in the event of a claim under the section in respect of death or theft will be either the sum insured for the animal or its market value (whichever is the lower). The cover for 'inability to perform' would provide a payment of either 50% of the sum insured or 50% of its market value immediately before the claim (whichever is the lower). There is a further limit for the payment of veterinary fees usually expressed as an amount for each course of treatment.

In the event of death or theft the claim payment will obviously mean there is no further cover provided by the policy. The policy normally makes it clear that this is true also of the disablement benefit.

The conditions of this cover require the insured to arrange for a veterinary surgeon to attend and treat the animal in the event of an accident or disability. If the animal should die, the insured is responsible for disposal of the carcass although any amount raised from its disposal belongs to the insurers. This supports the principle of indemnity. You will recall that subrogation requires that if there is any remedy open to the insured to recoup money from another source, the insurer is entitled to stand in the place of the insured to avail himself of any such rights or remedies.

Equipment

There may be an extension to the basic cover to provide for accidental loss of or damage to saddles, bridles and riding tack which is owned by the insured, and in addition accidental loss of or damage to any non-motorized horse box identified in schedule.

The exclusions that apply to this cover are those you would expect to find in any 'all risks' insurance. The only additional exclusion for the equipment cover may be loss by theft from a riding establishment. So far as the horse box is concerned there may be an exclusion of loss or damage unless the horse box is immobilized and not attached to the towing vehicle.

A limit applies to the saddles etc. item which may be a standard figure according to the particular insurer. So far as the horse box is concerned a specific sum insured needs to be stated by the insured.

Third Party Liability

There are special liabilities that relate to the ownership or use of animals.

The basic cover provides an indemnity in respect of liabilities expressed as any amounts the insured becomes legally liable to pay for:

- accidental bodily injury, death or disease of any person (other than a member of the family or an employee); and

- accidental loss of or damage to property (other than property owned by or in the custody or control of the insured).

Cover includes any vehicle being drawn by the animal and legal liability for ownership or use of any land or building for stabling or grazing the animal. The legal liabilities of other people who use, or have custody of, the animal are insured provided they are not insured by another policy. A limit of indemnity applies to this section which may be as much as £1,000,000 in respect of any one incident and the usual third party extension applies in respect of other cost expenses and solicitor's fees which need to be paid provided the insurers agree to this in writing.

Other Considerations

Underwriting

We have described in this section cover that applies to animals used for private purposes. If any wider use is needed then insurers would consider this upon receipt of further information. Features of particular interest to insurers are the age and condition of the animal and any previous history of injury, illness or disability.

Claims

Repairs are paid at cost, or the insurers may opt to replace any item damaged less a deduction for wear, tear or betterment.

11.8   Benefit Policies

There is a variety of policies that entitle the policyholder to receive benefit in certain circumstances.

Personal Accident Insurance

Background

This form of insurance dates back to the mid-1800s. Its introduction was prompted by the potential dangers and perceived risk of injury inherent in travelling on trains. From these beginnings it has developed into a class of insurance business that relates to all kinds of accidents, not merely those associated with travel. There still remain the special travel policies, as we shall see later.

You will already know from your study of this subject that personal accident policies issued to individuals are not contracts of indemnity - they are benefit policies. The sums that become payable are not geared to actual earning capacity. Often the benefits are set as 'standard' sums by the insurer. The following amounts of each benefit are illustrative only. They do, however, serve to show the different categories of benefit.

Policy benefits and cover

£10,000 capital sum for death.

£10,000 capital sum for loss of one or more limbs or eyes.

£10,000 capital sum for permanent total disablement.

£50 per week (maximum 104 weeks) for temporary total disablement.

£20 per week (maximum 104 weeks) for temporary partial disablement.

The first important thing to note about this cover is that there must be an 'accident'. Various wordings are used to achieve this but they all seek to ensure that the cause is:

● external;

● violent (although the degree of violence need only be slight);

● accidental so far as the insured is concerned.

Insurers are also keen to make sure that the event giving rise to the claim is independent of other causes. (See Unit 6 regarding proximate cause.)

A mere inability to attend work will not in itself satisfy the policy conditions. There needs to have been an event giving rise to the claim.

The death benefit has a time limit attached to it. It is often defined as needing to occur within 12 months of the event giving rise to the claim. So far as the loss of limb(s)/eye(s) benefit is concerned, this item may also include loss of **use** of limbs or eyes. Where actual loss is referred to, the definition for limbs will usually be 'physical severance at or above the wrist or ankle'.

There is obviously a clearly demonstrable claim in the event of death or loss of limbs or eyes. However, there may be more of a subjective judgment needed in relation to the three 'disablement' benefits. For this reason, insurers will wish to see (sometimes frequent) medical reports. In straightforward cases, the insured's own doctor's report will suffice; in others insurers may ask for an independent medical report completed by an approved medical examiner.

Permanent total disablement is a category of benefit that in the past used always to refer to an inability to carry out **any** occupation. This is still the case with most policies, although there has been the tendency for a relaxation of this definition to include only the insured's usual occupation.

The maximum period during which weekly benefits will be paid may be fixed at different periods up to a normal maximum of five years. Some insurers offer different options; others have a standard fixed period.

Claims

Payments are made under only one of the capital or weekly benefit items for a single event giving rise to a claim.

When a claim payment is made, even under a weekly benefit item, the insurer will wish to pay a single sum once the total amount is established. An interim payment may be possible, but for two major reasons insurers may wish to resist this. The first is that it is administratively inconvenient and it is less expensive to pay a single sum; the other major reason is that a single payment reduces any potential tendency to malinger on the part of the insured.

Underwriting considerations

There is an age limit (often 16 to 70 years) for eligibility. The state of health is important. Insurers will first of all establish that the proposer is not overweight (this may suggest potential heart problems), or underweight (which may be the sign of a wasting disease). Height, age and sex are taken into account and it is normal to allow a 20% variation on 'standard' weights shown in a table used by the insurer. It is rare to find that an insurer will automatically refuse to offer insurance to a person on grounds of being overweight or underweight unless the condition is very significant. What is more likely is that an insurer may call for a medical opinion, provided at the proposer's expense, to consider the matter further. In cases of overweight the insurer would be looking for confirmation that the weight is evenly distributed, blood pressure is not high, and so on. In the case of serious underweight an insurer would wish to be confident that it is not caused by a medical condition or linked to anorexia nervosa. Existing illnesses or disabilities are relevant. Some of these may involve refusal of the proposal. Conditions in this category might include a serious heart problem - not because the heart problem itself will give rise to a claim under the policy, but linked to the fact that if an accident does occur, the recovery period may, at the very least, be extended.

Other conditions may result in the insurers seeking to restrict cover in relation to similar future problems. An example would be a back injury such as a slipped intervertebral disc. In this case insurers may be perfectly content to cover other accidents but will endorse the policy to exclude claims arising from or exacerbated by the existing condition.

The insured's occupation will affect the rate to be charged (especially for the weekly benefits) and, as we have said, the occupation may affect the eligibility for a permanent total disablement benefit related to the insured's usual occupation. A scale of premiums normally applies - at the lower end of this scale there will be clerical occupations and at the upper end the more dangerous occupations such as builders, spidermen and steeplejacks.

This class of business is annually renewable. This means that the insurer has the option of inviting renewal or not. If there has been a series of claims or a particular problem has been identified, the insurer may not wish to invite renewal of the policy. This is in sharp contrast to permanent health insurance. That class of business, as we shall see, is a long-term and permanent contract which may be cancelled only at the option of the insured (provided that the premium payments continue to be maintained).

You will appreciate that as with many other classes of insurance there are a number of simplifications in the procedure that is adopted. Many insurance schemes require little or no information regarding height, weight, medical conditions and so on. There is normally a declaration on a very limited proposal form which requires information regarding visits to the doctor in the past, say, three years. These schemes tend to be insured on the basis of a bulk premium measured against costs plus expenses. It is for this reason that less information tends to be requested. There would, of course, be a declaration of good health in a proposal form and any inability to confirm good health would need to be followed up. In order to maintain the profitability of schemes it is clearly in the interest of both insurer and scheme operator that appropriate underwriting measures are taken to ensure that individuals are paying a fair premium into the insurance pool.

Accident, Sickness and Unemployment Insurance

As with many classes of insurance various brand names are given to these products, but for our purposes we will refer to them as **payment protection plans**. Typically, this class of business provides cover for a mortgage in the event of the borrower being unable to follow his normal occupation as a result of an accident or illness, or having been made redundant. The policy is geared to pay the monthly repayments to the building society or lender over a period normally not exceeding 24 months. There is a deferment period of one, two or three months before payment is made under the policy. Some policies have a further form of cover built in which repays the loan in full should the borrower become permanently totally disabled as a result of accident or illness.

The amount of cover that can be effected under the policy relates directly to the loan repayments, but a number of schemes allow for an increase of this figure in order to cover additional monthly outgoings, which may include gas and electricity bills, and poll tax up to a specified limit above the monthly figure for loan repayment.

Normal exclusions are:

- any previous illness or injury;
- pending or known unemployment before taking out the insurance;
- the first 30, 60 or 90 days of each and every claim;
- wilful acts;
- death of the insured.

In common with certain of the temporary benefits under a personal accident policy, all claims must be supported either by a medical certificate, or by evidence of unemployment, usually on a monthly basis.

From April 1995, anyone with an existing mortgage who became unemployed received no financial assistance from the DSS for the first two months, 50% of the interest for the next four months, and 100% thereafter. Any new borrowers after 1 October 1995 who became unemployed would receive no financial assistance for the first nine months.

This measure has led to a significant increase in the availability of redundancy insurance in the market, which is now even more essential to provide peace of mind to new borrowers in particular.

Since April 1996 all benefits from these policies have been tax-free.

Travel Insurance

Most travel insurances are purchased as part of a holiday package by an individual. It is relatively convenient and quick. However, it is often surprising how many individuals, while they acknowledge the need to purchase insurance, do not realize the extent of cover provided by the particular arrangement on offer. They merely buy the package 'with insurance'.

Of course there are other kinds of travel insurance need - there are many business trips that require some form of cover - but for this course we shall concentrate on travel in connection with holidays.

Travel insurance cover

The normal policy offers the following range of possibilities. Bear in mind that a number of these are grouped together for special package arrangements - others are available as a menu of options:

- **Cancellation, curtailment and change of itinerary** - this provides for the fact that the insured may be forced to cancel, cut short his holiday or have to change the itinerary due to injury, illness or death of a relative, close friend and certain other categories of persons.

- **Missed departure** - this provides cover in respect of late arrival at a port or airport so that a connection is missed through accident or breakdown of an individual's car, or industrial action or strikes affecting public transport.

- **Travel delay** - if an aircraft or ship journey is delayed because of strike or industrial action, or indeed mechanical breakdown, a specific amount will be paid. There is a proviso here that the delay needs to be for a set number of hours (typically 12).

- **Personal accident** - this provides cover for accidents during the journey and pays out fixed sums under the headings described earlier in this unit.

- **Medical and emergency travel expenses** - this is designed to provide for the cost of medical treatment if an insured person becomes ill during the journey, and it will also pay for the necessary additional travel expenses.

- **Hospitalization benefit** - a daily amount is provided towards the cost of admission to a hospital. This is occasionally included in the general medical and emergency travel expenses item.

- **Personal baggage** - cover under this section is provided for loss or damage to luggage (this may often be removed if cover is already provided under an individual's household contents policy). The cover for this sections is 'all risks' and therefore subject to the usual range of exclusions.

- **Delayed baggage** - sometimes baggage may be delayed to such an extent that it is necessary to purchase additional clothing and other necessities. There is a fixed amount payable for this item which may be set at, for instance, £100.

- **Personal money** - an amount of up to £500 per person will be paid in the event of loss of money or credit cards immediately before and during the holiday. This is not a flat sum payment. In the event of a claim, the payment is limited to the amount actually lost.

- **Passport indemnity** - there are additional expenses incurred (possibly additional travel) if a person's passport is lost. This item provides compensation for such additional costs.

- **Personal liability** - normally subject to a limit of £500,000 or £1,000,000, cover is provided for events giving rise to claims for sums that the insured may become legally liable to pay in respect of death or bodily injury to third parties or damage to their property.

Additional covers available from certain insurers include:

- Breakdown cover - provided in respect of private motor cars for the cost of towing and repair.

- 'Get you home' cover - some insurers have arrangements with particular companies that offer specialist facilities in order to ensure that an air ambulance service is available.

Proposal form and risk factors

Proposal forms are normally straightforward and request the following information:

- Name and ages of persons to be insured (normally restricted to a simple family on one proposal form). The definition 'children' normally covers those under 14 years of age. Often the premium charged for children is half the adult equivalent.

- The countries being visited - the rating of the risk is directly related to this factor, e.g. Northern Europe presents less of a risk than does Africa. On the other hand medical costs in the USA are on a significantly higher scale and this is reflected in premium levels.

- The length of holiday or journey - much of this business is written as scheme business and so various combinations of package arrangements have been developed by different insurers and scheme operators. A number of these offer prices in 'bands' which cater for different groups of holiday periods.

Permanent Health Insurance

This type of insurance resembles life assurance in many respects. It is a permanent contract.

By this we mean that provided the premium continues to be paid, once it is in force it is cancellable only at the option of the insured. Unlike personal accident insurance, the insurer has no right to impose terms at renewal or to decline to renew.

As the name suggests, permanent health insurance is concerned with medical conditions that render the insured unable to carry out his or her business or occupation. There is often a substantial excess period (waiting period before claims become payable) which may be 6 months or 12 months. There is also an upper age limit written into the contract.

Underwriting

A detailed proposal form is needed for this class of insurance because of the obvious long-term commitment being entered into by the insurer. Premiums for this class of business are very high when related to personal accident type premiums because of the much wider cover.

Claims

Documentary evidence is required in support of claims, normally in the form of monthly doctor's certificates.

Student Activity 2

Before reading the next section of the text, answer the following questions and then check your answers against the pages indicated.

1. What is the maximum term for payment of a sickness benefit under a permanent health policy?   *(page 263)*

2. What does a payment protection plan cover ?   *(page 261)*

If your answers are basically correct, then proceed to the next section. If significant parts of your answers are wrong, then study the whole of the relevant sections again in detail. Note your areas of weakness, and be prepared for further questions on these areas in the self-assessment section at the end of this unit.

11.9   Mortgage Indemnity Guarantee Insurance

Definition of Cover

Mortgage Indemnity Guarantee (MIG) insurance provides additional security for lenders where a high percentage value of the property is advanced.

It ensures **the lender** against loss on repossession and subsequent sale, for the amount of the loan that it advances above its 'normal' 75% or 80% loan to valuation ratio. It does not provide any protection for the borrower should he have to sell at a loss.

This means that the lender limits its own risk to 75% with the insurance company covering the top slice of the loan. If the lender has to realize its security by selling the property, the insurance covers any deficit arising on that part of the advance over 75%.

The premium is a one-off payment charged to the borrower, and some lenders allow this to be added to the loan. A typical premium for MIG cover in 1995 was:

Loan to valuation up to 90%

= (Total advance - 75% of valuation) x 5%

Loan to valuation of 90% to 95%

= (Total advance - 75% of valuation) x 7.5%

Historical Perspective

MIG insurance has existed in some form since at least the 1930s. By the 1970s, insurance companies discovered that providing guarantees was more lucrative than direct mortgage exposure. At this stage the business was underwritten on a loan-by-loan basis.

Within a short period of time the insurers gave delegated authority to lenders to act as agents and to arrange residential MIG insurance on a block basis without referral to the insurer.

Lack of profit in the mid-1980s led to premium increases, and the housing 'boom' led to a record amount of business being underwritten. Loans for house purchase were readily available and lending criteria were less stringent. The fact that lenders were able to rely on insurance for the top slice of mortgage risk, and that it seemed inconceivable that house prices should decline by more than 25%, exacerbated the problem that was soon to emerge.

Repossessions

In 1988 the onset of recession led to a slump in the property market and a fall in house prices. Recession, unemployment, high interest rates and slow economic recovery led to a record number of repossessions.

The severity of each MIG insurance claim was increased by the collapse in house prices. It is estimated that the average loss to a building society on the sale of a repossessed property in 1991 was £10,000, with a further £16,000 claim under MIG insurance. The Building Societies Commission issued new regulations on loss provision and the calculation of arrears.

Changes to MIG Policies

Insurers reacted strongly in a variety of ways:

- tightening up policy conditions, for example imposing exclusions in respect of fraud or dishonesty by the lender or anyone acting on its behalf;

- reducing cover by imposing a claim limit for any one loan and specifying more precisely the costs and charges that will or will not be covered by the policy;

- introducing the 20% co-insurance clause to align the interests of lenders and insurers more closely, both in underwriting and arrears administration;

- increasing premium rates by up to 60%;

- restricting the type of lending they are willing to insure, for example, the exclusion of all self-certified, non-status products and equity release schemes;

- specifying requirements for regular management information on the quality of mortgages underwritten to allow the insurer to assess more accurately the risks covered;

- withdrawing from the MIG market altogether.

Although it is understandable that action had to be taken, many lenders feel that insurance companies imposed too many restrictions and went too far. In time, this situation will no doubt change.

Alternatives to MIG Insurance

Lenders do have alternative options available to them, and these include:

- Dispensing with MIG cover altogether by changing lending policy to rebalance the risk profile of the lending portfolio. This would involve restricting all lending to a maximum loan to valuation ratio of 75% or 80%.

- Use of a captive insurance company to underwrite MIG business. This would allow access to the lower cost reinsurance market and premiums are deductible for tax purposes. This course of action is subject to strict rules.

- Self-insurance, perhaps by including an amount to pay for mortgage credit risk in its rate margin. This could be achieved by setting differential interest rates for higher-risk borrowers. Lenders can then establish an 'internal fund' with or without excess of loss protection.

- Approach alternative providers of MIG insurance, for example Lloyd's or particular US insurers, to negotiate different levels of cover.

Self-assessment Questions

Short Answer Questions

1. What underwriting factors are relevant for buildings and contents combined insurance?

2. How do insurers maintaining sums insured at proper values?

3. How is underinsurance dealt with in the event of a claim under a household policy?

4. What is meant by 'accident' under a personal accident policy?

5. What is the main difference between personal accident and PHI contracts?

6. Who is protected under a mortgage indemnity guarantee insurance policy?

7. When was MIG insurance first in existence?

8. At what point is MIG insurance required by most lenders?

9. Who pays the premium for MIG insurance cover?

10. Why have policy conditions for MIG insurance been tightened in recent years?

(Answers given in Appendix 1)

Specimen Examination Question

Outline the cover usually provided under the buildings section of a household policy in respect of:

a) storm, tempest and flood;

b) subsidence;

c) fees;

d) personal liability.

(Answers given in Appendix 1)

12

Private Car Insurance

Objectives

After studying this unit, you should be able to:

- outline the basic requirements of the Road Traffic Acts in relation to motor insurance policies;

- identify the range of covers available for private motor risks;

- describe the nature of certificates of motor insurance and cover notes;

- state the basic policy conditions found in a motor policy;

- explain the way the green card system operates;

- provide the key rating factors for private car insurance;

- know the claims procedures for dealing with motor accidents.

12.1 Introduction

In this unit we shall look at the statutory requirements for motor insurance, the types of cover and the basis of rating.

12.2 Compulsory Car Insurance

There are relatively few classes of insurance that are compulsory in the United Kingdom. As we saw earlier, the most significant (in terms of numbers of people affected) is motor insurance. The most important piece of legislation in this connection is the Road Traffic Act 1988. This act brought together the requirements of legislation that had previously operated (the 1972 and 1974 Road Traffic Acts). It also extended the requirements of the previous legislation, as we shall see later.

What does it mean when we say that motor insurance is compulsory? It means that it is illegal to drive (or be in charge of) a vehicle on a public road unless there is in force a policy of insurance that covers certain liabilities towards others and the property of others. Note that the law is not concerned with the actual risk of damage to the vehicle itself. This is entirely a matter for the individual to decide upon. Let us examine precisely the amount and extent of cover required by law.

A policy that complies with the terms of the 1988 Act will cover (at least) the following:

- liability for death or bodily injury to any person arising out of the use of the motor vehicle,

  - in the United Kingdom;

  - in any other EU country;

- liability for death or bodily injury to any passenger in the vehicle;

- liability for loss or damage to property belonging to other persons for a sum of at least £250,000;

- emergency treatment of injuries arising out of the use of the vehicle.

These are the minimum requirements. Most policies go beyond this. Particular points to bear in mind are that the liability for death or bodily injury (including passenger liability) must be unlimited in amount. Liability for third party property damage was introduced at the beginning of 1989 to comply with an EC directive which made such insurance compulsory but for a lesser sum than the £250,000 introduced in the United Kingdom. The emergency treatment fee is payable regardless of negligence. Any payment under this section does not affect the no claims discount.

All member countries of the EU agree to abide by directives issued by the EU. It is not an 'imposed' situation in the way you might suppose because their decision is reached by those same member countries who vote on these matters with a view to harmonization of local legislation. The normal procedure is to allow a certain passage of time before it is necessary to legislate in any particular country. In the case of the EC directive relating to third party property damage, this was known years in advance of its compulsory introduction in the United Kingdom.

In practice there is a variety of basic policies offered by insurers. Theoretically insurers could offer Road Traffic Act only cover. This was certainly an option exercised by some insurers before the advent of compulsory third party property damage. Nowadays, however, the marginal difference between Road Traffic Act cover and third party only cover has rendered the former redundant for all practical purposes.

12.3   Third Party Only Cover

Third party only cover for private car policies provides the following :

- legal liability for third party personal injury (including injury to passengers) and third party property damage, which is unlimited in amount;

- emergency treatment fees for those injured or requiring hospital treatment.

The major point to note is that the third party property damage (as well as the personal injury) cover is unlimited in amount. This therefore goes beyond what is required by law.

12.4   Third Party, Fire and Theft Cover

Third party, fire and theft cover, in addition to what is covered by a third party only policy, also includes:

● damage to the vehicle itself by fire, theft or attempted theft.

12.5   Comprehensive Cover

As the name suggests this is a much wider form of cover than third party, fire and theft. The most notable addition is the provision of accidental damage cover to the vehicle itself. The term 'comprehensive' may be somewhat misleading in the sense that there is no policy that provides totally comprehensive cover. However, it is not just the cover to the vehicle itself that is provided by this form of policy, there are a number of other benefits.

Extensions to Cover under a Comprehensive Polciy

The basic cover provided by a comprehensive policy can be extended in a number of ways, considered in turn below.

Injury to policyholder and/or spouse

Most insurers offer a limited amount of personal accident cover to the policyholder and/or spouse. Some insurers offer special personal accident benefits to the policyholder only; a few omit this section altogether. The amount offered by insurers ranges usually between £1,000 and £5,000 if the policyholder or spouse dies or loses the use of one or more limbs or eyes. The accident must be connected with a car. The car may belong either to the policyholder or to someone else. Other terms follow the general pattern of personal accident policies (see Unit 11, section 8).

Medical expenses

Under this section insurers undertake to make a payment towards medical expenses incurred in treatment of the policyholder, or the driver or any occupant of the insured car as a result of an injury received in direct connection with the insured car. The insurers pay up to a certain amount for each person - often £50 or £100. Payment is made to the policyholder even if the claim relates to passengers. This should not be confused with the emergency treatment clause which relates to hospital charges under Section 154 of the Road Traffic Act 1988.

Rugs, clothing and personal effects

The policy provides a limited amount of cover if personal items belonging to the policyholder or to passengers are damaged by theft or accidental damage. There is a limit to the amount payable for such items, normally £50 or £100. Payments are usually made to the policyholder even if a lost item belongs to a passenger. Any 'own damage' excess would not apply to this cover.

There are two groups of exceptions:

- money, stamps, tickets, documents or securities;
- goods and samples carried in connection with a trade or profession. These items could be particularly attractive to thieves, or easily damaged by fire or accident.

If cover is required a separate insurance policy is necessary - possibly as an extension of a household contents policy.

It is worth noting the situation with regard to radios in cars. If a radio is fitted permanently into the car, insurers consider it as part of the car and the policyholder should take account of the value of the radio in stating the value of the car. This also means that any claim for damage to a radio would be subject to any policy excess. However, theft cover is not subject to the provisions of an excess clause as we shall see later, and if a radio which is permanently fitted to the vehicle should be stolen this would be dealt with as a theft claim in the usual way. However, if the radio is not permanently fitted to the vehicle then it is subject to the limitations of the section for rugs, clothing and personal effects; the most relevant of these will be the overall limit of value.

12.6 Certificates of Motor Insurance

We have already mentioned the Road Traffic Acts and the fact that these stipulate a minimum level of cover that has to be provided by every private car policy issued in the United Kingdom. There are also regulations regarding the issue of certificates of motor insurance and these must be complied with by law. The regulations provide, among other things, that:

- Where a policy relates to a specified vehicle and extends also to cover the driving of other vehicles, the insurers must issue a second certificate on the demand of the insured.
- Insurers must keep records of certificates issued for at least one year from the date of expiry.

There are specific headings that must appear on certificates of insurance. These are:

- Registration mark of vehicle (or description of vehicles).
- Name of policyholder.
- Effective date of the commencement of insurance for the purposes of the relevant law.
- Date of expiry of insurance.
- Persons or classes of persons entitled to drive.

- Limitations as to use.

Certificates end with a statement signed by an official of the authorized insurers: 'I hereby certify that the policy to which this certificate relates satisfies the requirements of the relevant law applicable in Great Britain, Northern Ireland, the Isle of Man, the Island of Guernsey, the Island of Jersey and the Island of Alderney.'

12.7   Cover Notes

A cover note is, in effect, a temporary policy of insurance. It is issued pending preparation of the permanent document, but it also fulfils the function of a temporary certificate of motor insurance. It contains:

- a statement to the effect that the insured is held covered in the terms of the insurer's usual form of policy for the risk subject to any special terms noted on the cover note;

- terms of cancellation - usually 24 hours upon written notice being given;

- the date and time of commencement of cover;

- the duration of cover - often 30 or 60 days, although a shorter period can be specified when appropriate;

- the registered number of the vehicle and its make, or a description of vehicles covered;

- the name and address of the insured;

- the purposes of use of the vehicle;

- any special terms - such as driving limited to the insured, or an excess;

- a certified statement that it is issued in accordance with the provisions of the Road Traffic Acts.

It is very important to note that a **cover note cannot be backdated**. For example, if a person buys a vehicle one day but for some reason does not arrange insurance cover until the next day, the cover note can commence only from that later date. The person may not drive the vehicle until that time. If he does, he will be driving without insurance and committing an offence under the Road Traffic Acts.

When a 'permanent' certificate is issued to supersede the cover note, it is in order to date the certificate from the earliest date shown on a cover note provided there has been no 'break' of cover.

12.8   Policy Conditions

Regardless of the extent of policy cover, there are certain policy conditions common to all private motor insurances.

Notification

This standard condition covers three basic requirements:

- The insured or his legal representatives must tell the insurer as soon as possible about any incident which might give rise to a claim.

- The insured or his legal representatives must forward immediately to the insurer all written documents (letter, claim, writ, summons, etc.) which the insured receives as a result of the incident.

- The insured or his legal representatives must advise the insurer in writing immediately they have word (written or oral) of any prosecution pending, or of an inquest (in England, Northern Ireland or Wales) or of a fatal accident enquiry (in Scotland).

Control of Claims and Subrogation

This particular condition gives the insurer the right to handle the claim in order that it may be dealt with to the best advantage. The condition modifies the common law rule. You will recall that insurers have the automatic right to stand in the place of the insured **after** payment of a claim. This condition provides the insurer with opportunity of exercising the right**before any payment is made**.

Cancellation

The insurer is entitled to cancel the policy giving (normally) seven days' notice by registered letter to the insured at his last known address and in this event the insurer will return to the insured the premium less the *pro rata* proportion for the period the policy has been in force.

In practice this condition is rarely invoked. The circumstances in which insurers may decide to issue notice of cancellation are where they may suspect that the risk is totally different from what had been expected originally, or if the insured has been guilty of a breach of utmost good faith although there is no acceptable evidence that would stand up in a court of law. The Road Traffic Act states that insurers must recover the Certificate of Motor Insurance within seven days.

Contribution

The contribution clause follows the normal pattern of such clauses stating that if there are any other existing insurances covering the same loss, damage or liability, the insurers should not pay more than their rateable proportion of any loss, damage, compensation costs or expense.

You can imagine that there are a number of situations where more than one policy would cover the same event.

Example

If a driver were to drive a friend's car then there are likely to be two policies in force covering third party personal injury and property damage. The first is the owner's policy and the second is an extension normally granted under a private car policy that the user would have, giving cover for the driving of other vehicles not owned by him. Since 1976 motor insurers have agreed voluntarily that claims in such circumstances are paid by the insurers of the vehicle involved, although in accordance with the terms of the policy the driver should still notify his own insurers of the accident.

Maintenance and Examination

This condition underlines the insured's obligations to act as though he were uninsured. It relates to the maintenance of the vehicle in an efficient condition and gives insurers the right to examine the vehicle. In practice this right is rarely exercised unless there are very unusual circumstances.

Arbitration

The arbitration clause is intended to deal with any disputes that arise as to the **amount** to be paid in settlement of a claim under a policy. If there is a dispute as to whether liability exists or not, this is not a matter to be dealt with by the arbitration clause. Provided that liability is admitted under the policy then any difference in amount is referred to an arbitrator to be appointed by the two parties in accordance with current statutory provisions.

12.9   No Claims Discount

One of the major features of motor insurance is the incentive given to those policyholders who do not make a claim during the preceding year to reduce the level of premium charged for the forthcoming year. There are many arguments as to whether the no claim discount system provides an incentive to policyholders to drive safely or whether it merely creates administrative work for insurers. Some insurers have tried to abolish the practice for certain types of motor insurance. Others have abolished it where private motor insurance is offered as part of a personal insurances package. Nevertheless, the idea of a motor premium reducing annually in the absence of claims remains popular with the motorist.

The no claim discount is exactly what its title indicates. If a policyholder completes a year of insurance without making a claim, a discount is allowed on the premium when the policy is renewed. Claims cost insurers money, regardless of whether the policyholder was to blame for the accident. Much ill feeling arises because motorists feel that they should not be penalized when an accident was due to circumstances beyond their control; that is to say they feel that the discount should be a 'No Blame Discount'. More than ten years ago one insurer produced such a scheme but it proved unsuccessful.

It is true that insurers will reinstate a no claim discount provided any uninsured losses are recovered from elsewhere.

Example

Mary Smith has driven up to a crossroads and indicates she wishes to turn right. She applies the brake and the car stops. While she remains stationary, Bill Jones misjudges the distance between the two cars and crashes into the back of the stationary car. It is quite clear who is to blame and the insurers of Miss Smith's car pay for the damage which has been inflicted but not the £50 excess which applies to her policy. She in turn claims this £50 from Mr Jones' insurers who pay the amount in full to Miss Smith. Miss Smith's insurer reinstates her no claim discount.

In practice, of course, there are many situations that are not as clear-cut as this. In these circumstances, where blame may be apportioned between the two parties, both lose their no claim discount. We shall look at the major agreements which exist between insurers later in this unit. There are also those circumstances where no fault attaches to the insured but there is no means of recovery available. Typically this arises when a vehicle is damaged while parked and it is not possible to trace the guilty driver of the other car which caused the damage. If a claim is pursued there is no potential for recovery of the insurer's outlay and the no claim discount is therefore forfeited.

No claim discount schemes are many and varied. In private car insurance, the no claim discount increases in most cases over a period of between three and six years, the majority of scales spanning four or five years. Discounts range in most cases from 20% to 65% and it normally takes four years to build up to the insurer's maximum discount. Should a policyholder make a claim, the no claim discount is usually reduced by two stages. This means that if a policyholder is earning first or second year discounts, he will revert to full premium after a claim. On the other hand, if he is earning a larger discount, he will still be allowed some reduction of the next renewal premium. Because of the sensitivity of motorists to any loss of no claim discount there is a trend among insurers to offer what is called a 'protected no claim discount'. This may be known by a number of different terms. Its purpose is to cushion the effects of the occasional claim and to encourage the policyholder to remain with his existing insurer. It does this by allowing the discount to continue but identifying in some way on the renewal notice the fact that there has been a claim, often by showing 'number of claims free years - nil'. This may make it difficult to transfer to another insurer at renewal while maintaining the higher discount level. Some insurers have introduced this feature at standard premium rates, others make a small charge for it.

12.10 The Green Card System

The Green Card is an internationally recognized certificate of motor insurance. It guarantees that the motorist to whom it has been issued has an insurance that complies with the compulsory motor insurance requirements of the country he is visiting.

The system is administered by a network of bureaux. Each country subscribing to the Green Card System sets up its own bureau. In the United Kingdom it is the Motor Insurers' Bureau. It is this organization that is responsible for controlling the issue of Green Cards in each individual country and also settling claims that arise from accidents involving visiting motorists. Each bureau has reciprocal arrangements with every other bureau. After settling a claim, the bureau concerned asks the bureau that issued the Green Card for reimbursement. The latter then asks the insurer of the motorist responsible for the accident for reimbursement. In practice, this rather clumsy chain of settlements is short-circuited, and the insurer often deals with the third party direct through his local agent or branch.

Insurers normally charge an additional premium when they issue a Green Card. This is not a charge for the Green Card itself - because at the same time as requesting the issue of a Green Card most policyholders require the full policy cover to be extended to the territory to which they are travelling.

Theoretically there is no need to have a Green Card for travel in any EU member country. In practice it still seems advisable to carry one to ease otherwise difficult administrative problems. For instance the motorist may be asked at any time while in another country to produce evidence of insurance. This is particularly likely after an accident. The Green Card is recognized immediately by the police and possibly also by other nationals of the country. On the other hand, the motorist may have difficulty convincing the police that his ordinary certificate of motor insurance is an acceptable alternative.

Spanish Bail Bonds

Although Spain is a member of the EU and subscribes to the Green Card system, the visiting motorist who is involved in an accident may still face considerable difficulties. There has been a tendency for a presumption of fault on the part of the driver in cases of third party personal injury. The result of this is that the motorist may be taken into custody and his car impounded. The only way of obtaining release is to produce bail for a considerable sum.

For this reason insurers issue Spanish bail bonds. The bond provides a guarantee, usually for £500 or £1,000, upon which a motorist can call in the event of being taken into custody and/or having his car impounded. On production of a bond the Spanish bureau in Madrid, or the insurer's local branch, will give the police a guarantee or, if necessary, deposit the amount of money required as bail, provided it is within the amount of the bond.

Insurers make this money available simply as bail. If the authorities retain any of it as a fine, the motorist must reimburse the insurer. The bail bond is obtainable only before leaving the United Kingdom. Most insurers make a small charge for the facility.

12.11 Days of Grace

For the vast majority of general insurances, insurers allow days of grace. This means that there is a period beyond the date when the policy has technically expired when the insurers will be prepared to accept the renewal premium and treat the policy as if there has been no break in cover. The normal period of grace for, say, a householder's policy is 15 days. Motor insurances is different. **There are no days of grace for motor insurance.** If the premium is paid after the renewal date, a new certificate must be prepared showing the date of payment as the effective date. To issue a certificate which was effective from the previous renewal date would amount to backdating cover if it had not actually been issued until after the renewal date. That would be an offence.

This clearly creates difficulties for insurers who may wish to treat the insurance as being continuous. For this reason most insurers print a temporary cover note on the back of their renewal notices. This is effective for 15 days and gives only the cover necessary to comply with the Road Traffic Acts.

If the renewal premium reaches the insurer within this period a certificate dating from the first day of the new period of insurance can be issued. There has been no 'break' in cover.

The alternative method adopted by some insurers is to print the temporary cover note as an addendum to the main certificate of insurance. This is designed to achieve the same objective.

If however, the policyholder obtains cover elsewhere or takes some action which implies that he does not intend to accept the renewal offer, he cannot then take advantage of the temporary certificate. If the policyholder does not receive the renewal notice or, having received the notice, remains unaware of the temporary certificate of a motor insurance, he cannot accept an offer of which he was unaware.

Student Activity

Before reading the next section of the text, answer the following questions and then check your answers against the pages indicated.

1.   What is the compulsory requirement for motor policies?   *(page 268)*

2.   What personal effects are usually covered under a motor policy?   *(page 270)*

3.   Why does a no claims discount system cause problems for insurers?   *(page 274)*

If your answers are basically correct, then proceed to the next section. If significant parts of your answers are wrong, then study the whole of the relevant sections again in detail. Note your areas of weakness, and be prepared for further questions on these areas in the self-assessment section at the end of this unit.

12.12 Trailers

Private motorists sometimes use their cars to tow a broken-down car or trailer. The trailer could be a boat trailer, a small open cart, a trailer tent or a trailer caravan. Whatever it is, insurers regard it as part of the car while it is attached to the car. It is therefore covered against the risks of causing injury to third parties or damage to their property in exactly the same way as the car. There is, however, no cover for damage to the trailer itself, or to its contents.

12.13 Underwriting

There is a great deal of agreement between insurers as to the important factors to be considered when deciding upon the rate to charge for a particular risk. They broadly fall into three categories. The first is the scope of cover required, the second is the frequency with which claims are likely to occur and the third is the severity of a claim if it should occur. Frequency and severity are very important criteria in assessing the level of premium.

Type of Car

You will know from your own experience that there is a wide variety of cars being driven about the public roads in the United Kingdom - everything from the very small family saloon car through to the very expensive, customized, high-performance vehicle. Insurers tend to use a points system in order to arrive at a premium - each of the major components is represented by a number of points which are then added together, and the consequent number of points related to a chart of premiums.

There are some exceptions to this general rule about methods of rating. The most common of these would be the policies offered to particular market segments. Many insurers have special flat rates for those, say, over 50 years of age who meet certain requirements regarding claims history. Nonetheless by far the most common method of rating is the points system. The points rating is applied to each of the different models and there is a grouping of different types of car according to a variety of factors which will include:

- the cost of the vehicle;
- the cubic capacity of the engine;
- the performance of the vehicle;
- the ease with which repairs may be carried out;
- the attractiveness to thieves;
- the availability of spare parts.

This will give you a picture of the factors relevant for rating purposes in relation to the car itself.

Age of the Driver

Most insurers regard anyone under the age of 25 as 'young'. This means that the scale of basic premiums charged become less as the insured gets older. Insurers are able to extract a variety of sophisticated statistics which demonstrate the relative claims costs and frequencies for different age groups. These are reflected in the points allocated for this feature.

Rating District

The area in which a policyholder keeps his car and the area in which he uses his car are not always the same. Insurers base their premiums on the district in which the policyholder garages or keeps his car because it is a recognizable factor and it provides a reasonable guide as to the area in which the car is likely to be used. It would be extremely difficult to take account of all the variations in areas in which the policyholder may drive. However, if it is known for instance that a vehicle is used for commuting to London each day, insurers may well wish to apply a loading to the 'normal' rating which would be produced merely by looking at the garage district. A scale of district rates applies. The lowest rated are the islands off the coast of Great Britain, for example Anglesey, and the highest rated are the cities, especially London. With the increasing sophistication of rating structures many insurers use the post code as a rating factor and have a significant number of different rating districts. This is especially true of the 'direct' writers.

Cover

The greater the amount of cover, the higher the premium. Comprehensive cover is more expensive than third party, fire and theft, for the same insured.

Use of the Car

You will remember when we looked at the various headings in the certificate of insurance that one of these was the class of use. Generally speaking insurers have three or four classes of use. The first, and generally the least hazardous, is social domestic and pleasure purposes only. Not all insurers have this restricted class of use as their normal minimum. Many include the business use of the policyholder and/or the policyholder's spouse, although some have these as a second or third class of use. There are, however, restrictions even under this form of cover. It does not allow for commercial travelling. If cover for commercial travelling is required a different class of use is used, and the premium adjusted accordingly. Each of the classes of use is designed to reflect the likely exposure of the vehicle in terms of the number of miles and amount of time it is on the road. It is not an exact science, but it would be extremely unusual for a commercial traveller to drive fewer miles in a year than an individual who was using the vehicle solely for pleasure purposes.

Occupation

There are certain occupations that require specific underwriting action. Some occupations are regarded by certain insurers as rendering the risk undesirable or altogether unacceptable. In this category are those in the armed services, members of the entertainment profession and betting shop proprietors. Certain other occupations require special underwriting consideration. The most notable of these is a person who is engaged in the motor trade.

A standard extension is provided to a normal private car policy that allows the policyholder to drive another motor car or motor cycle not belonging to him (it provides cover for third party risks).

Age of Car

We have already looked at the type of car as being relevant in rating terms. It is also true that the age of the car is a relevant factor. Most insurers allow sometimes quite substantial discounts for cars that are more than, say, seven to ten years old. It is difficult to be precise in this area because insurers have fixed their discounted figures at different levels and different ages of car.

Rating Summary

It cannot be emphasized too strongly that in underwriting an individual risk and deciding upon the rate it is necessary to look at all the factors in combination. Individually they may not pose a problem, but taken together they may produce a different picture.

The options available to an underwriter when considering a proposal are as follows:

- to decline the proposal altogether;
- to increase the premium that would normally be charged (or reduce it if there are specially favourable features);
- to apply some form of restriction to the cover (an 'own damage' excess or a restriction of cover for those aged under 25, for example);
- to restrict the driving (to the insured only, or to the insured and spouse);
- to accept the risk on normal terms.

12.14 Claims

The claims condition of the motor policy requires notification of a claim or an event likely to give rise to a claim in writing as soon as possible. This is so even if the insured does not intend to make a claim on the insurer.

Example

Jim Brown is reversing his car in order to park the vehicle and in doing so slightly misjudges the position of a stationary vehicle already parked at the kerbside. The result is minor damage to the bumper of the parked car and Jim wishes to pay for the damage himself in order that his no claim discount should not be prejudiced. He must still complete an accident report form for the insurers making it clear to them that he does not intend to make a claim under the policy.

You should be aware that this is an area that has caused a number of disputes between insurer and insured in the past. The main problem likely to arise is that the insured, having agreed to deal with the payment, finds that the amount of the damage is considerably more than had at first been thought. At the point where this is discovered he may feel that he would rather his insurer had dealt with the claim. However, from the insurer's viewpoint, their position may well have been prejudiced because of the inability to carry out the normal investigations associated with the settlement of a claim. It is important when providing advice that it is made clear to any insured who wishes to settle a matter of this sort himself, the potential problems associated with this course of action.

Most motor insurance claims for damage to the vehicle are settled on a repair basis. The process for settling claims would normally be as follows:

- an accident occurs between two cars (with no personal injury being sustained) but both vehicles are damaged and in need of repair;

- the insured fills in an accident report form which will ask for details such as:

    - description of how the accident happened;

    - the weather conditions at the time of the accident;

    - the speed of the car just before the accident;

    - full names of any independent witnesses.

The other information requested is normally similar to that asked on the proposal form itself:

- an estimate of the repair costs is requested by the insurers. This can be obtained fairly quickly and should be sent to the insurers;

- any other relevant correspondence such as letters from the other party should be sent to the insurer;

- most insurers would require at least two estimates of repair costs unless the insurer has recommended a particular repairer;

- the insurers would ask a specialist (either an independent loss adjuster or their own specially trained motor assessor) to check the vehicle and confirm that the damage is consistent with the claims details that have been submitted before giving authorization that the repairs can proceed;

- once repairs have been authorized and the work carried out, insurers will pay the final account direct to the garage less the amount of any excess that may apply.

In this section we have looked at the special considerations that apply to motor insurance claims. The claims department would also carry out the usual functions of establishing that the policy is in force, that the type of damage is covered by the policy and that notification of the claim is within the prescribed period.

Self-Assessment Questions

Short Answer Questions

1. What is a motor cover note?

2. What is the purpose of a green card?

3. How many days of grace are allowed under motor policies?

4. Which is the least hazardous class of use for a motor policy?

5. What is a Spanish Bail Bond?

(Answers given in Appendix 1)

Specimen Examination Question

Explain the different rating factors used in private motor insurance and the significance of each.

(Answer given in Appendix 1)

13

BUILDING SOCIETIES ACT 1986

Objectives

After studying this unit, you should be able to:

● describe the effect of the Building Societies Act 1986.

13.1   Overview of the 1986 Act

There are two general characteristics of the 1986 Act you should understand. First, it is essentially enabling in nature. It is up to each individual building society to decide which of the trading powers permitted under the act it wishes to exercise beyond the principal purpose of a building society (this term is considered in the next section). Do not assume, therefore, that what one society chooses to do is necessarily the same for any other society, particularly when you are answering examination questions.

Secondly, the 1986 Act has been drafted deliberately to be flexible and to permit continuous change and development of building society legislation. Within the 1986 Act there are 78 occasions where amendments may be made by way of regulations, order, rules or directions. This point is illustrated by the fact that the Act has been amended or changed by 12 statutory instruments in 1986, 25 in 1987, 12 in 1988 and 10 in 1989 which are still in force. From an examination point of view this means that it is very important to keep up to date; however, you are not required to know about any legislation that occurs within six months of the examination, although due credit can be given where appropriate.

Before delving into the detail and specifics of the 1986 Act it is useful for us to look at a summary of its general features and the framework within which building societies operate:

● Building societies continue to retain their mutual status, being owned essentially by their members.

● Building societies may only undertake activities permitted by the 1986 Act and subordinate legislation.

● The predominant trading asset must be first mortgage advances to owner-occupiers secured against their home.

- At least 60% of funds raised must be from the retail savings sector and at least 50% of funds must be from shares as opposed to deposits.

- The maximum proportion of total assets that may be liquid assets (i.e., investments and cash) is 33.33%.

- Building societies have enabling powers (subject to certain restrictions) should they wish to exercise them to:
    - form and hold shares in corporate bodies;
    - offer a range of financial services;
    - hold other trading assets, e.g. unsecured loans, residential land.

- Building societies are supervised by the Building Societies Commission, which has substantial powers both of control and in formulating subordinate legislation.

- Building societies must comply with seven prudential management requirements, one of which is to satisfy minimum capital adequacy criteria set by the Building Societies Commission.

13.2   Structure of the 1986 Act

The Building Societies Act 1986 is divided into 126 Sections contained within 11 Parts, together with 21 Schedules. These are set out below for your information.

Part	Sections	
I	1-	The Building Societies Commission
II	5-	Constitution of Building Societies
III	10-	Advances, Loans and other Assets
IV	24-	Protection of Investors
V	34-	Power to Provide Services
VI	36-5	Powers of Control of Commission
VII	58-7	Management of Building Societies
VIII	71-	Accounts and Audit
IX	83-	Complaints and Disputes
X	86-	Dissolution, Winding Up, Mergers, Transfers of Business
XI	104-126	Miscellaneous and Supplementary and Conveyancing Services

Schedules

1   The Building Societies Commission.

2   Establishment, incorporation and constitution of building societies.

3	Authorization: supplementary provisions.
	Advances: supplementary provisions.
5	The Building Societies Investor Protection Board.
6	Insolvency payments: trusts and joint or client account holdings.
	Investors: special provisions.
8	Powers to provide services.
9	Directors: requisite particulars of restricted transactions.
10	Requisite particulars of income of related business.
11	Auditors: appointment, tenure, qualifications.
12	Schemes for investigation of complaints.
13	Schemes for investigation of complaints: recognition, accession, etc.
14	Settlement of disputes.
15	Winding up supplementary provisions.
16	Mergers: supplementary provisions.
17	Transfers of business: supplementary provisions.
18	Amendments of enactments.
19	Repeals and revocations.
20	Transitional and saving provisions.
21	Provision of conveyancing services by recognized institutions and practitioners.

Throughout this unit any reference to Sections or Schedules will mean the 1986 Act unless it is otherwise specifically stated.

This Act is dealt with in detail in the Law and Practice subject. However, it is strongly recommended that you obtain a copy of the 1986 Act for your own reference.

13.3   Subordinate Legislation and Case Law

Subordinate legislation consists mainly of statutory instruments, which we shall now consider.

Statutory Instruments

Statutory instruments have already been mentioned on several occasions but require further explanation. Statutory instruments, or subordinate legislation, enable an act of parliament to be 'modified', i.e. updated, amplified or amended, provided its principal act contains provisions for such changes to be made.

Examples of the uses of statutory instruments include:

- to fill in detail not covered in the 1986 Act itself (for example, the assets a society may hold in liquid form, the definition of residential use for the classification of an advance as class 1, etc.);

- to alter the various quantitative limits or to widen the powers of societies up to the full extent of the 1986 Act, to take account of market developments;

- to make adjustments to the 1986 Act that become necessary over time, either as a result of market changes or perhaps because of interpretative difficulties;

- to provide for certain detailed matters that need to be revised on a regular basis, for example, regulations governing the form of annual accounts.

It is important that you understand the concept of subordinate legislation and are aware of the major changes that such facilities can bring about. For example, Schedule 8 to the 1986 Act (the Schedule that sets out details of the financial services that building societies may provide) was replaced by a statutory instrument that brought in a completely new Schedule 8.

Statutory instruments are 'coded', for example, 'SI 1988 No. 1197', and are then followed by a title and commencement date.

'SI' indicates statutory instrument, 1988 indicates year of origin, and 1197 indicates numerical sequence in year (from which it will be obvious that across the entire spectrum of legislation many hundreds of statutory instruments are issued every year).

Schedule 1 states that the Statutory Instruments Act 1946 shall apply to all powers of the Commission of making statutory instruments under the act as if the Commission were a Minister of the Crown.

Statutory instruments can be divided into three main types:

- Those made by the Commission alone, generally on points of detail.

- Those laid before each House of Parliament which automatically come into effect unless they are put to a vote and lost (the negative resolution procedure). These are usually made by the Commission, usually with the agreement of the Treasury, or by the Treasury alone.

- Those that have to be approved by each House of Parliament (the positive resolution procedure). This procedure is generally required for the more important changes. These are usually made by Treasury and may be in consultation with the Commission.

Most statutory instruments are instigated by the Building Societies Commission, a fact that once again emphasizes the importance of the Commission both in controlling building societies and in developing the regulatory framework.

Case Law

As with many different areas of law, a body of case law exists in relation to building societies. This can also be referred to as common law, i.e. law resulting from court decisions which establish precedents. Quite often these cases relate to disputes between building societies and individuals or companies and may involve interpretation or reinterpretation of particular statutes or previous case law. However, these are not dealt with in this course.

Prudential Notes

Prudential notes are documents issued by the Building Societies Commission which, as the name implies, provide guidance to building societies concerning their management and financial performance. Their key purpose is to assist building societies in making sure that they do not contravene the requirements of the 1986 Act, subordinate legislation or necessitate the Commission to exercise its substantial powers of control.

Thus if a building society complies fully with a prudential note on a particular matter then it will have satisfied the Building Societies Commission that it has not contravened the 1986 Act. If, however, a building society has not complied with a prudential note then clearly the Commission may give consideration to whether it should exercise any of its supervisory powers over the building society. The moral for building societies is therefore clear; it disregards or contravenes a prudential note at its peril!

Prudential Notes are issued by the Commission from time to time and, for example, those currently in force include two issued in 1986, six issued in 1987 and five issued in 1988.

Student Activity

Before reading the Summary, answer the following questions and then check your answers against the pages indicated.

1.   What is meant by the term mutual?   *(page 283)*

2.   Who supervises building societies?   *(page 284)*

If your answers are basically correct, then proceed to the Summary. If significant parts of your answers are wrong, then study the whole of the relevant sections again in detail. Note your areas of weakness, and be prepared for further questions on these areas in the self-assessment section at the end of this unit.

Summary

The 1986 Act is enabling, i.e. it is for building societies to choose what new powers they wish to exercise.

The 1986 Act is deliberately designed to enable considerable change and development of building society legislation without necessarily requiring the passing of a new Act.

The main sources of legal authority on building societies are:

- the 1986 Act;
- statutory Instruments;
- case law.

Self-assessment Questions

Short Answer Questions

1. What is a prudential note?
2. Is the Building Societies Act 1986 an enabling act or a statutory instrument?

(Answers given in Appendix 1)

14

THE FINANCIAL SERVICES ACT 1986

Objectives

After studying this unit, you should be able to:

- outline the background to the Financial Services Act 1986;

- identify the scope of the Act;

- define the term 'investment' under the Act;

- describe the scope of membership of approved self-regulating organizations and recognized professional bodies;

- say how these bodies comply with the terms of the Financial Services Act 1986;

- state the rules regarding the provision of advice to clients in different circumstances and the use of client agreements;

- explain how complaints are to be handled.

14.1   Introduction

Before the regulations under the Financial Services Act 1986 came into effect, those offering advice in the financial services sector were subject to general laws on fraud, insolvency and, of course, theft. A number of statutes were in force which gave a limited measure of regulation and consumer protection, but the whole area of advice regarding intangible investment products was viewed by the government as one that required tightening up. There was not the same degree of protection available as for people buying things they could actually touch or see.

Professor L C B Gower was commissioned in 1981 by the then Secretary of State for Trade to carry out a review of the statutory protection of both private and business investors. What has emerged from that review is the Financial Services Act 1986.

14.2 The Financial Services Act 1986

This statute is,

> An Act to regulate the carrying on of investment business; to make related provision with respect to insurance business and business carried on by friendly societies; to make new provision with respect to the official listing of securities, offers of unlisted securities, takeover offers and insider dealing; to make provision as to the disclosure of information obtained under enactments relating to fair trading, banking, companies and insurance; to make provision for securing reciprocity with other countries in respect of facilities for the provision of financial services; and for connected purposes.

It applies to the whole of the United Kingdom. It has implications for businesses based both in the European Union and elsewhere if they pursue investment business in the UK.

Offences under the Act

It is a criminal offence to carry on investment business (which is defined later in this unit) in the United Kingdom without being either an authorized person or an exempted person.

In practice it is a business that seeks authorization and so it is only as a sole trader that an individual would seek authorization as such.

The penalties associated with this offence, and the offence of issuing an advertisement that has not been approved by an authorized person, are both criminal and civil and may involve imprisonment, a fine, or both.

There are powers for the appropriate agency to apply to the courts for injunctions to prevent the continuation of an offence and for restitution orders should profits accrue, or if it can be shown that investors have suffered loss. Knowingly making a misleading statement is also an offence.

The Act gives many powers to the Treasury but it is permitted to delegate to one or more designated agencies. The Treasury has delegated a great many of the powers to the Securities and Investments Board (SIB), the agency named in the Act.

The SIB has the power, in consultation with the Secretary of State, to recognize self-regulating organizations (SROs) and other bodies.

The SIB then has the duty to supervise the activities of these organizations and bodies which, in the main, are the source of authority to carry on investment business.

Unless a person falls foul of one of three offences specified in the Act (being unauthorized, issuing an unapproved advertisement or making a misleading statement), it is the rules made by the SIB or, more importantly, by the organization or body from whom authorization is sought that govern compliance with this legislation.

A person will commit a criminal offence if he continues to carry on investment business after authorization has been withdrawn.

The Financial Services Tribunal exists to consider appeals against certain notices that can be served under a few Sections of the Act.

Investments and Investment Business

The Act is about investments:

> *They include shares and stock in the share capital of a company; debentures; loan stock; Government and public securities; warrants or other instruments entitling the holder to subscribe for shares or securities; units in a collective investment scheme; options; futures; contracts for differences; long-term insurance contracts; rights and interests in investments.*

Authority or exemption is needed to carry on investment business. The list of those who are exempted is relatively short. It starts with the Bank of England and continues with other bodies that receive their authority from elsewhere, notably the Society of Lloyd's.

The Act says that 'an appointed representative is an exempted person for investment business carried on by him as such a representative'. It then goes on to define an appointed representative as a person who has a contract for services with another person (his 'principal') who is an authorized person under the Act. The principal is accountable for the investment business carried out by the appointed representative. An appointed representative can be a corporate person or an individual; it is the force of the contract which matters.

The Act does not refer to a company representative but the practice has been established that such person is an employee, a person with a contract of service with his company. The company is therefore responsible for his actions when he conducts investment business.

Formal authority (usually membership of an organization) will specify what can be done (and therefore by implication what cannot). There may be restrictions upon the business that is conducted.

Exceptions

There is a long list of exclusions (exceptions) to the definition of investment business. These are summarized below:

Dealing as principal

A person is not deemed to be engaging in activities constituting investment business when he buys and sells investments unless:

- he is willing to enter into transactions of that kind at prices determined by him generally and continuously; or

- he is in the business of buying investments with a view to selling them; or

- he regularly solicits members of the public for the purpose of inducing them to enter into transactions relating to investments.

The excluded activities do not apply so as to exclude activities in options, futures, contracts for differences etc., and long-term individual business.

Group and joint enterprises

Certain group and joint enterprises are exempt. For example, these include any transactions between firms in the same group.

Suppliers

Very broadly speaking, transactions by a supplier as principal, with a customer, are excluded where the supplier's main business is not investment business. This exclusion does not apply where the supplier holds himself out as engaging in the buying of investments with a view to selling them.

Employees' share schemes

In general, a corporate body may operate (as an excluded activity under the Act) an employee share scheme for its own bona fide employees or employees of another body in the same group, in shares or debentures of the employing company.

Sale of private companies

The provisions of the Act do not apply to the acquisition or disposal of shares in a private company, if they include shares carrying 75% or more of the voting rights attributable to share capital.

Trustees and personal representatives

The provisions of the Act relating to dealing in investments do not apply to a person by reason of his buying, selling or subscribing for an investment, or offering or agreeing to do so, if:

- the investment is, or is to be, held by him as bare trustee or, in Scotland, as nominee for another person;
- he is acting on that person's instructions; and
- he does not hold himself out as providing a service of buying and selling investments.

Also, in general, the provisions of the Act relating to arranging deals in investments do not apply to anything done by a person as trustee or personal representative with a view to a beneficiary under the trust, will or intestacy engaging in any such activity, unless additional remuneration is involved.

Dealings in course of non-investment business

The dealings in investments provisions do not apply to anything done by a person as principal or agent if it appears to the Secretary of State:

- that the person's main business is not investment business requiring authorization;

- that the person's business is likely to require dealing in investments;

- that it would be inappropriate to require him to be subject to regulation as an authorized person.

Advice given in course of profession or non-investment business

The Act does not apply to advice which is given in the course of a business not otherwise constituting investment business and which is a necessary part of other advice or services given in the course of carrying on that business.

This will not apply if it is remunerated separately from the other advice or services.

Newspapers

The provisions of the Act relating to investment advice do not apply to advice given in a newspaper or other periodical, if the main purpose of the publication is not to lead persons to invest in any particular investment.

Additional exclusions for persons without permanent place of business in the UK

The Act's provisions regarding dealing in investments do not apply to any transaction by an overseas person with or through an authorized person or an exempted person acting in the course of business in respect of which he is exempt.

The Securities and Investments Board (SIB)

The SIB is a company limited by guarantee and funded by the organizations it recognizes. These will subsequently be referred to as recognized bodies.

The SIB can directly authorize firms but it has set out to discourage this happening. The vast majority of firms are authorized by one or more of the recognized bodies.

The Act calls for the Treasury to make rules governing the conduct of business, but in practice it was the SIB which produced an all-embracing rule book covering all aspects of investment business as required by the Act. A directly authorized firm has to comply with this complex rule book.

The recognized bodies had to satisfy the SIB that their own rules provided protection to investors at least equivalent to the SIB rules. But there is no requirement for them to be identical. It does mean that rules can be written in a manner most suited to the types of business authorized by the regulatory body concerned.

The SIB may apply for a court order to deal with any breach, or likely breach, of its rules or of the provisions of the Act about misleading statements and market-making. Court orders can also be applied for to deal with aspects of cold-calling and issuing investment advertisements in the United Kingdom.

The orders for which the SIB can apply are an injunction restraining a firm from contravening the provision concerned, or an order requiring a firm to remedy a contravention. A receiver can be appointed to recover an investor's losses.

The SIB has the power to issue 'a disqualification direction' prohibiting firms from employing a particular individual without the SIB's consent, if it considers he is not a 'fit and proper' person.

Powers of recognition

Recognition of self-regulating organizations and of recognized professional bodies is dependent on the Secretary of State and the SIB being satisfied that they each have a constitution, rules and administrative capability to discharge their duties. There are provisions for continuous monitoring of capability.

The SIB maintains an up-to-date central register of authorized firms. The Central Register and Monitoring Service (CRAMS) is available to the public.

Advertising

The Act makes it a criminal offence for anyone except an authorized or exempted person to issue an investment advertisement in the United Kingdom unless its contents have been approved by an authorized person or it falls within one of the exempted categories. All advertisements must be vetted for compliance.

An investment advertisement is widely defined to include every form and every medium. A circular letter to a number of clients which is 'privatized' by an individual salutation is likely to be deemed to be an advertisement.

An investment advertisement is any advertisement that invites people to enter into an investment agreement or is calculated to lead to this.

The SIB rules cover all aspects of advertising. An advertisement must be clear, and not misleading, and it must be plain that it is an advertisement.

If there is the opportunity to cancel an agreement this must be mentioned.

In the fuller advertisements the fact that investments described may fluctuate in value and that any income may fluctuate in money terms has to be made clear if this is so. The fact that some investments may not be readily realizable has to be stated if it applies to the subject advertised.

The SIB provides a list of questions it is reasonable to expect an investor to be able to answer after studying the advertisement.

A firm's business documents, letterheads and business cards are a form of advertising and need to carry information showing which regulatory body has given the firm authorization.

Compensation

There are powers in the Act (Section 54/1) to set up a scheme for compensating investors. This is for those cases where persons who have been authorized are unable, or likely to be unable, to satisfy claims for civil liability incurred by them in connection with their investment businesses.

On the one hand the Act provides for rules to protect investors by defining rules of conduct. On the other hand it cannot actually prevent failure. It is very unlikely that a compensation claim could be sustained under this scheme if it were to originate solely in loss suffered through market movements. In any case a claim can be entertained only if a firm has to cease business (or be seen to be likely to do so). There are also provisions for the operators of the scheme to recover their due proportion of any money that might become available subsequently.

The SIB has set up a separate company to operate the Investors' Compensation Scheme. Its workings apply only to authorized firms for investment business transacted after 27 August 1988. The maximum claim is £50,000 and the maximum payout £48,000. It is described as the final safety net for the private investor. The cost is borne by a levy on all other members of the organization to which the defaulting firm belonged. In practice this covers the SIB and the SROs, because the recognized professional bodies have to have alternative equivalent arrangements to become recognized. The provisions of the Policyholders' Protection Act also cover life assurance policies.

Polarization

The concept of polarization is introduced in the SIB rules so that the private investor can be clear with whom he or she is doing business. Stated simply the investor must be clear as to who is acting as agent for whom. An independent intermediary should be holding himself out as an agent of the investor. The appointed or company representative is by definition acting on behalf of a company. Both are required to give best advice within the limitations imposed by their roles.

The purity of the idea is not complete because traditionally the independent intermediary is usually remunerated by commission paid by the supplier of the product rather than by a fee from the investor. Some of the problems associated with commission structure and debates on the way forward arise from this method of remuneration.

The polarization requirement affects the rules of the different authorizing bodies in different ways, reflecting the type of business being authorized. The proposed SIB principle specifies that: 'employees and appointed representatives of product companies who are authorized to canvass for business must be prohibited either by the contract governing their activities or by a specific restriction - empowered by Section 44(4) and (5) of the Act - to prevent them from canvassing for or advising about life policies or unit trusts emanating from outside the marketing group'. (Marketing group is defined in such a way as to bring together the various connected companies in a financial group.)

14.3   The Self-Regulating Organizations (SROs)

The SIB recognizes bodies in two major categories: the self-regulating organizations (SROs) and the recognized professional bodies (RPBs).

The SROs are shown below with details of the scope of membership of each.

The Securities and Futures Authority (SFA)

The SFA regulates firms dealing and arranging deals in securities of all kinds, futures, options and giving incidental advice and management in those areas. The securities include international bonds and equities, and related matters such as warrants and options both on individual stocks and commodities.

The SFA arose from a merger on 1 April 1991 of two previously separate SROs: The Securities Association (TSA) dealing with securities such as equities, and the Association of Futures Brokers and Dealers (AFBD) which regulated the activities of those dealing in futures and options.

Personal Investment Authority (PIA)

The PIA arose from a merger of Lautro and Fimbra in 1995. It regulates the activities of any individual or organization in the retail sector, which includes life assurance and pension companies and independent financial advisers.

Investment Management Regulatory Organization (IMRO)

Firms with investment management as their main activity, including the management and operation of regulated unit trusts, investment trusts and pension funds, fall under IMRO.

14.4   The Recognized Professional Bodies (RPBs)

The RPBs are those recognized because they have applied to the SIB and are able to comply with the 'equivalence of rules' requirement:

- Chartered Association of Certified Accountants;
- Institute of Actuaries;
- Institute of Chartered Accountants in England and Wales;
- Institute of Chartered Accountants in Ireland;
- Institute of Chartered Accountants of Scotland;
- Insurance Brokers' Registration Council;
- The Law Society of England and Wales;

- The Law Society of Northern Ireland;
- The Law Society of Scotland.

The Act defines one route to becoming an authorized person (for investment business) in the following terms:

> *A person holding a certificate issued for the purposes of this Part of this Act by a recognized professional body is an authorized person.*

It is important to recognize that mere membership of a professional body is not enough to be considered an authorized person. A certificate has also to be issued to cover investment business.

14.5 Authorization by Membership

In this unit the PIA rules have been used as an example because this SRO has the majority of independent financial advisers among its membership. Reference has also been made to other bodies. All rule books have to afford at least equivalent protection to investors as that provided by the SIB rules. A member of a self-regulating organization is an authorized person by virtue of his membership of that organization.

The PIA membership rule starts with a definition of the types of investments in which members may transact business and is a precise statement of the general description given in the list of SROs. This is followed by a sub-division into categories if, as PIA finds, the ways of doing business are sufficiently diverse to justify it. Categorization involves the applicability of some rules but not others and variation of financial resource requirements.

An applicant for membership must indicate into which category or categories the firm falls. Any subsequent change of category must be agreed beforehand with the regulatory body.

For advisers, the minimum PIA category is that of giving advice but nothing else. To this may be added arranging life and pensions policies and investments in unit trusts, but not handling clients' money.

A further addition is that of arranging deals in investments using the services of a clearing firm or, for instance, having this as a separate activity from life pensions and unit trusts. Managing clients' funds invested exclusively in broker funds is separately identified.

The widest category, which includes carrying out all services which may be authorized by the regulatory body, imposes the most onerous membership requirements. These relate to rules, financial resources, subscriptions and (not least) fitness and properness.

Fit and proper is interpreted by the SIB as honest, solvent and competent. An application form is designed to ascertain whether this is so. Such an enquiry cannot be divorced from the people in the firm: they also must be fit and proper.

A sole trader or firm with only one registered individual must specify what arrangements will exist, if membership is granted, in the event of holidays, illness etc.

Compliance Procedures

Any authorized firm must establish and maintain internal rules and procedures to ensure compliance with the rules of the regulating body.

Student Activity 1

Before reading the next section of the text, answer the following questions and then check your answers against the pages indicated.

1. What does PIA stand for? *(page 296)*

2. To whom is SIB responsible to for the FSA? *(page 290)*

If your answers are basically correct, then proceed to the next section. If significant parts of your answers are wrong, then study the whole of the relevant sections again in detail. Note your areas of weakness, and be prepared for further questions on these areas in the self-assessment section at the end of this unit.

14.6   Dealings with Clients

In dealing with a client it must be clear at all times what is the basis of the intermediary-client relationship: whether it is that of an independent intermediary or not; and whether the client is an execution-only client, in which case he or she will lose some protection, or a 'professional' who may be deemed capable of looking after himself; and whether the client agrees and understands these special distinctions, if they apply.

Know your Client

In advising and dealing with the usual private client there is a requirement to 'know your client'. If the client refuses to cooperate the intermediary may proceed with the transaction but will be well advised to make sure that the record is clear as to what happened.

Know your client means that you must take reasonable steps to ascertain the personal and financial circumstances of a client before performing any service for him or her.

The next part of the rule requires that you must be satisfied, having taken all reasonable steps, that the client understands the nature of the risks to which the proposed investment is subject (not in the case of an execution-only client). This duty is extended, in the case of providing a discretionary management service, to taking all reasonable steps to ensure that a client understands the risks to which he or she will be exposed. This rule is termed understanding of risk. The extent of the duty will depend upon your powers of discretion, the objectives of the management agreement, and the extent to which you are supplying expertise that the client does not have. These are demanding requirements.

Best Execution

Best execution is not difficult if it is kept separate from best advice, as it should be. 'Best execution' means that all reasonable steps must be taken to ensure that a transaction is effected on the best terms available at the time, on the market generally, for transactions of the same size and nature, with reliable counterparts. PIAA rules make it clear that the 'best execution' rule does not apply to life policies, pension contracts and collective investments (unit trusts).

Best Advice

The 'best advice' rule is perhaps the area of greatest distinction between the requirements of the SROs. Broadly speaking, a tied agent is bound to give advice relating only to that member's own products. The advice is therefore 'best' only within that constraint. There is no requirement to point out to a client the benefits of a specific competitor's product although he is bound to identify situations where he himself has no product that will meet the client's need.

The independent adviser, on the other hand, must be aware of all available options and this section therefore concentrates on the duties imposed upon the independent adviser.

'Best advice' is concerned with suitability of the product or range of products recommended.

Taking together the rules on know your client and understanding of risk, best advice summarizes the process of giving best advice. You must take reasonable steps to know your client. In the light of knowledge gained and any other relevant information you ought reasonably to know, you must then determine, taking reasonable care, what is a reasonable investment for your client. (The repetition of the word reasonable implies that there is not necessarily a unique solution in each case.)

The guidelines may be summed up by saying:

- The objective is to give considered advice that has been arrived at conscientiously.

- Because there is not necessarily any single recommendation that would constitute best advice at any given time, and there is an element of subjective judgement in most recommendations, members must ensure that judgements are made on a well-informed basis. For a tied agent there could well be a single best solution, depending upon the product range.

- If a client refuses to supply information an adviser has to be especially careful because he may not have a complete picture.

- The investment markets are so diverse that information sources selected need to be relevant and up to date.

- For routine cases there is merit in compiling a short list of recommended products for each class of investment product, but of course this must be subject to continuing review.

- It is important to avoid suggesting that cash or percentage returns achieved in the past will or may be achieved in the future, but consistency of past performance may be important in assessing future relative performance.

- Compliance visits and analysis of any complaints received will form a basis for judging whether a member firm has taken the steps needed to inform itself about its clients, the markets and the suppliers used.

- Undue reliance on a restricted list will have to be justified.

- Record keeping is clearly essential. Adequate records help to demonstrate that relevant information used to give advice was all that should have been reasonably known at that time.

- The record keeping requirements cover appointed representatives and any registered individuals as well.

- There is a special standard of care needed if a 'connected person' is involved. Essentially this relates to an association, such as some form of common ownership, involving the member and the supplier. In this case some sort of vested interest might be suspected in a recommendation and the product must then be superior to any other product from another source. This is sometimes referred to as 'better than best' requirements. Clearly the company representative is in a different position although there are rules designed to achieve the same end of putting a client's interests first.

Remuneration of an Authorized Firm

Before you execute any business for a client you must explain how your firm (and any person connected with your firm) is to be remunerated. From 1995, both tied agents and 'independent intermediaries' must disclose the exact amount of commission payable in respect of the product recommended.

Unsolicited Calls ('Cold Calls')

A cold call refers to a personal visit or communication made without express invitation.

In general such calls are prohibited. However, actually making a cold call does not constitute an offence; it is the fact that a contract resulting from such a call is unenforceable which poses problems. Furthermore, if the client has parted with any money it can be recovered.

However, SIB has made some exceptions to this rule. The exceptions appear in the regulatory body rules. They relate firstly to life policies or insured pension contracts, the sale of collective investments (unit trusts) or contracts to manage the assets of an occupational pension fund. Secondly a cold call may be made on someone who has expressly consented to such calls being made. This may arise if a person has responded to an advertisement, for instance, which makes it clear that a call may follow any response to the advertisement.

Anyone making a permitted cold call must observe a detailed code which ensures that calls are made in a reasonable manner and also at a reasonable time of day, and that the name of the firm and of the caller is stated at the outset and repeated as necessary, together with the genuine purpose of the call. If at any time the caller makes an offer which if accepted would result in the making of an investment agreement, then the consequences of acceptance must be given.

Recommendations

Recommendations must be made with all reasonable care to include sufficient information to provide a client (actual or potential) with an adequate and reasonable basis for deciding to accept the recommendations.

Benefits and gifts of any kind in recognition of special sales performance are now generally banned. There are some minor exceptions such as diaries. More substantial items are subject to an overall limit.

Documentation

The important documents are:

- terms of business letter;
- client agreement;
- discretionary investment management agreement.

Terms of business letter

A terms of business letter contains:

- a statement of the investment services provided;
- a reference to the rules of the regulatory body;
- a statement that the firm is bound by an undertaking not to transact business in which the firm has a personal interest without disclosing the fact (a general disclaimer may be used);
- a statement about remuneration;
- a statement that the firm is not authorized to handle clients' money, or details of how clients' money will be handled;
- a statement on the safe keeping of clients' assets and of the clients' rights of inspection and that the records will be maintained for seven years (this period may be less in some cases);

- details of any locum arrangements;

- a statement as to whether or not professional indemnity insurance is held.

If business is being transacted as a result of an off-the-page advertisement, the letter may be sent as a first response.

Client agreement

A client agreement, rather than a terms of business letter, is required for regular services that amount to more than advice or a transaction relating exclusively to a life policy, or pension contract or collective investments. A client agreement does not apply to broker bonds. It is not required in the case of an execution-only client (provided that the client is aware of his execution-only status).

Further details are required, in addition to those for a terms of business letter.

Discretionary investment management agreement

This is the most elaborate of the investment agreements that may be made. It must contain all the details required in the terms of business letter and the client agreement, but it can do so by making references to current agreements.

In addition it must specify the limits of discretion within which the manager will operate. Where the services to be provided include the management of broker funds, details of the arrangements between the firm and the relevant life office must be included. The basis of fees to be charged is to be stated, as is whether there are any other benefits payable to the firm (these need not be quantified).

14.7 Record Keeping

In general, records need to be kept for at least six years. In many cases longer periods of time are specified, particularly where Inland Revenue requirements are involved, and seven years is a common time period given. It cannot be overemphasized that record keeping is at the heart of compliance and avoidance of regulatory problems.

A client has the right of inspection of a record that relates exclusively to him or her. The specific records for each client must be made up as soon as possible after receipt of instructions. They must be timed and dated.

Complaints

A member will keep copies of each complaint relating to the conduct of its investment business made to it in writing by or on behalf of a client, or to which the member responds in writing, together with a record of any action taken in response to that complaint.

The firm must inform the complainant of his or her right to complain to the regulatory body, which is also required to investigate the complaint.

Accounting Records

Records must be kept that are sufficient to show and explain a firm's transactions and disclose with reasonable accuracy, in relation to any point in time, the financial position of the member firm at that time.

They must show entries from day to day of all sums of money received and expended by the firm and record all assets and liabilities including any contingent liability. There must be internal rules and procedures for the control and conduct of business in accordance with the regulatory body's rules.

Student Activity 2

Before reading the next section of the text, answer the following questions and then check your answers against the pages indicated.

1.   Distinguish between appointed representatives and company representatives.

(page 291)

2.   What document must be given to the client at the start of an interview before any advice is given?   *(page 301)*

If significant parts of your answers are wrong, then study the whole of the relevant sections again in detail. Note your areas of weakness, and be prepared for further questions on these areas in the self-assessment section at the end of this unit.

14.8   Monitoring

The reporting requirements on membership form the first level of monitoring of compliance with the rules.

The auditor's report delivered at the same time as the annual accounts provides a second level because the auditor has to satisfy himself that adequate record systems are in place to sign an unqualified report.

The third level of monitoring is provided by the system of random checks carried out by the SRO compliance officers. The frequency is determined by the type of business being transacted. In addition specific visits may be initiated by the checking of routine reports or by the receipt of complaints by the SRO.

SROs retain the right to make such visits unannounced, but a short period of notice (say 48 hours) is usually given by telephone.

It is clearly in everyone's interest that records are clear and up to date so that there is the least possible disruption to the business by the visit.

Powers of Direction

A serious problem, which might well lead to disciplinary action, may call for immediate action in the interests of investor protection.

In the case of PIA the Chief Executive, acting with the agreement of at least two members of the Council, may prohibit a firm or registered individual from entering into transactions, from soliciting business, from carrying on business and from disposing of assets or liabilities. He may require the transfer of some or all of the member's assets to a trustee. The Chief Executive may vary a directive or publish a direction or variation as he sees fit. If a direction is made to a member, the member has a right to request consideration under the Disciplinary Scheme as a matter of priority. The Council may have recourse to the courts to compel compliance with a direction. A Disciplinary Panel has at its disposal a number of sanctions.

Disciplinary Panel sanctions

The Disciplinary Panel may terminate a firm's membership or remove an individual's registration. It may impose conditions on a firm's membership, require the member to remedy the breach that caused disciplinary action to be taken or reprimand the member. No order may take effect or be publicized until an appeal is heard if such an appeal is made in due time.

Appeal Tribunals

An Appeal Tribunal is an *ad hoc* body set up to hear a particular appeal. Appeals are not made to the Financial Services Tribunal set up under the Act for other purposes.

The Chairman has to have legal qualifications and experience. The two other members must be independent of the SRO.

The SRO does not have a right of appeal to its tribunal.

Self-assessment Questions

Short Answer Questions

1. Under the FSA, to do investment business without authorization - is it a criminal offence OR a civil offence?

2. Which of the following are covered by the FSA?

    a) bank and building society deposit accounts;

    b) gilts;

    c) mortgages;

    d) permanent health insurance contracts.

3. What is the full name of IMRO?

4. What is meant by best advice?

5. What is meant by execution only?

6. What is the term used where all reasonable steps must be taken to ensure a transaction is effected on the best terms available at the time?

7. What are the three ways of obtaining authorization under the FSA?

8. How long must records be kept for under the FSA?

9. What is a cold call?

10. What is the maximum payout under the Investors Compensation Scheme ?

(Answers given in Appendix 1)

Specimen Examination Question

Discuss the extent to which protection and access to unbiased advice has been provided by the FSA.

(Answer given in Appendix 1)

Appendix 1

ANSWERS

Unit 1

Short Answer Questions

1. The identification, analysis and economic control of those risks that can threaten the assets or earning capacity of an enterprise.

2. Small fires.

3. Large fires.

4. A risk with which there is the possibility of a loss or break-even result.

5. A fundamental risk.

6. Association of Risk and Insurance Managers in Industry and Commerce.

7. A method of risk transfer that involves the parent company forming a subsidiary to underwrite certain risks.

8. A risk transfer mechanism.

Specimen Examination Question – Model Answer

Risk management can be defined as 'The planning, arranging and controlling of activities and resources in order to minimize the impact of uncertain events'. It involves the identification, evaluation and control of risks. Businesses are used to dealing with speculative forms of risk, but it is only over the past few decades that they have moved to a managerial response to pure risks.

The identification of risks and their subsequent evaluation allow a business to:

- decide whether the risk, or its cause, can be removed (risk avoidance) or its potential effect reduced (risk reduction);

- make a decision as to whether it is economic for a risk to be controlled;

- make an informed decision as to exactly how the risk should be effectively controlled, whether this is physical or financial control;

- assess the advantages and disadvantages of risk transfer mechanisms such as insurance;

– ensure that the future of an organization is not jeopardized by sudden events.

In particular, insurance as a risk transfer mechanism has the following benefits for the business:

– exchanges uncertainty of loss and its effect for certainty in the form of a known premium to the insurer to provide cover;

– enhance the security of a business by ensuring that once insured, the business can recover from a loss;

– provide a stimulus to business activity and peace of mind;

– wider social benefits, for example, after a loss insurance will ensure that jobs will not be lost, goods and services can still be sold, and the effects on the community can be minimized.

A risk management strategy including insurance allows a business to identify, evaluate and find economic ways of controlling risks. Without such a strategy, the potential risks and their effect are unknown, and there will be no plans in place should such a risk occur.

Unit 2
Short Answer Questions

1. Risk transfer.

2. Peace of mind, loss control, social benefits, investment, invisible earnings.

3. Different vehicles will be in their control at different times.

4. Industrial life assurance.

5. Any five from: storm, tempest, flood, riot, burst pipes, malicious damage, earthquake, explosion, aircraft, impact.

6. Cover for compensation that a director may be liable to pay and defence costs.

Specimen Examination Question – Model Answer

The individual benefits from insurance in the following ways: transfer of risk gives peace of mind; protection of assets; uncertainty of frequency and severity of risk is replaced by certainty of premium; and loss reduction and prevention from the insurance process.

The State benefits from a thriving insurance industry because:

– Insurance companies have a large accumulation of funds for investment and this provides a source of money for government and industry and commerce.

– The insurance market is a world financial centre attracting business from abroad.

– The industry contributes to the balance of trade through invisible earnings.

– It allows government to use insurance to deal with responsibilities that would otherwise fall on the state, e.g. industrial injuries, redundancy.

- The benefits from loss prevention and control enhance business confidence.

- Insurance provides funds to meet losses to assist business recovery and job security.

Unit 3

Short Answer Questions

1. Individuals, industry and commerce.

2. An agent of an industrial life office or friendly society who collects premiums at policyholders' homes.

3. Individuals and corporations (from 1994).

4. Mutual.

5. Protection and Indemnity Club.

6. Insured's details, period of cover, inception date, perils covered, insured property, sums insured, special conditions, expected premium.

7. Any three from: Lloyd's List, Lloyd's Shipping Index, Lloyd's Loading List, Lloyd's Law Reports.

8. Institute of risk managers.

Specimen Examination Question – Model Answer

A major bank subsidiary developed the successful selling of private motor, household and mortgage products by telephone during the late 1980s using the latest telecommunications technology, and this has been copied by many other insurance companies. Most composite insurers now often have direct writing subsidiaries which accept business from the public direct and bypass the intermediary. This growth in direct writing has had a major effect on personal lines business.

However, this distribution method tends to be suitable only for simple products which need minimal advice. More complicated products such as pensions would be difficult to market in this way. It is interesting to note that some of the direct writers have started to offer simple pension plans to the public on the back of their success in other areas. In most cases, advice is not available and it remains to be seen whether the public is prepared to buy these types of products with information rather than advice being given. There is still a reluctance by some customers to buy complex products over the telephone. This distribution method is not suitable for commercial insurances where the services of a broker are invaluable in researching the market and placing the risk. Direct insurance means a loss of the services and expertise of the broker

Advantages:

● Use of the latest technology in telecommunications and telesales techniques means that the new direct writers do not require extensive branch networks to service their business.

● Their administration and underwriting centres can be located anywhere in the country. Cost of office accommodation can therefore be kept to a minimum.

● There is no commission payable to an intermediary.

● Contact with customers is simply subject to the cost of a telephone call and postage of documentation.

● The customer often buys insurance based on price alone, and the reduction in fixed costs listed above allows insurers to provide a low-cost product.

● No communication problems or delays: the customer deals direct with the insurer and often the process is dealt with wholly by telephone.

Unit 4

Short Answer Questions

1. ECU.

2. It must be maintained at all times and is a specified sum or one third of the solvency margin.

3. Insurance Brokers Registration Council.

4. To allow a buyer of an investment product 14 days to change his mind.

5. Any three from: employer's liability, public liability for riding stables, public liability for nuclear installations, professional indemnity for solicitors and brokers, public liability for ships carrying oil, and public liability for owners of dangerous wild animals.

6. Nationalization.

Specimen Examination Question – Model Answer

See Section 5: Reasons for State Regulation of Insurance.

Unit 5

Short Answer Questions

1. The legal right to insure, arising out of a financial relationship, recognized at law, between the insured and the subject matter of insurance.

2. It limited liability for loss or damage to guests' property to £50 per article, £100 per guest.

3. 'Let the buyer beware', which means the seller must ask all relevant questions and

'utmost good faith' where there is a positive duty to disclose whether a question is asked or not.

4. Fraudulent non-disclosure.

5. Clearing rubbish away at night, maintenance of an alarm system, storage of dangerous chemicals.

Specimen Examination Questions – Model Answers

1. Mr Smith can take out a policy on the life of Mr James for the amount of the loan plus interest because there is a debtor-creditor relationship. However, Mr James cannot take out a policy on the life of Mr Smith because the mere expectation of having to repay the loan early is not enough to create a financial relationship. Should the loan be repaid early, Mr Smith will not have to cancel the policy because, for long-term insurances including life assurance, insurable interest need only exist at the start.

2. The words 'see your records' should put the underwriter on enquiry and if he chooses to waive the information then the proposer has done everything necessary to bring these facts to the insurance company's attention. They will be liable for the claim.

Unit 6

Short Answer Question

1. Insured, uninsured, other.

2. The condition that details of and proof of the loss must be delivered in a certain time or in a certain way.

3. 'An exact financial compensation'.

4. Cash, repair, replacement, reinstatement.

5. The principles apply only to contracts of indemnity and are there essentially to ensure that the insured does not profit from a loss.

6. Where a person sustains damage and is indemnified, his insurers have a right to recover their outlays from the policy authority.

7. Two or more indemnity policies; common interest; common peril; common subject matter; each policy liable

Specimen Examination Questions – Model Answers

1. Proximate cause of loss is theft; the indirect cause is war because it only provided the opportunity for theft. Therefore the loss would be covered by the insurance policy. Case is *Winicofsky v. Army & Navy General* (1919).

2. Average applies because the property is underinsured. Calculation is sum insured divided by full value times loss, i.e.

$$\frac{12,000}{16,000} \times 9,000 = £6,750$$

Unit 7

Short Answer Questions

1. To give the insurance company the necessary information to assess the risk, issue terms and prepare the policy.

2. The operative clause.

3. The insured, his address, nature of the business, period of insurance, premiums, sums insured, policy number, special exclusions or conditions.

4. Motor and employer's liability.

Specimen Examination Question – Model Answer

Proposal forms are used to supply the insurance company with the necessary information to assess the risk, issue terms and prepare the policy. There are some aspects of all proposal forms which will be similar for all types of insurance:

– name and address of proposer;

– details of past claims or other insurances;

– type of policy required;

– term of policy.

The other questions relate specifically to the type of insurance being offered and ask detailed questions about the risk. For example, motor proposals ask full details about the car, drivers, their history and any convictions, whether or not the car is garaged, what type of use is required, voluntary excesses required, etc. A life assurance proposal asks for the full medical and occupational details of the life assured, any hazardous pursuits, and residence and travel.

The proposal forms for various classes of business also vary in length. A travel policy proposal form is very short due to the nature of the risk, whereas a life or permanent health proposal is more lengthy because the information the underwriter needs is much more detailed. It is also important to remember that life, PHI and critical illness cover is long term, i.e. the insurer is accepting a risk for 20 or even 30 years and cannot cancel once accepted. A motor or household policy is only for 12 months so the amount of detail required is considerably less.

Unit 8

Short Answer Questions

1. Concerned with the extra risk posed by the attitude of the insured rather than the physical aspects of the risk.

2. Mortality, investment, expenses, contingency.

3. An original copy of the death certificate.

4. Occupational Pensions Advisory Service.

5. Any dispute relating to the sale of investment products and any other dispute where the life office elects for the PIA Ombudsman to deal with such complaints.

6. An informal method of resolving disputes between insurers and insureds.

7. a) No b) Yes up to £100,000.

8. 1981.

Specimen Examination Questions – Model Answers

1. The steps involved in assessing a claim can be lengthy, time consuming and require considerable expertise. There is a limit to the number of staff an insurance company can employ to deal in house with claims and the level of expertise would be costly in terms of recruitment and training. The insurance company can employ an outside expert to assess and deal with claims and these experts are chartered loss adjusters.

   Their role is to process the claim from start to finish, to ensure that the interests of the insurer are preserved, and to minimize the extent of the loss if possible. The loss adjuster can also be of considerable help to the insured, and has the knowledge and experience to advise on loss minimization, rebuilding and repair.

   The loss adjuster's report covers: basic facts about the insured and the loss; estimated claim amount for reserve purposes; comments on adequacy of cover; full description of the premises; steps taken in handling of the claim. His final report gives details of exactly what has taken place, and gives the final settlement figure.

2. The policyholder's first course of action is to approach the company to discuss the problem direct. This is often the easiest and fastest way of sorting out the problem and means that it can be discussed amicably.

   If this cannot be resolved, the next action is to approach OPAS through the Citizens Advice bureau. OPAS has a network of 250 regional advisers plus a central panel of experts and is able to give help and advice on all different types of pension schemes, except the state scheme.

   If not satisfied, or if still unresolved, he can go to the Pensions Ombudsman, whose decision is legally binding. The complaint must be referred to the Pensions Ombudsman within three years.

Appendix 1 – Answers

Unit 9
Short Answer Questions

1. a) Family income benefit is the cheapest form of protection but level-term assurance could also be suggested.

    b) Convertible-term assurance.

    c) Unit-linked endowment.

    d) Reversionary (contingent) annuity.

2. **Unit Trusts and Investment Trusts Compared**
    Unit trusts

    - A trust regulated by the Financial Services Act 1986 with an independent trustee.

    - An open-ended fund. The number of units increases or decreases in accordance with customer demand.

    - Units can be bought and sold only via the trust manager.

    - The price of units is determined by the net asset value of the underlying investments held.

    - The open-ended nature of a unit trust means the manager must have regard, in respect of investment decisions made, to the possibility of redemptions. Cash or other readily accessible assets must be available.

    - An annual management fee of 1% to 1.5% of assets is usual, although other fees are payable by the trust.

    - A unit trust cannot borrow money.

    - Annual meetings are not normally held.

    - Investment by the unit trust outside the recognized stock exchanges is strictly controlled.

    - Cannot issue different classes of units.

    - Income is usually distributed, although accumulating units will have income added.

    - Marketing is usually quite easy via the manager.

3. a) Permanent health insurance covers inability to work because of sickness or accident and thus provides a regular income to replace that which the insured is no longer able to earn for himself.

    b)
        i) To replace 50 to 60% of average income;

---

ii)   deferred period of four weeks;

iii)   term is to cover until the expected retirement age.

Multiple Choice Questions

1.   d)

2.   c)

Specimen Examination Questions - Model Answers

Life assurance as a means of providing cover in the event of death has been used for protection purposes for many years and in this area it has no serious competitors.

The cheapest form of protection is a term assurance-type contract.

Full definition of the following types of term contract could then be discussed in your answer: Level term assurance, increasing term assurance, renewable term assurance, convertible term assurance, RICTA, family income benefit.

A mortgage protection policy is also available and can be used to protect the amount outstanding under a repayment mortgage.

Whole-of-life contracts are more expensive but provide permanent protection. The following policy types could be explained here: non-profit, with-profit, unit-linked, flexible whole life, low-cost whole life.

Endowments should not be viewed as a protection policy because the main aim is investment. However, the built-in life cover provided by an endowment effected alongside an interest-only mortgage does provide protection for the family in the event of death.

A life policy for protection purposes can very easily be effected under trust. Both Married Women's Property Act 1882 and non-statutory or discretionary trusts can be used. The advantage is that the life policy proceeds are paid direct to the trustees without the delay involved in obtaining probate AND the proceeds do not form part of the deceased's estate for IHT purposes. In addition, the policyholder can appoint himself as one of the trustees to retain a degree of control over the policy.

2   **Regular premium endowment**
    Advantages

- built-in life cover;

- savings locked in until maturity unless surrendered, therefore reduces temptation to take money out;

- choice of companies and funds;

- past performance figures available;

- no tax on proceeds as long as qualifying policy.

Disadvantages:

- low surrender values if encashed early;

- client may not need built-in life cover;

- built-in life cover has to be paid for;

- higher charges to pay for management of funds and commission to intermediary;

- life assurance fund is subject to tax.

Regular Unit Trust Savings Plan
Advantages:

- choice of companies and funds;

- collective investment with advantages of spread of risk and expertise;

- past performance figures available;

- flexible payments;

- can encash at any time without any specific penalty;

Disadvantages:

- not designed for short-term investment;

- unit values can go down;

- charges for fund management including a bid-offer spread;

- no tax advantages - income tax on dividend and CGT on any capital gain above annual exemption.

Regular General Pep
Advantages:

- fund and proceeds are completely tax free;

- choice of companies and funds;

- collective investment with advantages of spread of risk and expertise;

- choice of investment in unit trusts, investment trusts or directly in shares;

- past performance figures available;

- flexible payments;

- can encash at any time without any specific penalty;

- can take an income or reinvest dividends.

Disadvantages:

- not designed for short-term investment;
- unit and share values can go down;
- charges for fund management;
- limit of £6,000 and only one Pep per tax year.

Before giving advice

A full fact find should be completed and this would enable the adviser to 'know your client' as required under the FSA before giving advice. The additional information required would include: personal details such as name, number of dependants, marital status, occupation; financial details such as income and outgoings; assets and liabilities such as investments and mortgages; objectives and attitude to risk.

Unit 10

Short Answer Questions

1. Basic old age pension and Serps.

2. Exempt approval.

3. The Pension Schemes Office (PSO).

4. 35% of net relevant earnings.

5. A personal pension that has been approved to be used to contract out of Serps.

6. 25% of the retirement fund excluding protected rights but including dependant's benefits.

7. A final salary scheme that guarantees a proportion of salary at retirement.

8. It is written under a discretionary trust.

Specimen Examination Question – Model Answer

1. A member of an occupational scheme is able to top up the benefits from that scheme in a number of ways. He cannot use a personal pension, but can take out an in-scheme AVC, buy added years (if available) or effect a FSAVC. Alternatively he can save using a Personal Equity Plan or other investment vehicle.

   If he uses an AVC of any sort, he is limited to a maximum contribution limit of 15% to all of his occupational schemes. Therefore a contribution of 5% to the main scheme would mean that he can pay 10% to an AVC. The benefits from all occupational schemes must not exceed Inland Revenue limits.

   - In-scheme AVC : employers must offer these by law if they offer an occupational scheme. They are money purchase schemes with no guarantee as to the benefits on retirement. Charges are very low and often subsidized by the employer. However, he is limited to the employer's choice of provider and fund, and may not be able to vary contributions. If he leaves the main scheme the AVC is treated in the same way as his main benefits and he must stop paying contributions.

- Some employer's schemes offer the facility to buy added years, which means that the pension on retirement is guaranteed. This would suit someone who expected his salary to increase considerably or who requires the guarantee. However it is very expensive.

- Free-standing AVCs are independent contracts taken out with insurance companies where the choice of provider and fund is made by the individual. However, charges are not subsidized by the employer. The plan is portable on moving jobs and as long as the individual joins his new employer's scheme, he can continue contributing to the FSAVC.

Unit 11

Short Answer Questions

1. Construction, claims history, convictions, sum insured, security precautions.

2. Index linking at renewal.

3. Underinsurance can be ignored but some insurers are applying average clauses to their policies.

4. External, violent and accidental so far as the insured is concerned.

5. PA contracts are annually renewable, PHI are long-term contracts.

6. The lender.

7. 1930s.

8. When the loan to valuation ratio exceeds 75%.

9. The borrower.

10. Because the number of repossessions have increased and house prices have fallen.

Specimen Examination Question – Model Answer

Cover is provided for damage or loss caused by storm and flood; some insurers also use the term 'tempest'. Damage caused by frost, subsidence or landslip is excluded under this section. Destruction of or damage to gates hedges and fences is also excluded. There is usually an excess under this section.

Cover is for subsidence or heave of site or landslip. This section excludes the bedding down of new structures; coastal erosion; damage resulting from the movement of solid floor slabs;

damage to swimming pools, patios, terraces, footpaths, drives, gates, fences, etc. unless there is damage to the building at the same time; the use of defective materials or faulty workmanship in constructing the foundations. An excess of £500 normally applies.

Reasonable legal fees and architects' and surveyors' fees necessarily incurred in the reinstatement of the buildings following loss or damage are included. The cost of demolition and shoring up the property and removal of debris from the site are also included. This does not cover the insured's costs in preparing a claim.

The owner of the property is protected against all sums he shall become legally liable to pay for

● accidental bodily injury to or disease contracted by any person other than a member of the insured's family permanently residing with him;

● accidental loss of or damage to property not belonging to nor in the custody or control of the insured or member of his family (as above).

Unit 12

Short Answer Questions

1. A temporary policy and certificate of insurance.

2. It is proof that cover that complies with at least the minimum requirement for cover in the country visited is in force .

3. None.

4. Social domestic and pleasure.

5. A guarantee that the motorist can call upon £1000 in the event of being taken into custody or having his car impounded.

Specimen Examination Question

1. The important factors to be considered when underwriting and deciding on a premium for motor cover can be split into three broad categories :

● the scope of cover;

● the frequency with which claims are likely to occur;

● the potential severity of a claim should it occur.

The following should be discussed in detail, referring to section 12.13 Underwriting in Unit 12 and giving examples where possible :

● type of car;

● age of driver;

● rating district;

- cover;
- use;
- occupation;
- age of car.

Unit 13

Short Answer Question

1.   A guidance note issued by the Building Societies Commission.

2.   The Act itself is an enabling act. Further detailed rules issued subsequently are statutory instruments.

Unit 14

Short Answer Questions

1.   Criminal.

2.   Only gilts are covered by the FSA.

3.   Investment Management Regulatory Organization.

4.   Recommending the most suitable product to fit the client's needs.

5.   The client requests a particular product and no advice is given.

6.   Best execution.

7.   Direct with SIB; through an SRO; through an RPB.

8.   Six years.

9.   A personal visit or communication made without express invitation.

10. £48,000.

Specimen Examination Question – Model Answer

The FSA was designed to make the investment area 'a clean place to do business' through regulation and control of providers, informing the customer and removing biased advice.

Protection is provided in the following main areas (each should be discussed in detail):

- authorization, giving clear identity to the customer about who is selling and allowing the authorities to remove any unsuitable providers or advisers;

- polarization, specifying that all advisers had to be either completely independent or tied to one particular company;

- three-tier structure of rules, which includes know your customer, best advice, disclosure, complaints procedures;

- training and competence rules and standardized examinations (Macdonald Report);

- compensation through the Investors Compensation scheme;

- powers of the PIA and fines levied on authorized persons for failure to comply.

Clear choices are provided mainly through the polarization and disclosure rules. Polarization allows the customer a choice between an independent and tied adviser. His status must be disclosed at the start of an interview or contact over the phone by a verbal statement, usually a business card and a terms of business letter. Disclosure of commission, product particulars and charging structure details allow the customer to make informed choices. The key features document must be clear and understandable and show the amount that the adviser will receive as a result of the sale. The reason why letter, post-sale information and cancellation notice give the information in a different format and allow the customer 14 days cooling off.

Some argue that the FSA has caused customer confusion and lack of understanding but overall the FSA has provided both protection and choice.

Appendix 2
GLOSSARY OF INSURANCE TERMS

ABI

Association of British Insurers

AIRMIC

Association of Insurance and Risk Managers in Industry and Commerce

All risks

Wider protection usually for specific goods or expensive items

Annuity

Fixed annual/monthly payment to a person for the rest of his life in return for a lump sum payment

Assurance

Cover for an event that will happen at some time, e.g. death

Average

Used where there is underinsurance to reduce the settlement to an amount commensurate with the premium paid

Basic state pension

Flat-rate pension available at state pension age to all those who have paid NI contributions for 90% of their working life

Best advice

Recommending the most suitable product for the client's needs

Best execution

Taking all reasonable steps to obtain the best terms for a product recommended

BIIBA

British Insurance and Investment Brokers Association

Bona fide

In good faith

Broker

Agent whose full-time occupation is advising clients on their insurance needs. Registered with IBRC

Buy-out bond (Section 32 Fund)

Individual plan to which occupational scheme benefits can be transferred after leaving service. The guaranteed minimum pension that corresponds to Serps is preserved

Business interruption

Policy that reimburses a business following an event such as a fire where the damage results in a loss of profit

Captive

Method of transacting risk transfer where the parent company forms a subsidiary to underwrite

Catastrophe risk

The possibility of an exceptionally heavy loss, e.g. a 'freak event' such as the San Francisco earthquake and fire of 1989

Caveat emptor

Let the buyer beware

Cold calling

An unsolicited call or visit subject to strict FSA rules

Commission

The remuneration paid to an agent for the introduction or renewal of business, usually in the form of a percentage of the premium

Composite company

An company that transacts more than one class of business

Convertible term

Provides a death benefit, but also the option to convert to an endowment or whole-of-life contract at any time during the currency of the policy, without further medical evidence

Cover

Range of events that a policy insures against

Deductible

A very large excess; used in commercial insurance

Directors' and officers' liability

Insurance cover for compensation for legal liability for errors and omissions made by a director or officer of a company, plus defence costs

Endorsement

The means by which policies are kept up-to-date

Employer liability

Cover for employees who are injured or fatally injured at work; compulsory for employers to take out such a policy under the Employers Liability (Compulsory Insurance) Act 1969.

Execution only

Where no advice at all is given or sought

Executive pension

A money purchase scheme provided by the employer usually for directors and key employees. They are subject to occupational scheme rules but have the advantage that they can provide different levels of benefits for different members

Excess

An amount of each and every claim not covered by the policy

Ex gratia

As a favour

Family income benefit

Provides a tax-free income on death which continues until the expiry date

Fidelity guarantee

Insurance against loss caused by a dishonest employee

Final salary

A scheme provided by an employer where the benefits at retirement are based on final 'pensionable' salary, number of years' service and the scheme accrual rate

Fundamental risk

Impersonal in origin; widespread in effect

Goods in transit

Cover for damage or loss of goods while in transit

Grantee

The assured under a life policy

IMRO

Investment Management Regulatory Organization

Indemnity

The principle that an insurance claim provides the value of loss, neither more nor less

Industrial life

Insurance for the masses; small sums assured and small premiums

Insurable interest

A legal or financial interest in property or in the happening of some event

Insurance

Financial protection against an event that may happen, e.g. fire, burglary, accident

Insured/assured

Person or objects protected

Intermediary

Agent or broker appointed to advise clients on a company's behalf

Legal expenses insurance

Cover for costs of defending and taking certain court actions

Lloyd's underwriter

Underwriter who works in a syndicate in the Lloyd's building. Is personally responsible for accepted risks. May be contacted only via a Lloyd's broker

Low-cost endowment

A combination of an endowment with profits and a decreasing term assurance; commonly used for mortgages for house purchase

Low-cost whole-life

A combination of a whole-life with profits and a decreasing term assurance. It is used to provide a high death benefit at minimal cost

Money insurance

Cover for loss of money from premises, home or in transit to/from the bank

Money purchase

A defined contribution pension scheme where the contribution level, investment return and annuity rate at retirement determine the eventual pension

Moral hazard

The hazard that attaches to the attitude of the insured or proposer

Mutual company

An insurance company owned by its policyholders; it has no shareholders

Mutual indemnity association

Originally accepted business from a particular trade, e.g. P and I clubs for marine insurance

New-for-old cover

Claims are settled on the basis of the cost of replacing items as new.

No claims discount

Available to policy holders with motor or household insurance who do not make a claim in a policy year

Particular risk

Personal in both cause and effect

Personal accident

Benefit of a lump sum on injury, death or loss of limb as a result of accident

Personal lines business

Types of insurance an individual would hold, e.g. motor, personal accident, household

Personal pension

A money purchase pension scheme available to the self-employed and those who are not in an occupational scheme

PIA

Personal Investment Authority

Polarization

An adviser must either be completely independent, or tied to one particular company

Policy signing office

All risks accepted by Lloyd's syndicates must be closed electronically through LPSO, who prepare accounts

Premium

The consideration paid for insurance cover

Products liability

Cover for legal liability for injury or death arising out of products supplied to the public

Proposal

Document used to ascertain details of the risk to be insured as well as the type of cover required

Proprietary company

An insurance company owned by shareholders

Proximate cause

The 'active efficient' or dominant cause of a loss

PSO

Pension Schemes Office; approves pension schemes

Public liability

Insurance to cover legal liability for death or injury to the public

Pure risk

Possibility of a loss or break-even situation as a result of a situation

Reinsurance

Insuring the insurer

RICTA

Renewable Increasable Convertible Term Assurance; a very flexible term assurance with the option to increase, renew or convert the policy without medical evidence

Risk management

The identification, analysis and economic control of those risks that can threaten the assets or earning capacity of an enterprise

Serps

State earnings-related pension; available at state pension age to employees, which is based on 20% of average revalued middle band earnings for those retiring after the year 2000

Self insurance
The setting aside of funds to meet insurable losses within the organization itself

SIB
Securities and Investments Board

SFA
Securities and Futures Authority; regulatory organization for stockbrokers under the FSA

SSAS
Small self-administered scheme; an occupational scheme for fewer than 12 members where the pension fund can be used to 'self-invest' in the company's property or assets. Loans can also be made to the company. Subject to strict rules and must have a pensioner trustee

Solvency margin
A minimum relationship between assets and liabilities that must be maintained

Special perils
Extra perils such as storm and explosion which can be added to a standard fire policy

Speculative risk
A risk that can result in a loss, break-even or a gain

Subrogation
The right of the insurer to stand in the position of the insured and claim any rights and remedies available

Sum assured
The amount payable by the insurers under a policy

Term assurance
A sum assured on death within the term. The sum assured remains level throughout the contract

Tied agent
An appointed representative or company representative who is allowed to sell only the products of the company to which he is tied

Underwriting
Assessing the risk

Universal whole-life

A unit-linked whole-of-life plan with the option to vary the sum assured to meet changing circumstances

Uberrima fides

Utmost good faith; a duty to disclose all material facts

INDEX